JOHN T. MALLOY'S
NEW
DRESS
FOR
SUCCESS

WARNER BOOKS

A Warner Communications Company

Copyright © 1988 by John T. Molloy

Warner Books, Inc., 666 Fifth Avenue, New York, NY 10103

A Warner Communications Company

Printed in the United States of America

First Printing: January 1988

10 9 8 7 6 5

Book design: H. Roberts

Library of Congress Cataloging-in-Publication Data

Molloy, John. T.
  John T. Molloy's new dress for success.

  Rev. ed. of: Dress for success. 1975.
  1. Men's clothing. 2. Grooming for men.
I. Molloy, John T. Dress for success. II. Title.
III. Title: New dress for success.
TT618.M64 1987   646'.32   87-2098
ISBN 0-446-38552-2 (U.S.A.)

TEST YOUR IMAGE I.Q.

•

1. What is the most effective raincoat color?

2. For which professionals are bow ties acceptable—and often preferred—attire?

3. What tie color makes men look sexy?

4. Should today's executive wear pants with cuffs—or without them?

5. Are shirts with contrasting collars acceptable in conservative companies?

6. "Old money" Americans are most likely to distrust a man who (a) has disheveled hair, (b) is wearing a wrinkled suit, (c) is wearing shoes that are unshined or worn at the heels, (d) drives an old car.

7. Should suspenders always have button fasteners?

8. Should you wear stripes or solids if you are going to appear on television?

9. If you are a small man, will a dark, pinstripe suit make you look smaller and ineffective?

•   •   •   •

PRAISE FOR THE ORIGINAL
Dress For Success

ANSWERS: 1. beige **2.** waiters, clowns, college professors, and commentators **3.** bright red **4.** with cuffs **5.** Yes, Lee Iacocca made them acceptable. **6.** (c) **7.** yes **8.** solids **9.** No, with the right accessories it will do the opposite.

ALSO BY JOHN T. MOLLOY

•   •   •

How to Work the Competition into
the Ground and Have Fun Doing It

ABOUT THE AUTHOR

In addition to his books and his highly successful image consulting business, John T. Molloy writes a column on business dress syndicated by the *Los Angeles Times*, has a call-in radio show on the ABC Network, and is a contributing editor to *Success* magazine. He also has appeared on over seven hundred radio and TV shows, gives numerous presentations and speeches per year to business groups, and has written thousands of articles for business magazines and newspapers.

I wish to express my enduring appreciation to Thomas Humber whose collaboration in the first edition of *Dress for Success* was invaluable to its development and to its success.

Contents

JOHN T. MOLLOY'S
NEW
DRESS
FOR
SUCCESS

Introduction:
Why Men Dress
For Failure and What
to Do About It

When I tell conservatively dressed businessmen that most men dress for failure, they generally agree. They all know men who wear ill-fitting polyester suits, wash-and-wear shirts and garish ties and they know that in their companies these men have no chance of getting to the top. However, when I tell them that many of them in their conservative suits, shirts and ties are dressing for failure as well, they are incredulous. They find it difficult to believe that dressed that way they could be doing their careers and their companies more damage than the fellows in their polyester suits, but the research is overwhelming; they are.

The reasons that businessmen dress for failure are many. The chief ones are:

1. They let their wives or their girl friends choose their clothing.

2. They let their favorite sales clerk choose their clothing.
3. They let designers choose their clothing.
4. They let one of the new breed of image consultants choose their clothing.
5. They let their backgrounds choose their clothing.

There is a way to avoid making any of those mistakes and to dress for success instead. Let research choose your clothing. My research is unique in concept, scope and results. It has been conducted over a period of twenty-six years and includes the opinions and subconscious reactions of over sixty thousand executives in all phases of business, as well as those of a wide cross section of the general public.

This research is based on the very reasonable premise that the two great behaviorists Pavlov and Skinner are right: We are preconditioned by our environment—and the clothing we wear is an integral part of that environment. The way we dress has a remarkable impact on the people we meet professionally or socially, and greatly (sometimes crucially) affects how they treat us.

It is possible, through the skillful manipulation of dress in any particular situation, to evoke a favorable response to your personality and your needs.

And it is possible for me, based on the research I have done, to teach you to dress for success.

I do not ask you to accept these conclusions immediately; I do hope that you will accept them when you have finished this book.

I will never ask you to concede that it is fair or just or moral for a man's success or failure to depend, to a large extent, on how he dresses. But that is very much the way the money-oriented sectors of our culture work; and it is my contention that in matters of individual striving, it is far more rewarding to let reality be your guide, to use the system rather than ignore or flout it.

Many critics charge that my approach to successful dress is snobbish, conservative, bland and conformist. They may further charge that I am encouraging the executive herd-instinct. To these charges I must plead guilty, for my research documents that in matters of clothing, conservative, class-conscious conformity is absolutely essential to the success of the American business and professional man. Executives do, in particular, constitute a herd, and those who understand how to cope rather than fight are much more likely to emerge as leaders than as casualties.

FACT: People who look successful and well educated receive preferential treatment in almost all of their social or business encounters. And since I came to the conclusion long ago that every man wishes to be treated as if he is important, I assumed that the reason that most men do not dress in a manner that commands respect is lack of money. Later, when I became involved in research that proves that money is not the issue, and that, with a little care and effort, the average man can easily create the look of success, I endeavored to find out why he does not make this attempt. That was when I discovered the five reasons listed at the very outset of this book.

• • • • • • • • • • • • • • • • • •

WHY IMAGE CONSULTANTS ARE DANGEROUS

You can only understand why image consultants are dangerous if you know something about their history. The image-consulting industry as we know it really started with the publication of *Dress for Success*. When the book became a best-seller, a number of people decided to become instant image consultants. The best qualified were college professors who for the most part, thought because they had Ph.D.'s in sociology or psychology that they could take my research and explain it as well or better than I could. These men stayed in the field at most two or three years because they came to realize I had not published all my research and without access to it they could not compete.

The second group who went into the field were not interested in research. They claimed that because of their backgrounds or their special sensitivity, they were able to dictate the clothing a businessman should wear to work. Most of them came from fashion backgrounds; they were former clothing buyers, retailers or models. Interestingly, the people I considered the best qualified of this group were the buyers, but, like the college professors, they usually stayed in the field for a short period of time, and then decided they could not compete and left.

The people who remain in the field today are mainly ex-models. They are a living tribute to the power of image. They succeeded, not because they knew what they were talking about, but because they *looked* like they knew what they were talking about. Many are still lecturing about clothing today when their only qualification is that they look beautiful when they are wearing it.

For the first two or three years several of these people followed me from city to city and speech to speech, carefully recording every word I spoke.

When they thought they had enough information they developed their own presentations and started speaking to companies and groups around the country. Although initially the reaction to their presentations was very good, after my book became a best-seller people started asking them why anyone needed them when you could simply read *Dress for Success* on your own. The way most of them chose to answer this question was to say that they were not John Molloy disciples; they agreed with me on some things and disagreed with me on others. The minute they took that position, they had to fight my research. And when they fought the research, they often got into trouble—and so did their clients.

The second problem they faced was that while *Dress for Success* contained information that individuals would find useful, I did not publish data that would be useful to companies in general. Therefore, when they were asked questions about how a particular company should dress, they were forced to guess at the answers. Sometimes they guessed right, other times they guessed wrong—and when they were wrong the results were often disastrous.

The classic example of a consultant fighting the research took place in San Francisco about three years ago. I was asked by a large accounting firm to speak at their annual West Coast meeting, but I had a previous engagement and had to decline. They so liked the subject that they hired a local "expert" to give what they referred to as a *Dress for Success* presentation. The consultant told the accountants that since twenty percent of their clients were in the movie industry, they should shed their conservative suits, shirts and ties because the people in the movie industry related best to a casual look.

The head of the Los Angeles office disagreed with the advice the consultant gave, but he assumed that an expert hired by the people at headquarters would be a real expert, so he told his men that if they wanted they could leave their suits, shirts and ties at home. He rescinded his order two days later after receiving a dozen complaints from clients. The complaint that really caught his attention was from one of his more famous clients, an actor, who said he wanted a real accountant, not an actor, to take care of his taxes.

That consultant caused only a slight disruption in the office procedure, but do not underestimate the amount of damage an unqualified image consultant can do.

A large Midwestern industrial giant bought a small high-tech firm on the Coast several years ago. They did so, not because they were interested in the products or the profit of that firm, but because the firm was on the cutting edge of a technology they badly needed.

As soon as they took control they sent a vice-president out to run the operation. When he arrived he took one look at the employees and decided he would have to clean up their act. He sent for an image consultant he had known in the Midwest who had worked for the mother company and had done a terrific job. The consultant had talked to several groups of industrial salesmen and told them, if they would dress conservatively they would sell more, and sure enough they did. When the consultant arrived at the California firm she took one look at the engineers and gave them the same message. She also told them to shave their beards and mustaches. When several employees objected to this directive and went in and complained to the vice-president, he told them he stood behind the orders. They packed their bags and left. Four of them were research people, two were top sales people and one was an accountant. To make matters worse, three of the engineers and the accountant opened a competitive firm, and convinced a dozen of the best employees of the old firm to follow them. According to the president of the Midwestern firm, that consultant's advice cost his firm anywhere from one million to four million dollars, depending on who does the calculating.

When an individual firm hires a consultant they should check on three things. First, the consultant's background. Second, the consultant's track record and, third, the source of the consultant's information. If you hire a lawyer, a doctor or an architect you know that they have been trained in their fields, but if you hire an image consultant you cannot make that assumption.

• • • • • • • • • • • • • • • • • • • •

WHY WOMEN FAIL THEIR MEN

I realize that a large number of women are now saying to themselves, "I am not a villain. I love my husband and always want him to look good."

Certainly, women are not conscious villains, but the result of their efforts is the same. The fact is that for years women have been indoctrinated by the fashion industry to believe that anything new, up-to-date, innovative and different is desirable. Most women, regardless of their status, would like to be leaders in fashion, and they transfer this desire to their husbands when they choose or influence their husbands' selection of clothing. They want their husbands to look good to them, and time and again they select a garment that is fashionable in the female sense of the word. Unfortunately, the reality—that is, the attitude of the American corporate establishment—militates almost totally against such a look for top executives.

My evidence is overwhelming. In one survey I conducted, ninety-two percent of the executives who were questioned said they would not hire a man who presented himself for a job interview wearing high-fashion clothing. In another survey, eighty-seven percent of the executives questioned said they would reprove any subordinate who continually dressed in that manner.

If any doubting Thomasinas are reading this, I can only ask that they visit any top-league executive office and look around, making careful mental notes on how the men are dressed. Then these women should ask themselves a question that could be worth a lot more than $64,000 to their husbands' careers: "Would my husband, dressed in the clothes I have chosen for him, fit in with these successful men?"

Most women would be forced to answer "no."

• •

HOW SALESMEN SABOTAGE THEIR CUSTOMERS

The next group that leads men down the path to sartorial slaughter are sales clerks. I mean no offense, and there are certainly some qualified exceptions, but most men's clothing store salesmen come from limited backgrounds and possess limited education, limited personal resources and limited knowledge of the business world. Little or no formal training is required for the job, and even the major stores that do have training programs generally teach their employees how to sell, rather than how to serve.

Their job is to move the merchandise they have, not to provide you with the clothing you should be wearing. If they did know what you should be wearing, they would not be in the relatively menial positions that they are locked into. Do not let them lock you into the position you are in.

• •

WHY FASHION DESIGNERS ARE DANGEROUS

The final villain who can be named is the fashion designer or consultant. A designer's name on a garment is supposed to represent quality and good taste. But more often than not, all a designer's label on a garment means is that he is getting a slice of the take. Even when quality is present, it is usually accompanied by an exorbitant price and foreign design, neither of which should be an inducement to buy.

The trouble with fashion designers, many of whom come from Rome, is that they do not export the maxim, "When in Rome, do as the Romans do." They ignore the fact that America is largely run by men who dress in a specific, traditional way, and they imply that we are all tasteless peasants who must be guided for our own good. Their condescension is not only insulting, it is also foolish. It is evident from the statistics I have already cited that a high-fashion look is rejected by the American business establishment—the very men whose clothing budgets could make designers richer than they ever dreamed, if only they would design clothes suited to people's needs, rather than clothing that feeds their own egos.

There are, of course, some fashion designers who are American. But remember, male fashion designing was not exactly a chic profession in this country until very recently. Consequently these men are, by and large, products of the lower middle class, and regardless of their income, their lower-middle-class taste lingers on.

Although fashion designers have been responsible for many positive changes in men's clothing in recent years, and some liberalization of style, patterns and colors have taken place, this trend is basically confined to leisure wear. For corporate and professional clothing, the loudly proclaimed radical changes in acceptability are more fashion fantasy than business fact. The truth is that business styles change with glacierlike slowness, and there is no point in risking career, income and social position by gambling on passing—and very expensive—fads. The only bank accounts that are fattened by a new fad are those of the designer and manufacturer who created it.

Even if designer clothes reflect quality and sophistication, as some very definitely do, the seductive manipulations of most fashion designers should still be viewed with suspicion, and for a more fundamental reason. They are advisers and associates of the manufacturer, not of the buyer. And their best interests are not necessarily his.

I am the consumer's man. My interests are his because I

like it that way and because it is he who pays me. My interest in clothing begins where that of the designer, the manufacturer, the retailer and his clerks leave off—at the point of sale. For a decade and a half, I have thoroughly researched what effect clothing has after the buyer puts it on. Through this research, I am able to engineer a man's wardrobe to elicit almost any desired effect.

• • • • • • • • • • • • • • • • • • • •

WHAT RESEARCH CAN DO FOR YOU

I can help you look successful, fatherly, honest, sexy, or even use clothing to mask or overcome detrimental physical characteristics or quirks. I have successfully applied these techniques on behalf of national political figures of both parties, executives of many of America's leading corporations, diplomats of foreign governments stationed in the United States, foreign executives seeking to do business here, television personalities, salesmen, courtroom lawyers, defendants in major criminal trials, professional associations and, of course, private individuals.

• • • • • • • • • • • • • • • • • • • •

GETTING DOWN TO CASES

A woman teaching in a black Chicago ghetto after reading my books decided she would package according to my guidelines the young people who came through her class. During the first year she called me half a dozen times and asked my assistance. After that I did not hear from her for eight years. Then, two years ago, she wrote me a letter telling me she was retired now, but wanted me to know that before getting her hands on my book, sixty percent of the young people who graduated from her high school were unemployed for at least six months to a year and many longer. After teaching them the principles of *Dress for Success* the number of youngsters in her class who were unemployed dropped to less than ten percent. She said that between us we had saved a lot of lives. It is the highest compliment I have ever received.

Item: A few years ago, a Midwestern politician running for a minor office called me in as a consultant when the political pros told him he had no chance of achieving even that lowly position because he lacked charisma. I changed his dress and his image and today he is governor of his state.

Item: I was hired by two firms on the same day. The president of each firm told me he had an image problem with a new employee. The first company was in Boston and the man who had the problem came from Jackson, Mississippi. He was a terrific marketing man but he dressed in a manner that made him unacceptable to his Boston colleagues. He was overweight, his suits did not quite fit, and he thought of himself as having a good ol' boy relaxed image. In fact, he looked as if he slept in his suits. The president of the company wanted the other employees in the firm to listen to this man, but he could not command their respect.

Since I was dealing with an intelligent man, I told him what the president perceived as his problem and offered to help him pick out a wardrobe. Only after I explained to him that the company was willing to pick up the price of his new wardrobe did he go along, and even then he did so reluctantly.

Two days later I was working with the new controller of a large Midwestern firm. He had until six months earlier been a resident of Greenwich, Connecticut, a very fashionable suburb of New York. He had lived and worked in the Northeast all his life, and was a graduate of a prestigious Eastern school. He was the epitome of an Eastern establishment gentlemen and dressed the part. When I explained to him that his wardrobe turned off and antagonized many of the men he had to now work with, he agreed to allow me to help him pick out a new wardrobe, although he expressed some doubt about its effectiveness.

Six months later I met the two men at an industry meeting in Chicago. Both admitted that when I changed their wardrobes I made their jobs easier. Since they were attending the same meeting, I went out of my way to introduce them to each other, and told them that what I had done was give each the other's dress code. I pointed out that if they had been the same size, they could have switched closets, and everyone would have saved a great deal of money. When I left they were joking and giving each other suggestions on how to do better in their roles.

Obviously there is no one *Dress for Success* look. It varies from place to place and from company to company, and a truly sophisticated businessman is one who adapts his wardrobe to suit his environment.

Item: I regularly consult with a major New York law firm and dress the young lawyers when they are hired. Within the first six months to a year of their employment, I conduct a seminar for them on effective dress in and out of the courtroom. After one of these seminars, during which I had casually and somewhat playfully mentioned that a man could be made to look sexy, one of the young men stayed behind to ask if I would help him. He did not want to become a swinger, he said, but wanted to settle down and get married. The problem was that he was not at all successful with women. I gave him copies of my research on what clothing appeals to women, and did not see him again for about a year. When I did see him, I asked if my research had helped.

"Yes," was his emphatic and cheerful reply, "so much that I no longer want to get married."

Item: About six months ago, I was hired by an accounting firm to establish a dress code for their accountants who did audits in their clients' offices. Several of the senior partners of the firm pointed out a particular employee to me. They said he was a brilliant accountant, but dressed so badly that they could not send him out to important clients. He did dress very poorly, and even though he had received strong hints to change his ways, he ignored them. Unless he changed soon, he was on his way out, rather than up. I had a short, frank talk with him, but he resolutely refused to believe that clothing could make any difference to his career.

Going back to the senior partners, I said, "Look, if I can get him to dress correctly, at least when he goes out on business, will you give him several important clients?" They agreed, and I finally was able to persuade this young man to follow my advice just as a test. I think he really went along only to get me off his back.

Yet six months later, his salary had been increased by $12,000 a year; his clients could not have been happier with him and he was well on his way to becoming a partner in the firm. I now choose all his clothing and have a three-year contract with him.

Item: Several years ago, I was approached by a self-made millionaire. Here was a man who had pulled himself up from poverty and achieved the American dream—except for him and his family it had become a nightmare. He had moved into a wealthy, sophisticated suburb of New York, and while he had the money to buy and sell just about anything with no significant effect on his bank balance, the neighbors had some assets that his money could not buy—class, education and sophistication. It was not so much that the neighbors were nasty or snobbish; they simply had nothing in common with these products of the lower classes. His wife and children had no neighborhood friends. They were lonely and the children were failing in school.

In this millionaire's case, dress was not enough to overcome his family's massive social problems. But it was the starting point. Once I had them looking like their neighbors, we set about getting him and his wife into night courses where they acquired the cultural refinements they needed to talk with their neighbors on an equal footing. Today, they are one of the most respected and best-liked families in the community.

•   •   •   •   •   •   •   •   •   •   •   •   •   •   •   •   •   •

HOW TO OVERCOME YOUR OWN BACKGROUND

As in the case of the lonely millionaire, helping people to overcome their own backgrounds, that great impersonal killer of careers, has always been my primary goal. In twentieth-century America, this is particularly difficult to achieve because most of us forget that when the Founding Fathers declared that all men are created equal, they did not mean that we are literally born into equal environments. Democratically, but foolishly, we bristle at the concept of training a man to move from one class to another and dismiss this need as a nineteenth-century Dickensian notion. Unrealistically, we expect the mere acquisition of position and money to move men socially. We try to ignore the fact that people who possess wealth and education, our great social yardsticks, do carry themselves differently and do set themselves apart from their poorer, less-educated neighbors by distinctive patterns of speech and dress.

Successful dress is really no more than achieving good taste and the look of the upper middle class, or whatever is perceived by the greatest number of people to reflect these qualities. Historically, in Europe, there were men and organizations who taught the upwardly mobile man how to acquire the necessary manners and taste of the class to which he aspired. When those Pygmalions came to America, they generally treated America as a country without classes and without class. Neither conclusion is correct, and so their input was of no value.

• • • • • • • • • • • • • • • • • • • •

WHY SUCCESSFUL DRESS IS NOT ALWAYS EXPENSIVE

My input would be just as valueless if cost were the only factor in determining the socioeconomic associations that are evoked by clothing, because the bottom line would always be how much money a man has to spend. In fact, upper-middle-class shades of color and patterns and textures have been available in relatively inexpensive clothing for years. With the improved technical abilities achieved by the clothing industry in recent years, you can get at moderate prices almost all the variations of color, pattern and texture that were once the exclusive province of the upper-middle-class man. If a man knows how to choose his clothing—and after you finish this book you will—he can, without substantial increase in his clothing expenditure, look right on all occasions.

There are times and places, however, when the amount of money you spend on your clothing can be a critical factor. You have to understand that the people who spend $600 or more for their suits, and $30 or more for their ties, usually do so because there is a difference between the more expensive and the cheaper models and believe the more expensive clothing is a sign of success. Obviously, these people are more likely to trust, believe, hire and promote men who look affluent and successful, because they correlate this look with achievement and competence.

If you visit the business district of any major city, you will notice that the men are dressing better today than they did ten years ago. Where before, elegance was evident only in executives' offices in ten percent of American corporations, it is easily the hallmark of the top executives in one-third of American corporations today. Therefore, the amount of time you put into selecting clothing is much more likely to be a critical factor that will affect your chances of success today than when the first edition of this book was first published eleven years ago.

Keep in mind that care in selection is a more important factor than the amount of money you spend. Most of the people at the top, even the more sophisticated, usually cannot spot the value of every item you are wearing. Most of them would not be able to tell the difference between a $300 suit and a $600 suit if the $300 suit was carefully chosen and carefully tailored and worn with other suitable items. And because that is so, you will see as you read through the book that I have come up with a very simple set of do's and don'ts that will allow you to look like a success—and greatly improve your chance of becoming one—without spending a fortune.

Naturally, successful dress cannot put a boob in the boardroom, but incorrect dress can definitely keep an intelligent, able man out.

The first rule of dress is common sense. This means that if you are a Wall Street stockbroker, you would be wise to go to work in a conservative, three-piece suit. If you are an art director in a Madison Avenue advertising agency, a television talk show personality or someone working in any so-called glamour industry, you would be wise to avoid conservative clothing in favor of more flamboyant, fashionable and with-it gear.

Not only individuals, but industries, professions, specific jobs, geography and climate dictate a natural clothing range that is easily identified through common sense. For example, if your boss never went to college and hates anyone who walks, talks and looks as if he did, it would be wise to avoid the Ivy League look. If you live in California or Florida, naturally you would not wear the heavy flannel suits common in most other areas of the country. You would wear lighter, brighter colors, for reasons of comfort, if for no other. In short, although this book is filled with rules, not every rule can work for every man in every situation or locality. Every rule must be measured against every individual's own specific circumstances and adapted accordingly.

So, while this book may not be able to do all things for all people, it can:

- Make movement up the social ladder easier for some.
- Make it easier for many men to sell everything better—including themselves.
- Make the right wardrobe less expensive.
- Give women a simple, sensible guide to buying men's clothing.
- Teach men how women like them to dress.
- Permanently change the way men look at clothing.
- Make a large number of people in the fashion industry angry as hell.

1

A Twentieth-Century Approach to Men's Clothing

If you asked me to divide the history of the world into two time periods, I would set the break early in the seventeenth century, when Francis Bacon introduced the scientific method of observation, deduction and induction. It is only because of the acceptance and the application of this method of reasoning that it became inevitable that sooner or later men would land on the moon, that hearts would be transplanted, and that in the future cancer will be conquered. It was also inevitable that someone would come along and apply valid scientific research methods to dress and its effects.

Those of you who are, at this point, saying that fashion is an art form and not a science are making a common mistake. While I do not contend that fashion is an absolute science, I do know that conscious and unconscious attitudes toward dress can be measured and that this measurement will aid men in making valid judgments about the way they dress.

19

After all, if we look at the reasons man puts on clothing, there are only three: to protect himself from the elements; to obey whatever his laws of modesty happen to be; and to look good to the people around him, to the people in his world in general. And when we say that clothing can make a man look good, we are really saying that it makes him look authoritative, powerful, rich, responsible, reliable, friendly, masculine or any other trait that is meaningful to us and meets with our approval.

There are men in the fashion industry who try very hard to make men look good. We know they are trying hard because their livelihoods depend on their success, but their attempts are made ineffective because they use subjective methods. A designer sits alone in a room and decides that a particular garment will make men look good. He does not bother to ask other men their opinions of the garment; he does not measure what the world thinks of it. He does not apply any scientific principles to arrive at his decision, and therefore his judgment has no validity; it is articulate, it can be systematized, it can be defended in all ways except before the avalanche of evidence. And I believe that this book is the first rumble of that avalanche.

Before going further, I think it is important to explain how I came to conduct experiments in fashion. I should like, of course, to claim insight, brilliance, even genius. I cannot. I was forced into it.

Twenty-six years ago, I was a young English teacher at a prep school in Stamford, Connecticut. The job paid *badly*, and after my first year I knew I could not afford to stay on. The owner of the school, wanting me to stay but knowing my economic problems, offered to find me a part-time job to supplement my income. I agreed, and that summer worked with a group of teachers who had received government funding to give remedial instruction to needy children in Connecticut and to do general research in education.

As my research project, I chose the effects of clothing on learning in the classroom. I was somewhat surprised when the idea was approved and I was given the go-ahead to undertake the study. I was also a bit frightened, because I was not at all qualified to conduct research of any type. But, needing the money, I immediately ran to the library and began reading everything I could find about research methods.

The outcome was that I conducted a series of experiments in Connecticut schools and proved that the clothing worn by the teachers substantially affected the work and attitudes of pupils. This was demonstrated in one case by two teachers who taught the same class in separate half-day sessions. One of the teachers wore rather casual clothing—penny loafers, a tie slightly open at the collar—while the other wore traditional lace shoes, always black, a conservative suit and a conservative tie. The students worked longer and harder for the teacher with the old-fashioned look.

Just at the time of my discovery, research funds were cut back by the government, and my project should have come to a halt. But I was hooked and started taking courses and doing research on my own. At the end of one year, I believed I had accomplished a breakthrough in education. In my report, I showed that clothing had a significant effect on discipline, work habits and attitudes in the classroom and that at different socioeconomic levels the pupils responded differently to various types of clothing.

When I took my report to my educator bosses, however, I was told that since the experiment was over, the report was not needed and that even if my results were valid, they would not know what to do with them. Frustrated and dismayed, I filed away my report and went on about my business as a teacher. But I was not to escape from my research quite so easily.

The following summer, again needing work, I applied for a part-time job at an elegant, expensive Fifth Avenue clothing store. The interviewer asked me how much I knew about clothing. After I had described my research project, I was assigned the task of coordinating the clothing purchased by the members of several law firms that sent all their members to the store.

I expected some difficulty in helping the lawyers, because I had never met them. I would receive only a name attached to a suit that needed a shirt and tie to be matched with it. The complaints I received—and there were many—never argued with my ability to coordinate clothing, but were related to the appropriateness of a given outfit for a member of the legal profession.

Since there was no consistency to the complaints, I was puzzled and therefore wrote, in the name of my employer, to several of my biggest clients. I told them I had noticed their members were making judgments about clothing that I felt were invalid. I also included some background information on the experiments I had conducted in the classroom, where credibility is as much a factor as it is in the courtroom. I also offered to meet with a member of each firm and discuss what I thought was proper attire for a lawyer in the courtroom.

All of our clients accepted my offer, and we were getting along famously when the store discovered that I was giving the extra service and decided to charge the firms accordingly—but without giving me a raise. I became annoyed, then angry, and quit. To my delight, the law firms engaged me directly for my services and began spreading the word that I was a valuable man to know.

At that point, twelve years ago, I became America's first wardrobe engineer.

New Dress for Success is intended as a practical tool, not as an academic exercise. I am not (and you are not) interested in theory for its own sake. We will leave that to the educators.

If I were to describe the methodology and results of all my experiments, surveys and tests in order to substantiate every statement in this book, it would run several thousand pages and be absolutely useless to you. I will spare you that, but for those with backgrounds in research, I should state that I followed standard research techniques with several exceptions. There was virtually no review of the literature in the field, since there is no literature in the field. At the stage of creating a hypothesis, I refrained from making a researcher's prediction unless it had to be included in the formal statement of the hypothesis (these predictions can become self-fulfilling prophecies, I believe).

When designing the data-gathering instrument, I often had to limit my objective since I found that corporations were unwisely frugal when appropriating funds for this essential work. But I never undertook a new project without testing and retesting the reliability of the testing instrument, and the only validity I considered adequate was predictive validity. While this is the validity measure that is least often used in the social disciplines, it is by far the best. Naturally, I ran pilot projects when needed and set up control groups whenever possible.

I am now going to present a few examples of my research in a way that will make them clear to any reader who will bear with me, and will offer no more technical jargon.

• • • • • • • • • • • • • • • • • •

THE PROOF:
WHAT WORKS AND WHAT DOESN'T

Since I had very early on discovered that the socioeconomic value of a man's clothing is important in determining his credibility with certain groups, his ability to attract certain kinds of women and his acceptance to the business community, one of the first elements I undertook to research was the socioeconomic level of all items of clothing.

Take the raincoat, for example. Most raincoats sold in this country are either beige or black; those are the two standard colors. Intuitively I felt that the beige raincoat was worn generally by the upper middle class and black by the lower middle class.

First I visited several Fifth Avenue stores that cater almost exclusively to upper-middle-class customers and attempted to ascertain the number of beige raincoats versus black raincoats being sold. The statistical breakdown was approximately four to one in favor of beige. I then checked stores on the lower-middle-class level and found that almost the reverse statistic applied. They sold four black raincoats to each beige raincoat.

This indicated that in all probability my feeling was correct, but recognizing that there were many variables that could discredit such preliminary research, I set the second stage in motion. On rainy days, I hired responsible college students to stand outside subway stations in determinable lower-middle-class neighborhoods and outside determinable upper-middle-class suburban commuter stations, all in the New York area. The students merely counted the number of black and beige raincoats. My statistics held up at approximately four to one in either case, and I could now say that in the New York area, the upper middle class generally wore beige raincoats and the lower middle class generally wore black raincoats.

My next step was to take a rainy-day count in the two different socioeconomic areas in Chicago, Los Angeles, Dallas, Atlanta and six equally widespread small towns. The research again held up; statistics came back from the cities at about four to one and from the small towns at about two and a half or three to one. (The statistics were not quite that clear-cut, but averaged out into those ranges.)

From these statistics I was able to state that in the United States, the beige raincoat is generally worn by members of the upper middle class and the black raincoat generally worn by members of the lower middle class. From this, I was able to hypothesize that since these raincoats were an intrinsic part of the American environment, they had in all probability conditioned people by their predominance in certain classes, and automatic (Pavlovian) reactions could be expected.

In short, when someone met a man in a beige raincoat, he was likely to think him a member of the upper middle class, and when he met a man in a black raincoat, he was likely to think him a member of the lower middle class. I then had to see if my hypothesis would hold up under testing.

My first test was conducted with 1,362 people—a cross section of the general public. They were given an extra-sensory preception test in which they were asked to guess the answers to a number of problems to which the solution (they were told) could only be known through ESP. The percentage of correct answers would indicate their ESP quotient. Naturally, a participant in this type of test attempts to get the right answer every time and has no reason to lie, since he wants to score high.

In this test, among a group of other problems and questions, I inserted a set of almost identical "twin pictures." There was only one variable. The twin pictures showed the same man in the same pose dressed in the same suit, the same shirt, the same tie, the same shoes. The only difference was the raincoat—one black, one beige. Participants were told that the pictures were of twin brothers, and were asked to identify the more prestigious of the two. Over eighty-seven percent, or 1,118 people, chose the man in the beige raincoat.

I next ran a field test. Two friends and I wore beige

raincoats for one month, then switched to black raincoats the following month. At the end of each month, we recorded the general attitude of people toward us—waiters, store clerks, business associates, and so forth. All three of us agreed that the beige raincoat created a distinctly better impression upon the people we met.

Finally, I conducted one additional experiment alone. Picking a group of business offices at random, I went into each office with a *Wall Street Journal* in a manila envelope and asked the receptionist or secretary to allow me to deliver it personally to the man in charge. When wearing a black raincoat, it took me a day and a half to deliver twenty-five papers. In a beige raincoat, I was able to deliver the same number in a single morning.

The impression transmitted to receptionists and secretaries by my black raincoat and nondescript suit, shirt and tie clearly was that I was a glorified delivery boy, and so I had to wait or was never admitted. But their opinion of me was substantially altered by the beige raincoat worn with the same other clothes. They thought I might be an associate or friend of the boss because that is what my look implied, and they had better let me in. In short, they reacted to years of preconditioning and accepted the beige raincoat as a symbol of authority and status while they rejected the black raincoat as such.

This study was conducted in 1971. And, although more and more lower-middle-class men are wearing beige raincoats each year (basically because of improved wash-and-wear methods that make them much less expensive to keep clean), the results of the study remain valid and will continue to be for years to come. You cannot wear a black raincoat, and you must wear a beige raincoat—if you wish to be accepted as a member of the upper middle class and treated accordingly (among all other raincoat colors, only dark blue tests as acceptable).

I continue to test the beige raincoat each year in my multiple-item studies. In the field of clothing, multiple-item studies are those that incorporate an entire look. These studies usually are not geared to test people's responses to specific items, but if a particular item is not consistent with the rest, it will destroy the effectiveness of the study because the incongruous item spoils the total look.

In one multiple-item study, I sent a twenty-five-year-old male college graduate from an upper-middle-class Midwestern background to one hundred offices. To fifty of them he wore an outfit made up entirely of garments that had been previously tested as having lower-middle-class characteristics; to the remaining fifty he wore an outfit of garments that had previously tested as having upper-middle-class characteristics. Prior to his arrival at each office, I had arranged for the man in charge to tell his secretary that he had hired an assistant, and to instruct her to show the young man around. The executive also made sure that his secretary would not be going to lunch, would not be going home, and would not be overworked at the time of my man's arrival.

After being shown through the office, which took anywhere from fifteen minutes to an hour, depending on the secretary and the office, the young man made a series of requests. He first asked for something simple like letterhead stationery or a pencil and pad. The responses of the secretaries to these requests had no statistical significance, although the young man did note that there was a substantial difference in attitude. In upper-middle-class garb, he received the requested item with no comment, but pejorative comments or quizzical looks were directed toward him at least one-third of the time when he wore lower-middle-class clothing.

Once the first request sequence was completed, the young man gave each secretary a standardized order. Before going to each office, he had been given the names of three people in the files of the office. These names were written on a card, and his procedure was always the same. Putting the card on the secretary's desk, he would say, "Miss (always using her name) Jones, please get these files for me; I will be at Mr. Smith's desk." He would then walk away, trying not to give the secretary a chance to answer him verbally. The results were quite significant.

In upper-middle-class garb, he received the files within ten minutes, forty-two times. In lower-middle-class garb, he received the files only twelve times. When the files were brought to him, pejorative comments were directed at him twelve times while wearing upper-middle-class clothes, and eight times while wearing lower-middle-class clothes. This means that he received positive responses only four times while wearing lower-middle-class garb; but he received positive responses thirty times out of fifty when he was wearing upper-middle-class garb.

From this experiment and many others like it, I was able to conclude that in upper-middle-class clothes a young man will be more successful in giving orders to secretaries.

The experiment will give you an idea of why I have spent so many years and so much of my clients' money in determining what constitutes upper-middle-class dress. It is obvious from the experiment that secretaries, who generally were not members of the upper middle class, did in fact recognize upper-middle-class clothing, if not consciously then at least subconsciously, and they did react positively to it. The reactions of the secretaries indicate that dress is neither trivial nor frivolous, but an essential element in helping a man function in the business world with maximum effectiveness.

But does everyone react as the secretaries did?

For years, some companies have been attempting to increase the efficiency of employees by prescribing dress and establishing dress codes. Most of these schemes have proved ineffective because they have been created by amateurs who don't understand the effect clothing has on the work environment. Dress codes can work, as I will show later, but the assumption that clothing has a major, continuing impact on the wearer is erroneous. True, you may feel shabby when you wear shabby clothes, and your morale may perk up a bit when you splurge on an expensive tie. But clothing most significantly affects the people whom the wearer meets and, in the long run, affects the wearer only indirectly because it controls the reaction of the world to him. My research shows that in most business situations the wearer is not directly affected by his clothing, and that the effect of clothing on other people is merely controlled by the socioeconomic level of the clothing.

Let me say it straight out: We all wear uniforms and our uniforms are clear and distinct signs of class. We react to them accordingly. In almost any situation where two men meet, one man's clothing is saying to the other man: "I am more important than you are, please show respect"; or "I am your equal and expect to be treated as such"; or "I am not your equal and I do not expect to be treated as such."

• • • • • • • • • • • • • • • • • • • •

THE "PUSH TEST"

I tested this hypothesis by using what I call the "push test." I took two men, both in their thirties, both of average height and weight, and dressed one in lower-middle-class clothes, the other in upper-middle-class apparel. On the second day of testing, we reversed the clothes so that the men's personalities and physical characteristics would not interfere with the results. We then went into the street and created minor conflict situations.

First, the man in upper-middle-class dress stood to the side of a revolving door at the entrance to a building. When he saw someone coming, he attempted to pace his steps so that he and the approaching party would reach the door at exactly the same time. At that point, we would see which man stepped aside.

In fifty-eight out of eighty-six attempts, our man went through first without any confrontation whatsoever; the other party simply stepped aside. In twelve confrontations the other man looked at him and seemed to say, "Look, buddy, who do you think you are?" but eventually let him through. In the rest of the attempts, the other individual walked through first, indicating by his actions that he was more important.

When the same test was conducted sixty-two times with our man in lower-middle-class clothes, he was pushed aside more often; and on three separate occasions he was threatened with physical violence, each time by other men wearing lower-middle-class garb.

The next day, when we reversed the clothing, the statistics held up: The man in upper-middle-class garb was allowed to pass through the door first on an average of three to one times. The man in the lower-middle-class uniform was threatened with physical violence on two occasions. We became afraid that he would be punched in the nose if we continued, so we stopped the test after twenty runs.

In another test, I again gave two men lower- and upper-middle-class clothing, and had them alternate the looks every other day. Their procedure was to go into stores, of all types and socioeconomic levels, and select some merchandise. When it came time to pay, they would search their pockets, say they had left their wallets at home, and ask to pay by check.

Too many variables run through a test such as this to put any weight on a small statistical difference. But in both these cases the differences were enormous: My men were able to cash twice as many checks wearing upper-middle-class clothing as they did wearing lower-middle-class garb. This means that in many cases the store made the decision to pass up a sale rather than trust a man wearing clothing that looked cheap. Believe me: If you dress like a man of substance and integrity, you will, more often than not, be treated as such.

One of the most significant studies I ever did, from a business point of view, utilized volunteer executives from a company I had worked for with offices in New York, Chicago, Kansas City and on the West Coast. Each man—two from each office—went to two executive headhunter outfits in his city, applying for a specific position, and handling the interview as best he could. For his trip to the first headhunter, the volunteer wore a strict, correct combination of conservative upper-middle-class clothing. When he went to the second headhunter, applying for a similar job, he wore a basic combination of upper-middle-class clothing, but broke one rule: either wearing a lower-middle-class patterned tie; or a shirt that was a bit too bright; or a suit that was not as good as it should have been. One man dressed in his most expensive, classiest outfit, but wore his son's cowboy boots.

If anything, the men had a verbal advantage for their second interviews because they had just been through the same drill earlier in the day and knew what to expect. Yet in seven out of the eight cases, the executive reported that the interview had gone much better when they wore an unflawed wardrobe.

Four of the eight men actually received offers from four of the headhunters to arrange interviews with prospective employers. In each of those four cases, the offer was made by a headhunter who had interviewed a man wearing perfect upper-middle-class combinations. None of the headhunters who had interviewed the men in their flawed combinations made an offer.

• • • • • • • • • • • • • • • • • •

THE CASE FOR DRESS CODES

Most large industries are involved in the same major endeavor—making money—and anything that increases efficiency helps them to make more. Many of my client-sponsored studies have been directed accordingly. Several years ago, one large corporation hired me to conduct a study in two of its branch offices. In one office, a dress code was being enforced for all men in positions of authority—that is, men who had direct responsibility for someone under them. In the second office, there was no dress code, and a rather lax attitude of dress was typical of most of the executives.

First, I tested the relative efficiency of the offices. A time study yielded the following results: The secretaries and clerks in the non-dress-code office spent four percent less time at their desks, five percent less time actually at their typewriters or equivalent work, and they were absent or late three percent to five percent more often than the workers in the office where the dress code was enforced.

I then established a dress code for the non-dress-code office, and it was enforced for one year. The code was an unwritten one, never formally declared, but the word was passed down from above, and it took about six months for everyone to realize it was there. Once they did, most people adhered to it rather strictly. As an adjunct to the dress code, I was brought in on three separate informal occasions to lecture the executives on those colors, patterns and combinations that would help to make them most authoritative and most effective.

At the end of the year, I repeated the time study. In the first office, the performance level was virtually the same as it had been at the beginning of the year. In the second office, where the new dress code had gone into effect, a vast improvement had taken place. The workers now outperformed themselves in every activity I surveyed. They stayed at their desks one percent longer; they worked two percent longer; and their lateness and absenteeism were fifteen percent lower than when first tested.

In addition, the top executives, reporting independently, said that middle-management people were performing at a much better level than they had in the past. And the middle-management people, with one exception, reported that the people working directly under them were performing at a better level than they had in the past.

The significance of this study is not based on the erroneous assumption that clothing changes a man. It is based on the fact that a man's environment changes him, and the clothing worn by people around him is part of his environment. The man who claims he could work as well in his underwear as he could in a $400 suit is probably telling the truth. It's just that if everyone came to work in his underwear, the office wouldn't function as well as if everyone arrived in $400 suits.

• • • • • • • • • • • • • • • • • • • •

HOW TO COMPETE WITH IBM

One of the most intriguing clothing problems I've ever faced was handed to me by a company that competes with IBM in the computer field. Almost everyone in business knows that IBM—at one time officially and now unofficially—enforces a rather strict dress code, particularly for its salesmen, and one of the mandatory staples of this code is the standard white dress shirt. I was supposed to find out:

Is that white dress shirt important?

Does it have anything to do with IBM's spectacular success over competitors?

And if it does, how do you compete with it effectively?

I started out by questioning 106 executives, mostly from the company that had hired me, but also from other IBM competitors in related fields. This was important since initial research had shown that the backgrounds of the IBM executives, their competitors and the people who bought from them were almost identical. Generally, they were technically educated, holding bachelor degrees or better, and very conservative in their dress patterns.

With people of this type, it is most unwise to use any direct questioning method; they grasp what you are seeking much too quickly, and then they tend to tell you what they think you want to hear. So I buried my white shirt question in a twin test, using one set of pictures showing men in white shirts and another set of pictures with men wearing other shirts.

Instead of asking questions that would assign socioeconomic values to the shirts, I asked questions that would call for moral values. For instance:

Which men would be late for work more often?

Which men would be likely to overstay their lunch hour?

Which men were likely to cheat on their expense accounts?

Which men were better family men?

Because these were all men whose educational orientations told them to think analytically rather than subjectively, I was somewhat surprised that 87 of the 106 executives attributed greater moral strengths to the white shirt than to the other shirts.

I then questioned the executives directly:

Did they think that a white shirt was an asset to IBM salesmen? Ninety-two said yes.

Did they think that they or their salesmen should wear white shirts in competing with IBM? Eighty-six said yes.

After showing the men the results of my initial survey,

one hundred agreed that they should adopt the white shirt if they were to compete successfully.

Right?

Wrong?

I next conducted in-depth interviews with fifty-six executives who had in the previous twelve months made major purchases of IBM equipment and consequently had not made major purchases of my client's equipment. The purpose of the interviews was to determine their motivation for making that particular purchase. In all the interviews, the findings were approximately the same. The primary motivation for choosing IBM was a belief in IBM's moral—yes, moral—superiority. In fact, many of the men questioned used the same moral characteristics to describe IBM that were previously attributed to wearers of the white shirt in my twin test.

The men went further, however, and here was the real problem. While forty-six of them attributed moral positives to the wearing of white shirts by IBM salesmen, forty-two of them attributed negative characteristics to any of IBM's competitors wearing white shirts. They considered this an attempt to copy IBM.

All of this is not to say that white shirts were all that the buyers of IBM equipment mentioned. The word that cropped up most frequently was "service," a legitimate area of concern with computer equipment. However, the contracts in most cases were large enough to warrant having special service agreements written in, and my client had on many occasions offered to make special service arrangements with purchasers, who summarily ignored the offer.

I asked forty-two buyers of IBM equipment if they had as much technical knowledge about the products as the people who were selling the equipment to them. Thirty-six said no, so they were making other than a technical decision. And since the IBM equipment was at least as expensive (if not more so) as the equipment of the competition, the men were not making purely economic decisions.

Therefore, although each of the executives was able to cite complicated reasons for their purchases, the white shirt response was glaring in its importance, and I believed that the decision to buy IBM equipment over my client's was largely emotional—based on the positive moral characteristics attributed to the dress of IBM's salesmen.

An allied study that I had conducted on dress as it is used for photographs in advertising had shown that if you put a man next to a computer, the general public would associate the value of the machine with the value attributed to the man's appearance.

So my client still had to combat the superiority of the white shirt, and he was damned if he wore it, and damned if he didn't. After much additional testing, I finally came up with a look composed of a conservative pinstripe suit, a very crisp, narrowly pin-striped shirt and a traditionally patterned tie. The look said: "conservative," "reliable," "efficient," "morally upright." It did not say, "copy."

That research project was conducted twelve years ago at the height of the colored shirt craze when most salesmen other than I.B.M.'s were wearing colored shirts. Today that same client has a white shirt dress code for his salesmen because I.B.M. no longer owns the white shirt in the public's mind and as a result their salesmen appear as reliable, efficient and as morally upright wearing white shirts as their I.B.M. counterparts without looking like cheap copies.

• • • • • • • • • • • • • • • • • • •

HOW ONE HUNDRED TOP EXECUTIVES DESCRIBED SUCCESSFUL DRESS

Twelve years ago I surveyed one hundred top executives in either medium-sized or major American corporations about their attitude toward corporate dress. With updated pictures I reran the survey for this version of the book.

The first series of questions was designed to establish the most up-to-date attitudes on corporate dress.

I showed the executives five pictures of men, each of them wearing expensive, well-tailored, but high-fashion clothing. I asked if this was a proper look for the junior business executive. In the first survey ninety-two of the men said no, eight said yes. Today sixty-eight men said no, thirty said yes and two did not comment. I believe the reason for this change is not that men have become more fashionable but men's fashion has become more conservative.

I showed them five pictures of men neatly dressed in obvious lower-middle-class attire and asked if these men were dressed in proper attire for a young executive. In the original survey forty-six said yes, fifty-four said no. Today twenty-six said yes, seventy-four said no. Executives are far more image conscious today than they were only a few years ago.

I next showed them five pictures of men dressed in conservative upper-middle-class clothing and asked if they were dressed in proper attire for the young executive. In both surveys all one hundred said yes.

I asked them whether they thought the men in the upper-middle-class garb would succeed better in corporate life than the men in the lower-middle-class uniform. Eighty-eight said yes, twelve said no. There was no significant change in the answer.

I asked if they would choose one of the men in the lower-middle-class dress as their assistant. Ninety-two said no, eight said yes twelve years ago. Today ninety-eight said no, two said yes.

I next showed them pictures of four young men. The first had a very short haircut; the second had a moderate haircut with moderate sideburns; the third had a moderate haircut, but with fairly long sideburns; and the fourth had very long hair. I asked what haircut was the most profitable for a young man to wear. Eighty-two executives then, while ninety-six now picked the moderate haircut with moderate sideburns. Their concept of a moderate hair style has changed; today it is much shorter.

I next asked if they would hire the man with long hair. Seventy-four said no then, one hundred said no now.

To one hundred other top executives of major corporations, I submitted the following written questions:

1. Does your company have a written or an unwritten dress code? Ninety-seven said yes. Three said no. Only two had a written dress code. There was no significant change.

2. Would a number of men at your firm have a much better chance of getting ahead if they knew how to dress? Ninety-six said yes, four said no. They gave the same answer.

3. If there were a course in how to dress for business, would you send your son? All one hundred said yes then, only fifty-six percent said yes today. It is not that they think that dress has become less important, rather most of them think that their sons know how to dress. Several said that their sons had been required to read *Dress for Success* in school and they thought that that was enough.

4. Do you think employee dress affects the general tone of the office? All one hundred said yes on both occasions.

5. Do you think employee dress affects efficiency? Fifty-two

said yes, forty-eight said no. There was no significant change.

6. Would you hold up the promotion of a man who didn't dress properly? Seventy-two said yes, twenty-eight said no twelve years ago. Today seventy-eight said yes, twenty said no and two chose not to express an opinion.

7. Would you tell a young man if his dress was holding him back? Eighty said no, twenty said yes just a few years ago. Clothing has become a more important subject and one that they are willing to discuss. Today sixty-five said yes and only thirty-five said no.

8. Does your company at present turn down people who show up at job interviews improperly dressed on that basis alone? Eighty-four said yes, sixteen said no then. Today ninety-three said yes, seven said no.

9. Would you take a young man who didn't know how to dress as your assistant? Ninety-two said no, eight said yes. There has been no significant change.

10. Do you think there is a need for a book that would explain to a young man how to dress? Ninety-four said yes, six said no. There was no signifcant change.

11. Do you think there is a need for a book to tell people in business how to dress? One hundred said yes. I am very happy to report this answer remained the same.

Keep reading, fellows, you got it.

2

How to Get the Most Out of Investing in Suits

The suit is the single most important garment worn by men—not only because it is the most expensive and requires the greatest amount of time for selection and fitting, but because it is the garment on which most people judge the wearer's status, character and abilities. And, since it covers the upper torso, which is the focal point of most people with whom we communicate, it is the central power garment—the garment that establishes our position as inferior, equal or superior in any in-person business situation.

Suits are positive authority symbols, worn by the upper middle class—the people who make important decisions in our lives. We are much more likely to believe, respect and obey the man who wears a suit than the man who does not. Men who do not wear suits may have important functions in our society, but we do not normally accord them such in our minds. In any level of society, suits are associated with authority, with position, with power.

Because of their importance and because no item of clothing can be dealt with in isolation, suits will be the subject of commentary throughout this book. This chapter merely establishes the basics.

• • • • • • • • • • • • • • • • • •

HOW TO BUY A SUIT

Most men believe that a suit can be bought in a fifteen-minute period during which they go into a store, walk to a rack, select a suit, have it fitted and leave. They not only believe this; it's how they do it, and it's wrong.

If you have only fifteen minutes to buy a suit on a given day, don't buy one that day. Purchasing a suit should be planned in advance. Decide what you need: color, pattern, texture, weight, material and style. Know your approximate size. And decide how much, within a certain range, you are willing to spend. For any businessman, buying a suit should be a serious, thoughtful endeavor, not a casual splurge.

There is one important factor that should influence your choice of style: If eighty percent or more of the top men in your field or in your company favor one style you should adopt it. You may even find that all the top executives in your company buy their suits in one store. If that is true, you should do the same. If you don't know if most of the top men shop at one store, you should be able to find out after you are on the job for about a week.

If the leaders in your field wear a variety of suit styles you should choose a style that is most flattering to you, remembering that you must be very careful, that there is a very fine line you cannot cross. Eighty-eight percent of the executives we questioned thought that men who were put together carefully were more competent and able than those who were slightly disheveled. These same men described those they thought of as fashionable as incompetents or as "lightweights." The style they admire most is conservative, well coordinated, macho, high power, traditional.

When you are ready to buy a suit, wear the best-looking and best-fitting suit you already own. If you are going to buy a suit with a vest, wear a vest. Wear a dress shirt of the weight and style you believe you will be wearing with the new suit. It also helps if the shirt you are wearing is of a color that will be compatible with the color of the suit you intend to purchase. Wear a good tie of a color and pattern that will not clash tremendously with the color and pattern of the suit you hope to buy.

If you are going to buy a suit that has belted pants (as business suits should), wear a belt. Carry with you all items that you normally carry in your suit pockets. Wear the type of shoes that you expect to wear with the new suit.

On any Saturday, in any upper-middle-class men's store, you can see otherwise astute, affluent businessmen buying suits while they are dressed in jeans or sport slacks, heavy wool shirts or sweaters, and Hush Puppies, boots, topsiders or running shoes. That any of these customers are able to buy suits that are appropriate and well fitting when wearing such attire is a miracle, with which most of them are not blessed.

There is another important reason for being properly dressed when buying a suit, and in this case the female shopping instinct serves far better than the male. Any woman will tell you that when she goes clothes shopping, she goes dressed to the hilt. She does so because she knows that clothing store clerks will judge her and treat her according to the clothes she is wearing, and she wants and expects to be treated well. Men should do the same, for exactly the same reason.

The best way to locate a good men's store and a helpful clerk is to ask the best dressers in your office for their recommendations. The reason you must find a good store is that when you buy a suit you not only buy material and workmanship, but tailoring as well. And since only the best stores can afford to maintain a top-notch tailoring department you cannot buy a first-rate suit in a second-rate store.

The advantage of having a relationship with an experienced salesman is that if he knows his business he will look out for his steady customers. You may have noticed that the last time you entered the suit department of your local men's store the head clerk said "up" loud enough for the other clerks to hear. He was signaling the clerk whose turn had come to wait on you. If you had indicated that you wanted to be served by another clerk, that salesman would jump to the head of the line. Since on a slow day a salesman can wait up to two hours for a turn, and most salesmen are paid on commission, they value their personal customers. A good salesman will steer you away from the shopworn suit (which has spent two years on a hanger and will fall apart soon after you get it home). He will arrange for the most experienced fitter to take your measurements and, if he can, have the head tailor work on your suit. If when you go to pick up your suit you are dissatisfied, he will make every effort to see that your complaint is handled properly. Obviously, if you have already found one of these gems you should shop with him and no one else. Get to know his schedule or call before you arrive to make sure he is working.

Once in the store, properly dressed, if you haven't found a salesman you trust, you will sooner or later be approached by one. Let him know immediately that you, not he, are in the authority position and that you know exactly what you are doing. You do this by describing, as specifically as you can, the type of suit for which you are looking and your size. If you do this, the clerk will not try to push everything in the store on you; unless he is spectacularly inept, he knows that men who know what they are doing become annoyed by such tactics. If he does try to push anything on you, become annoyed, and show it.

Let the clerk lead you to the suits where your size is kept, then ask him to let you look through the rack on your own. Some salespeople will and some won't. If he insists on staying, let him—he may even turn out to be helpful—but do not let him distract you or pressure you. If you see no suits that meet your basic requirements, leave immediately. Do not settle for anything but the suit you are after. Before you leave you can have them order a suit, or ask to be notified when the suits you want arrive, but do leave.

If you do find a suit, or suits, that meet your basic requirements, begin to look at it very carefully. Feel the material, and know what it is. Read the label if you must. Look at the stitching behind the collar to see that it is neat, even and reinforced. Examine the lining, keeping in mind that it must be sewn securely enough to stand up to dry cleaning. With most winter and all-weather clothes, it is preferable if they are fully lined. Check for required interior pockets. Look at the workmanship of the buttonholes to make sure that the stitching will hold up for several years of wear. Look at the buttons. Are they cheap plastic or expensive bone? Are they sewn on securely?

If the suit has any pattern, regardless of what the pattern is, look carefully at every place where material is sewn. There is little that looks worse in a suit than a pattern that is improperly joined. It is an immediate tip-off of poor workmanship or an attempt to save material, neither of which you are going to pay for, I hope.

If all the above aspects and any others that are of concern to you are satisfactory, then you are ready for your final test. Grasp the sleeve of the suit jacket in both hands and twist it tightly for a few seconds. The clerk will probably have a heart attack, but this test must be done. If the sleeve immediately springs back to shape, it's a wearable suit. If wrinkles remain . . . well, you have just wrinkled a suit you are not going to buy. The suit will wrinkle the minute you sit down; you'll look like a bum most of the time; and your pressing bills will be enormous. Don't buy it.

•   •   •   •   •   •   •   •   •   •   •   •   •   •   •   •   •

EVERYTHING YOU NEVER KNEW ABOUT GETTING A SUIT FITTED

When you have tentatively settled on a suit, you now come to the big hurdle—the fitting. As the clerk is leading you to the fitting room, tell him in affable but firm language that you wish to be fitted by the head fitter, or, if possible, by the tailor who is actually going to do the work on the suit. Some salesclerks will be upset and antagonized by this, but if you are dressed as you should be, and if you have followed all my previous advice, by this time he should be attuned to the fact that you are accustomed to getting your way without compromise.

When the tailor or fitter arrives, take him aside, tell him you are very particular about your suits and ask him to give it some extra attention. Then slip him a few dollars. This introduces a new element into men's clothes buying: tipping the tailor. Since virtually no one does it, the tailor will be grateful; everyone likes money and you will be rewarded with superior service. I'll leave the amount up to you, depending on the quality of the store and the cost of the suit, but generally I would suggest no less than $10 and no more than $20.

You are now ready to try on the pants—and only the pants. When doing so, put on your belt and put into your pockets all those items that you normally carry in your suit pants. You should also wear your shoes, because pants cannot be measured properly without shoes.

Pants are always fitted from the top down, and the first area of fit you must check is the waist. The proper position for a man's pants waist is slightly above the navel, and exactly horizontal to the ground, all the way around. They should not be lower in the front than in the back. Fitters will often tell you to adjust your pants to the height you normally wear them. If you wear them wrong, then it is high time for you to change your habits, and for the best of reasons: There is a very definite tendency on the part of lower-middle-class men to let their pants droop and hang from the hips. Upper-middle-class men wear them correctly.

Men who are either tall and thin or short and heavy may find that suit pants will have waists that are either too high or too low, because all rack suits are made proportionate to the average man wearing that size. If the waist is too high or too low and cannot be corrected, take off the pants and do not buy the suit. You do not want to look like Lou Costello with his pants under his armpits, and you do not want to look like a member of the lower middle class.

Assuming that the height of the waist is correct, then it should be neither too loose nor too tight. It is too loose if it does not fit smoothly all the way around, and if material bulges under the belt. It is too loose if it slips at all when you move. It is too tight if you cannot comfortably slip the flat of your hand in and out at the waistband.

Moving down, the next area that must be fitted is the seat area. If your waist is proportionately larger than your seat area, frequently the pants will sag and be baggy; if your seat area is proportionately larger than your waist, the pants may be too tight. In either case, the problem should be corrected so that the seat area is smooth but comfortable when standing and sitting. If the seat area is too large, have the fitter pin it rather than chalk it. When material is taken from the seat area, this very definitely affects the way the bottoms of the pants hang, and the measurement that must be taken for the cuffs. This is also true of the crotch, which should also not be baggy or tight. If the crotch is too big, have the area pinned also, if possible, or at least have it held so that the cuffs may be measured accurately.

The decision of whether to finish the bottoms with turned-up cuffs or with plain bottoms is no longer a matter of personal choice. Today most top executives have cuffs put on their suit pants. If you prefer plain bottoms you are going to have to enjoy them with your leisure-time slacks.

The final aspect of the pants fit is the length the pants should break in front and be one-half to three-quarters of an inch longer in the back. When you have cuffs put on your pants, it is usually best if they are tailored so they hang exactly horizontal to the ground and there are no wrinkles or bulges when the cuff fold is made (see drawing on page 74).

Whenever I have a suit fitted, I always ask that the cuffs be made as long as possible without drooping or dragging the floor. I ask this explicitly because, despite all assurances to the contrary, almost all suit materials shrink after a few cleanings. Some knits stretch but since no one with even the slightest sophistication would buy a suit made of a knit material today, the question is academic.

If the pants fit you properly in the waist, seat and crotch and do not require pinning, you are ready to move on to the rest of the suit while you're still wearing the pants. If they do not fit you in the waist, seat or crotch and must be corrected, put back on the pants you wore into the store before you try on the rest of the suit.

If you choose a suit with a vest, and you may because you wish to be more conservative, more traditional or more authoritative, the vest must be fitted and pinned as well. There are stores who will balk at this, but remember a vest is an essential part of a suit and its fit is just as important as the pants and the jacket. Because of its appropriate closeness to the body, it is particularly important when fitting a vest that you wear the same type of shirt that you will wear with your suits. A vest should fit smoothly with no pulling or sagging when sitting or standing. The arm holes should be open enough for comfort but they should not sag. The back should have no wrinkles and not ride up and down during normal activity. A belt in the back which you can use to adjust the vest is not a substitute for tailoring. Its purpose is not to save the tailor work but to allow you to loosen or tighten the vest if you gain or lose a few pounds. When you pull this belt tight, make sure it does not throw off the line of the vest. A good vest has four pockets, two on each side, and it should be long enough to cover your belt, your shirt and your tie. Nothing should stick out underneath. It should lie directly on your pants. That is more difficult than it sounds because a gentleman always wears his vest with the bottom button opened. If your shirt shows underneath your vest, your vest is too short or you are wearing your pants too low. In most cases the vest is too short. If your tie shows, you are probably tying your tie too long. Although it is perfectly acceptable for your tie to hit the bottom of your belt buckle when you are wearing a vest, I suggest that you tie it so it hits the top.

After the vest has been pinned, do not put your jacket on immediately. Keep the vest on for a moment and move around until you're sure it's right. The collar should lie flat at the neck and smoothly against your chest without puckering or bulging. I've had tailors, even in good stores, tell me that vests do not have to be tailored that carefully. The fact is, they do. They should be fitted every bit as carefully as a jacket, in fact more carefully, since they must hug the body without restricting it. If the vest is not pinned, keep it on when trying your jacket. If it is pinned, put on the vest you brought with you. If you are buying a suit with a vest, particularly if the suit is made of a heavy material, insist on having the jacket fitted with the vest underneath; it can make a difference.

When most of us think of vests we think of conservative, dark pinstripe suits in either blue or gray, and most vests are sold with suits. However, our research indicates a vest is almost essential when you buy a light-colored suit. It's ironic that vests work better with summer suits than with winter suits because it's impractical to wear them in very warm weather. Nevertheless, from a psychological point of view, they do. If you add a vest to a dark blue or gray pinstripe, it only adds marginally to the authority of the wearer. However, if you add a vest to a light beige or a medium-range brown suit, it adds dramatically to the authority and to the credibility of the wearer. The less formal and the lighter color the suit, the more effective is the vest. The choice, I realize, is often a catch-22, but you should understand that it exists.

When you put on any suit jacket, the first and most important aspect is how it feels. I don't care how it looks; if it does not feel perfectly comfortable sitting, standing and moving around, then do not buy it. You are going to have to wear it a long time, and you may as well not start out wrong.

It is very difficult to describe exactly how a suit jacket should fit although a perfectly fitting suit is very easy to spot. If you want to see someone whose suits always fit perfectly, watch Johnny Carson. His colors and patterns are sometimes inappropriate for the average businessman, but the suits themselves are always impeccably fitted. They do not wrinkle or bulge; they do not gap or pull. If you can come even close to this look, then you are going to look good.

If you still have difficulty finding or getting suit jackets that fit, pick a talk-show host, a network television news reporter or a major political figure who is built like you and take careful note of how his suits fit. Pay particular attention to the style of his suit jackets, the type of shoulder, the way it hangs in front, whether it is vented on the side or in the back, and other details, and try to get one that is similar in style.

As with the pants, the fit of the jacket begins at the top. Look at the neck area carefully; if it does not fit absolutely flat, with no wrinkles or bulges, tell the fitter to fix it. Now there's something about this area you must know: When a custom-tailored suit is being made, the body of the jacket is made and fitted first. Only when that is perfect, is the collar fitted and attached.

On rack suits, to repair major problems in this area, the collar must be fully or partially removed, and tailors hate to do this since it is meticulous, time-consuming work. Consequently, many of them simply take in a tuck, and a great number of men—at least half of those reading this book—end up walking around with a bubble, or what I call a miniature knapsack on their backs.

If there is a problem in this area, tell the tailor you want it done right. If he knows you are likely to tell him to keep his suit if it does not fit, he will probably do it right the first time. Many men have this problem because they do not have perfect posture, and rack suits are manufactured for the man with perfect posture.

The jacket must next fit around the chest and waist. While being fitted for the jacket, you will, I hope, not have forgotten to put into the interior pockets those items—wallet, cigarettes and so forth—that you normally carry there. If the fitter asks you to remove them, as many will, tell him no, because that's the way you will be wearing it, and that's the way you expect it to fit. If he says it cannot be done, buy your suits elsewhere. The chest should fit smoothly all the way around, with no wrinkles or bulges and no gapping or sagging of the lapels.

If you have a thin waist, your jacket should be a bit more tightly fitted than if you are heavy. The reason is that when you sit, the jacket will tend to bulge if you have a bit of a stomach; but it won't if you don't. The best way to judge this is to sit down with the jacket buttoned after the tailor has pinned it, and see how it looks. If it pulls noticeably, have it adjusted.

The standard method used to determine if a jacket is the proper length is to stand straight with your arms straight down at your sides, your hands flat against the sides of the jacket. Now curl your fingers under the bottom of the jacket.

If the bottom just fits into the curl, it is correct. If it is visibly longer or shorter, do not buy that suit, it cannot be corrected. Naturally, if your arms are much shorter or longer than usual for a man of your size, make sure that the tailor takes this into account and makes the proper adjustments.

The tip of the jacket sleeves should come approximately five inches off the tip of the thumb, never more than five and one-half inches. If they are any higher, you will end up looking like a Broadway crapshooter, a fashion model or a dandy. If you intend to wear French cuffs with the suit, you should wear same to the fitting. Today, some suits will not accommodate French cuffs because the suit sleeves are too tight, and this is a severe limitation you should keep in mind.

Once you and the fitter have done the best you can with the suit, stand back and look at it. Walk around. Sit down—but watch those pins. If you decide to take it, give it to the fitter, making sure to tell him to save for you the material taken from the cuffs of the pants—for reasons I will discuss later.

Arrange for the date when the suit will allegedly be ready to be picked up. I say "allegedly" because, nine times out of ten, the suit is going to need more work to make it fit just right. If you must wear the suit on the fifteenth, do not plan to pick it up on the fourteenth. Try to pick it up on the sixth.

•   •   •   •   •   •   •   •   •   •   •   •   •   •   •   •   •   •

NOW THE SECOND FITTING

When you return, allow yourself enough time to see that the fit is absolutely correct. The man who wears tailor-made suits goes in for numerous time-consuming fittings. He knows how important it is or he wouldn't be spending that kind of time and money. The difference between a good fit and a bad fit is very often the second fitting, and too many men simply ignore this point. Don't. Insist on it even if it causes long faces and even if the suit is carefully wrapped up and ready to go.

The Right Suit (Left) and the Wrong Suit (Right)

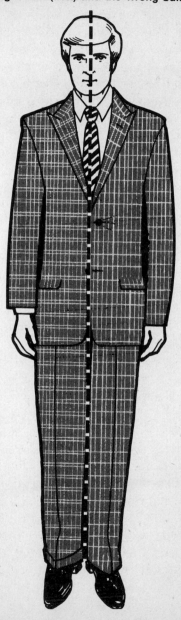

The procedure for the second fitting is exactly as before: pants first, vest next, then the entire suit. Start by standing in the five-way mirror and looking at each item, then the entire suit, from every angle. Then call over your wife, your friend, or whoever you have brought with you, and ask them for their opinion. You should bring someone with you for this second fitting. We had twenty-eight men take turns standing in a five-way mirror wearing the same suit. When we asked them if the suit jacket they were wearing was perfect, only two spotted an obvious mismatch in the plaids behind the collar. When we asked their wives to look at the same suits, twenty-two of them spotted the error. If there is anything, no matter how minor, that you do not like, tell the tailor you want it fixed. If he says it cannot be done, demand your money back and leave him the suit; if they sold it to you in the first place, then it can be fixed. You're paying for a suit that fits—so get it.

Even when you buy a suit from a good store you must take responsibility for how it fits, particularly if you are dealing with a clerk you do not know or with a large chain. About a year ago I went to pick up a summer suit that cost over $450 at one of the best stores in the country. When I tried on the jacket, the collar did not lie right, so I called over the tailor. At first he did not seem to see the problem, but after I explained it to him, he took the coat and told me not to worry, that he could fix it in a minute. Good to his word, he returned in about a minute and helped me on with the coat. When I pointed out to him that the collar still did not lie right, he adjusted—or more accurately pulled—the coat so the collar did lie flat. The minute I moved it was uneven once more. He said, "No, no, don't do that," and pulled on the jacket once more. Then, without taking his hands off my shoulders, he asked me if I was happy. I told him I was, but not with the jacket; I had always wanted a personal servant, and since the only way that suit would fit was for him to follow me around adjusting the collar, I assumed that he was volunteering for the job. He finally admitted that the suit could not be fixed, so the store replaced it and rushed the tailoring so I could take it with me on my next trip.

Two types of men go into restaurants and clothing stores. The first type is ignored; the other is served. The difference between the two is that the latter insists on service. I did not realize how few of us there were in this second group until I started telling that story to audiences. I've told it now to about fifty groups of businessmen in a variety of fields from every section of the country. When I ask if any of them have ever had a similar experience, over one-third of every audience tells me they have and ninety percent of that group admit they took the suit. If you are one of those men who in the past have been intimidated by clothing store clerks, it was probably because you knew little or nothing about clothing. After reading this book carefully you will have enough information to intimidate most of them; use it.

If, for any reason, you must take the suit to wear for a special occasion even though there are still problems that require adjustment, take it only with the understanding that it will be fixed later.

About a month or a month and a half after you have bought a suit and worn it and had it cleaned, put it on and look at it again carefully. If it has shrunk, or stretched, or sagged, or bagged, back it goes to the store for another adjustment. Most materials do have some change in fit after a time, and if this change is noticeable, it is your right and your duty as an aware consumer to take it back and have it fixed. If the store will not accommodate you, then you should no longer shop there.

One of the most important characteristics of a good suit is that it fits you and you alone—not everyone like you. Therefore, if you have any problems with size, you will be much better off if you buy your suits only in more expensive stores.

As I've mentioned already, the reason quite simply is that better stores have better fitters and tailors than less expensive stores. In the less expensive stores only minor tailoring services are offered at no extra charge, and even if you pay for more work, it probably will not be of satisfactory quality. Better stores usually charge extra for tailoring. Don't object. Although you may have to pay from $50 to $75 more for a suit, you are getting much more for your money in quality and fit. A suit that doesn't fit is wasted money, no matter how great a bargain it seems to be.

If you can afford a true custom suit, and are in the type of position where it is appropriate, I would suggest you buy one. There is nothing finer than a beautifully made custom suit. However, when you go to purchase a custom suit, you should realize that many of the places that advertise custom suits do not sell custom suits, they sell made-to-measure suits. There is nothing wrong with a made-to-measure suit. It can be a very fine garment; it may even be the ideal garment for you. Most of your better men's stores have made-to-measure departments, and if you buy a made-to-measure suit you will be able to choose fabrics, and styling, and make some requests for individual detailing such as functional button cuffs on the sleeve. (They will not want to do this, but it is one of the signs of a custom suit and you can get it done in a good made-to-measure store if you insist.)

Made-to-measure is ideal for the man who has a different size top and bottom. Over the years, I have had several clients who are weight lifters who were 44–46 jackets and have a size 32 or 34 waist. Obviously, if they want to buy a suit that fits them, they have to go to a good men's store before the season begins and ask them to order a suit from a manufacturer, with a jacket and pants that normally do not go together, a very tricky procedure at best. For these people and others who have similar fit problems, made-to-measure suits are ideal.

The people who buy full custom suits will be able to spot a made-to-measure suit from across the room, and you should be able to do so as well. The most obvious difference is that a full custom suit will be tailored to fit the arm in the same way it is tailored to fit the torso. You should also know that a good custom suit requires several fittings. If you go to a good custom shop, you will be fitted in a mock-up cotton pattern. Next, you will be fitted in a roughly cut suit without arms and, usually, without a collar. A good tailor wants to set the sleeves only after he sees how they fit. On the next visit the suit will have sleeves and probably the collar, but it will be very very rough. Two or three visits later you will have a final fitting and a beautiful suit. All of this takes eight or nine weeks and requires effort and considerable expense.

If you do decide to splurge and buy a full custom suit or a made-to-measure suit, you should know several things.

First, choose the best material you can. Ask the tailor for his assistance. A good tailor will act as your consultant. He will pick the best fabric for you. Since you're going to pay extra for tailoring, you might as well have a suit that lasts. A good made-to-measure suit should last seven or eight years and a custom suit may last even longer.

Second, avoid any extremes in design and avoid anything that is trendy. Stick with the traditional and conservative.

Third, if you go into a store that has only small swatches of material and you cannot envision what the suit will look like, ask to see bolts of cloth or a suit made of similar material.

Fourth, purchase your custom or made-to-measure suit only from a reliable dealer. Purchasing a custom suit from an unknown tailor from a distant city, whether that city be in America or in Asia, is very foolish. Unless you have had a personally good experience with a tailor, or know someone who has, it is simply too risky.

. . . .

HOW TO CHOOSE MATERIALS

The best material from which a suit can be made is wool. Wool takes dyes better than any other fabric. It does not snag; it fits well; it does not lose its shape; it is resilient; it lies better on the body; in winter, it's warmer; it outlasts any other fabric. It can also be woven into many different textures and looks.

The second-best suit fabric is a polyester and wool blend. The general rule is the more wool the richer looking the material and the better the suit. Avoid any suit made with less than forty-five percent wool, as well as those made of a blend that has the shiny look of polyester.

There is one advantage to blends—they do not wrinkle as easily as do wool suits in their price range. This makes them the suit of choice for men whose jobs require that their suits stand up to rough wear and who cannot afford high-quality wool models. I often recommend them for salesmen and others who work out of their cars, yet who must maintain a professional image. And, today, blends are found in all weights and can be worn both summer and winter. You are taking a risk however, if you buy a blend in a store you do not know, or without a label you recognize, because some blends that look wonderful when you purchase them look terrible after being dry-cleaned. Nevertheless, at least twenty percent of American businessmen would improve their image if they traded their inexpensive one hundred percent wool suits for carefully selected blends.

Texturized polyester suits can be fairly good or very bad, depending on the material. The only safe yardstick for the nonexpert is price in a reputable store. An acceptable texturized polyester can look like wool, be tailored very neatly, and hold its creases and shape remarkably well.

Polyester and custom blends are excellent in lightweight

summer suits, but because of their predominantly light colors, light linings and workmanship commensurate with their comparatively inexpensive price, they rarely last beyond one season of hard wear. The lightweight polyester and wool suit is just as comfortable in warm weather, looks richer to begin with and, in the end, is a better buy because it lasts longer.

Cotton suits and linen suits are extremely comfortable in warm weather, but any pure cotton wrinkles after only a few hours and so these suits are not practical for the man who must consistently look well groomed.

Suits are made from dozens more materials and blends but, all aspects considered, they are best avoided. Any suit with nylon or rayon in it is likely to be worthless, and suits with any percentage of mohair or silk rarely have an appropriate look for business wear. Corduroy and denim suits should be regarded as sportswear only.

The fact is that nine out of every ten good business suits are made from wool, and most successful men would not wear a blend. You too would do better if you never wore anything but wool.

· ·

PICKING COLORS AND PATTERNS

In addition to fit, the most important aspects of suits are color and pattern. The proper colors for a gentleman's suit are blue, gray, beige, brown and shades thereof. Any man who sticks within those categories and does not get into the hybrids (greenish blue or greenish gray), or weird, inappropriate shades like electric blue, will always be appropriately dressed. Blacks are hardly ever acceptable—avoid them.

Suit patterns are relatively simple. Solid suits, the staple of every man's wardrobe, should look rich and soft if they are standard business suits. Linen should look rich, but is rarely soft.

Two types of stripes are acceptable in men's business suiting. The first is a very narrow vertical pinstripe. The greatest majority of suits have white or blue stripes, and although other color stripes are acceptable, white is by far the most sophisticated. The only time a pinstripe will give you trouble is when it is orange, rust or purple. These colors are hell to coordinate with shirts and ties, and thus limit the use of the suit tremendously.

Chalk stripes are wider than pinstripes, generally about an eighth of an inch, and they are very tricky. A chalkstripe suit can label you a Wall Street executive or a Chicago gangster—and with only the slightest variation. If you think that a chalkstripe suit might look gaudy to your most conservative friend, don't buy it. You should buy one only if it looks very conservative and traditional and comes with a vest.

Several types of plaid suits are acceptable. The first is an almost invisible plaid. There is a plaid there, but you must look carefully in order to see it. The suit is usually of a dark color, with the pattern woven in threads of slightly lighter or slightly darker shades of the same color. This suit is always acceptable.

The next plaid is what I call the standard businessman's plaid. It is obviously a plaid, but it is subtle; you have to look carefully to see what colors are in it. This is traditionally a summer suit in lighter colors, but is also found in winter suiting.

The glen plaid suit is a discernible plaid, which has both definition and shape to it. It's an acceptable northern winter suit, but does not test well in the rest of the country. With this pattern, you must avoid (as you did with the pinstripe) shades of orange, purple or rust, not because they will make it a less acceptable suit, but, again, because they are so difficult to match with shirts and ties.

In the plaid category, a certain indefinable line separates acceptable business patterns from strictly sportswear patterns. Entire suits of the latter pattern should not be worn by any serious businessman. The only rule I can give is: If you think that the jacket of a plaid suit could possibly be worn separately as a sports jacket, then do not buy it.

Because we are far more conservative today than we were just a few years ago, most boxed patterns that were perfectly acceptable everywhere are now only acceptable in a few high-fashion industries and then only if they are simple with clean lines and appropriate colors. If you have any doubt about one of these avoid it—unless you were raised in a country club atmosphere. We found that those who came from blue-collar backgrounds, unless they had been in an upper-middle-class environment for at least ten years, almost always made the wrong choice.

The last acceptable pattern in suiting is really a combination of patterns lumped into the same group. I call it the beefy British look. The material is always wool and the patterns run from the traditional herringbone to the tweed and Donegal tweed. They are all basically the same in effect; they are only worn in northern climes, and they are very definitely a symbol of the upper middle class. The rule for wearing these suits is the follow-the-leader rule: If the men who run your company wear them, you may; if they do not, you may not. There are no exceptions to the rule—at least none we could find. We showed pictures of men in suits made of these beefy British materials to over one hundred executives and asked if they thought they were appropriately dressed for business. Everyone who worked in a company where they were worn by the men at the top said yes, and everyone who worked for a company where they were not worn by the men at the top said no.

While some other suit patterns might be acceptable for business wear, they are rare, tricky and should be avoided. If any man wishes to be safe, he will stick with the aforementioned. If you must have razzle-dazzle in your clothing, save it for sportswear.

• • • • • • • • • • • • • • • • • •

THE PSYCHOLOGICAL ASSOCIATION
OF SUITS

Because the suit is the central power garment in any business combination, it is the garment that will most influence any viewer's judgment of the wearer. It immediately establishes authority, credibility and likability—those qualities most important in any business interaction.

The darker the suit, the more authority it transmits. A black suit is more authoritative than a dark blue, although it is much too powerful for most men and should rarely be worn anyway because of its funereal overtones. The most authoritative pattern is the pinstripe, followed in descending order by the solid, the chalk stripe and the plaid. If you need to be more authoritative, stick with dark pinstripes. But if you are a very large man, or if you already have a great sense of presence, or if you have a gruff or swarthy appearance, it is best to trim down your authority so that people will not be frightened by you. This can best be accomplished by wearing medium-range teal blue, light gray, beige and brown.

Suits that will give you the most credibility with people of the upper middle class are dark blue and dark gray solids and pinstripes of both colors. The American Brahmins find men wearing dark teal blue pinstripes the most credible, followed by banker's gray. The navy-blue pinstripe which works with everyone else does not work too well with them, but that does not mean you should throw out your navy-blue suit. Only the dark blue solid will give you high credibility with the lower middle class.

If you must be authoritative and credible with both the upper middle class and the lower middle class at the same time—say you are a banker or a lawyer and must deal daily with a wide variety of people—light and medium-range blue, medium-range brown, and light gray accomplish this, although light blue is generally not considered an acceptable suit for the truly conservative businessman.

The suits in which men are more likely to be liked are, again, light gray and light blue solids and medium-range business plaids. Bright plaids are likely to turn off the upper middle class.

The following examples of the most important business suits provide more specific information. If a suit is categorized as "neutral," that means it will neither help nor hurt you, but is not recommended. "Before the public" means speaking before any group of people where television is not present.

Solid Navy: Every man should have at least one in his wardrobe. The upper middle class likes it. The lower middle class likes it and respects you in it. Large men should not wear it. Small men should not wear it unless they are going on television or on a stage. Heavy men should wear it. On thin men, it's neutral. Before the public, it's fine. On television it's fine. If you're a weak authority figure, it's excellent. If you're a strong authority figure, it's bad.

Solid Dark Gray: This is a strong positive with the upper middle class, a negative with the lower middle class. It is excellent for large men and negative for small men. It is good for heavy men, neutral on thin men. Before the public it is excellent, as it is on television. If you are a weak authority figure, use it. If you are a strong authority figure, it is neutral. If you are going to be dealing with high-powered executives that you have never met, and you have no idea of their backgrounds or style, it is your safest choice.

Dark Blue Pinstripe: It is positive with the upper middle class, strongly negative with the lower middle class. Very tall men should not wear it unless they plan to intimidate those they meet. Short men should wear it. Heavy men should wear it. Thin men should not wear it. No striped suit should every be worn on television; they look beautiful on the monitor, but if there is reception trouble at home, the pin-stripes jump all over the place and reduce concentration or attention. The pinstripe is an excellent suit for addressing the public. If you have authority problems, it is the best. If you come on too strong, it's bad. If you have a meeting with a conservative company for the first time this would be a good choice.

Dark Gray Pinstripe: The upper middle class likes it. The lower middle class does not; they are offended or intimidated by men in this suit. On tall and short men, it's neutral. On heavy men, it's positive, one of the better suits for them. On thin men, it's a negative. It's positive before the public. It's positive for men with authority problems, negative for anyone who comes on too strong. This is the ideal suit to wear if you have to deal with an American Brahmin or wish to sell yourself as an expert to American business.

Medium Blue Solid: This is a positive with all classes, a suit that can be worn anywere. Tall men should wear it and short men should wear it. It is neutral on heavy men, neutral on thin men and neutral before the public. On television, it is excellent. It is good for people with authority problems when they are dealing with subordinates. It works well for strong authority figures who wish to open the lines of communication between themselves and their subordinates.

Medium Gray Solid: This is positive with the upper middle class, negative with the lower middle class. On tall men, it is excellent. On short men, it is neutral. On heavy men, it is negative. On thin men, it is positive. It is neutral before the public and on television. If you have trouble giving orders, it is neutral. If you are a strong authority figure it's a positive, taking the edge off your aggressiveness. Women executives responded very positively to men wearing this suit.

Medium Gray Pinstripe: This is liked by the upper middle class, disliked by the lower middle class. It is a negative on tall men, positive on short men. It is neutral on heavy men, thin men and before the public. It is positive on those who find it difficult to give orders, negative on those who come on too strong. It is the favorite suit of the American Brahmins, and they respond positively to men who wear it.

Medium Blue Pinstripe: This is positive with the upper middle class, negative with the lower middle class. It is negative on short men, neutral on heavy men, negative on thin men, neutral before the public. It is good authority-boosting suit and also, surprisingly, positive if you come on strong.

Light Blue Solid: This is positive with both classes. It is positive on tall men and thin men, negative on short men and heavy men. It is negative before the public, not bad on television. If you have trouble giving orders, do not wear it. If you are too strong, it is good. It is also the trickiest suit to buy; men from both blue-collar backgounds and from middle-class backgrounds usually pick the wrong shades—and there are more wrong shades of light blue than right ones. Unless you come from an upper-class environment, and are sure of your taste, leave this suit alone.

Light Gray Solid: It is positive with both classes and on tall men. It is negative on short men, negative on heavy men, positive on thin men. It is negative before the public, positive on television. It is negative for those who have trouble giving orders, positive if you come on strong.

Dark Brown Solid: This is a positive with the upper middle class unless you are presenting yourself as a financial expert. The lower middle class likes, respects and trusts you in it. It is negative on small men. On thin men, it is neutral. It is a positive on big and heavy men. It is positive before the public and on television. It is neutral if you are trying to be more authoritative but positive if you are too authoritative. Although not as effective as traditional blue and gray, it is a newly accepted business suit. It is also an immediate and strong negative with people who are Jewish, particularly those over fifty-five, although I do not know the reason for this aversion.

Dark Brown Pinstripe: It is positive with the upper middle class, and neutral with the lower middle class. Tall men should not wear it. On short men it is neutral. Thin men should not wear it. Heavy men should wear it. It's good for men with authority problems, yet still neutral on men who come on too strong. It is a very high credibility suit.

Upscale (Obviously Expensive) Dark Teal Blue Solids and Pinstripes: These are the very best suits to wear if you are dealing with Brahmins. They also work well with upper-middle-class executives. They are neutral with blue-collar people, probably because they do not recognize them. Most expensive teal blue suits are only available in a very expensive material or at least they have been mainly available in those up to now.

Medium Brown Solid: This suit is positive with the lower middle class, the upper middle class and the Brahmins. Tall men should wear it and short men should wear it. Both heavy and thin men should avoid it. An excellent suit to wear when dealing with or speaking to the public, both on and off television when you are not dealing with very serious matters. It is not a good suit for people with authority problems, but it is the best suit for men who have a very rough appearance.

Medium Brown Pinstripe: The only pinstripe suit that tests well with all groups in our society. On tall and short men, it is neutral. Heavy men should wear it as, surprisingly, should thin men. It tests as neutral on both strong and weak authority figures. It is positive before the public, and negative on television. Like most brown suits, it does not work well when the wearer is dealing with a serious subject.

• • • • • • • • • • • • • • • • • • • •

THE SUIT VERSUS THE SPORTS JACKET

Sooner or later, most of my clients ask if it is ever appropriate to wear a sports jacket to the office. Some indicate that other men in their firm do. The answer is no, unless you work for a nonsuit company in a nonsuit industry. In every comparative test I have ever conducted in middle American industry, using such standards as integrity, ability or even "Which man would you want as a friend?" the suit has won hands down. The only exception is when the effect of an immediately recognizable upper-middle-class sports jacket, such as a camel hair worn with a pair of dark blue slacks, is measured against the effect of an obviously lower-middle-class suit. But, otherwise, the suit wins in all other comparisons.

In nonsuit companies, particularly high-tech companies dominated by engineers, most of whom come from blue-collar backgrounds, wearing a suit can mark you as an outsider. The sports jacket in that environment gives the wearer an advantage, in that it allows him to be part of the high-tech team, without adopting a negative authority uniform. If your immediate boss and your co-workers are not wearing suits, that does not necessarily mean that you work for a nonsuit company. You can be sure you are working for a nonsuit company if your CEO comes to work regularly without a suit. If he does, leave yours at home and you will be obeying the first rule of dressing for success; you will be following the leader.

There is an exception to this rule. If you are a lawyer or an accountant you must wear a suit and a very good one. Your clients, like the rest of us, have been conditioned to trust only suit wearers with important matters which they do not understand.

3

How to Maximize the Power of Shirts

In the Middle Ages, when a sovereign committed a crime that put him at loggerheads with the greatest power of the time—the Church—he would often expiate himself by putting on a hair shirt and prostrating himself before a cathedral. To all the other potentates in the area, he thereby signaled one of two developments: either he was working himself back into good graces, or his property was up for grabs. The shirt that you wear in the twentieth century can be just as significant a signal to everyone around you. It can either say that you're in good graces, or that your job, your power and your future are up for grabs.

CHOOSING MATERIALS

The most common and most acceptable material from which shirts are made is cotton. The advantages of a cotton shirt are substantial. It feels good to wear; it's soft and smooth; it looks very rich; and it breathes, making it comparatively cool in the summer and in stuffy office buildings. Unfortunately, cotton wrinkles like hell when you're wearing it. And if you must use a commercial laundry, you are undoubtedly well aware of how difficult it is to have a cotton shirt ironed well enough so that you don't start the day looking as if you slept in it. Nonetheless, a good-quality, well-tailored cotton shirt offers the look you should try to achieve.

You can find polyester and cotton blends that are suitable. The advantage of these is that they hardly wrinkle, and after long hours of wear they look better than does one hundred percent cotton. For most men who do not change their shirts during the workday and still want to look consistently neat, they are almost the perfect shirt. They do, however, tend to retain the heat and therefore are not as cool and comfortable as cotton in the summer.

The most popular of these blends is sixty-five percent polyester and thirty-five percent cotton. Although you can find dress shirts made of these 65–35 percent blends that are acceptable, most are not. In addition to being uncomfortable, they often look cheap. If you decide to buy a blend, buy one that is at least fifty percent cotton. The more cotton in a blend, generally the richer looking the shirt. Unfortunately, the best blend ever put on the market, eighty-five percent cotton and fifteen percent polyester, was dropped because it didn't sell. It was put out by the Arrow Shirt Company after they discontinued my favorite shirt, the one hundred percent cotton wash-and-wear model which they sold for three or four years. Obviously, I was not the only one who liked this shirt, because in the few years it was on the market it constituted twenty-five percent of Arrow's total dress shirt business. Unfortunately, the chemical they used to make the cotton

wash-and-wear destroyed the material; and they started getting too many complaints and too many returns, so they
discontinued it. Frankly, I wish they had not. If they come up
with a better replacement, which I'm sure they will, I will be
the first one to run out and buy it—and I would advise you, if
you travel for a living or your shirts must look as neat at the
end of the day as at the beginning, or you can't stand
polyester, that you do the same. In fact, I would advise the
Arrow Shirt Company to put that one hundred percent cotton
wash-and-wear shirt back on the market with a simple warning on the label telling buyers that it will wear out more
quickly than a regular cotton shirt. There are many businessmen who would be willing to sacrifice durability and dollars
for comfort and style.

You can, if you are already very rich and very successful,
or if you desire to have an affair with an Italian contessa, wear
silk shirts. If you fit into neither of the above categories, then
don't wear silk, I don't care how rich it makes you feel. A good
silk shirt will cost you $200. Once you've paid for it, if the
laundry doesn't ruin it on the first try, they will on the second.
Silk very rarely has an acceptable look for business purposes;
and when was the last time you heard of anyone asking for a
raise wearing a $200 silk shirt?

Always avoid any shirt that has a shiny look to it, as well
as all see-through weaves. No shiny shirt is acceptable for
business wear anywhere, and while the see-through shirt is in
excellent taste in parts of Europe, it is most certainly not so in
the United States. This includes some very expensive custom
voiles (a very lightweight cotton) that are sold in the best
shops in London, Rome and Paris.

• • • • • • • • • • • • • • • • • • •

READY-MADES, SEMI-CUSTOMS AND FULL-CUSTOMS

There are three types of shirts you can buy, in terms of method of manufacture: mass-produced (or ready-made), semi-custom (or made-to-measure) and full-custom. As little as six years ago eighty percent of the men in America fit comfortably into ready-made shirts. Shirts in standard collar and sleeve sizes were available in adequate variety and suitable quality in a number of price levels. Today this is no longer true.

The shirt manufacturers have introduced what they refer to as the average-length dress shirt. This shirt is made in fewer sizes. Obviously, this saves the manufacturers a great deal of money and it is wonderful for them, but it does not work too well for the consumer. By the standards the manufacturers themselves set for proper fit just a few years ago, less than one-third of American males can get a properly fitted shirt in most stores today. In the past, when a manufacturer produced a shirt with a 14½ neck size, he produced at least two sleeve lengths, 32 and 33. Now most manufacturers produce only one size which they mark 14½, 32–33, but which is in most cases a 14½ collar and a 33-inch sleeve. They have done the same with neck sizes 15–15½, which used to come in at least four sleeve lengths, 32, 33, 34 and 35. Now these shirts come in only two sizes marked 32–33 and 33–34. Once again, these shirts are actually measured to fit the man with the longer arm. About four months ago I actually saw a shirt marked 15 33–34–35. The makers of this shirt must think they are selling to Plasticman. When I measured the sleeve it measured 34½, which made it inadequate for a man whose actual sleeve length was 35 and ridiculous for the man whose sleeve length is 32. Men with larger neck sizes 16–16½ find themselves with the same problem. While at one time the shirts with that neck size came in at least two sleeve lengths, 34 and 35, today they have combined the two and, once again, the shirts fit only the man with the longer arm.

Those who happen to be lucky enough to fit into these shirts must wonder what men who have shorter arms do. Well, according to the manufacturers, they are supposed to button the second button in a horizontal two-button cuff. In fact, that is the characteristic of these shirts—they have a special cuff with two buttons. When the second button is buttoned, the cuff closes so tightly around the wrist that it piles the extra material above it. This means that the wearer has a bulge in his suit, no place to put his watch and, in most cases, a shirt that fits so poorly that he is embarrassed to take off his jacket.

The average-length dress shirt, however, creates more problems than just sleeves that do not fit. Shirt manufacturers in the past determined the size of the yoke and body of a shirt by looking at the neck size and sleeve length. When the neck size or sleeve size changed, the yoke and body size changed as well. They had quite a bit of research indicating that this was necessary, but of course today that is all thrown out the window. As a result, you can see men who pay good money for shirts with their shoulders running down their arms or up toward their necks. When I mentioned this problem to several men in the shirt industry, they said it would not make a perceptible difference. But I noticed each of them was wearing a shirt that fitted him properly.

If these average-length dress shirts were only found in inexpensive models there could be some excuse for it. After all, there has to be a correlation between the cost of manufacturing a product and the price. However, today you can go into very good department stores and buy expensive shirts, with designer names on them, that run at least $35 to $40 apiece with average-length sleeve sizes. That, of course, is ridiculous, because one of the hallmarks of the well-dressed gentlemen is that his clothing fits him and not everyone near his size.

Luckily, some of the better shirt makers are still making dress shirts in a full range of sizes. If you are easy to fit—if you can wear a standard collar size and common collar style, a standard sleeve length, and if you are neither too chunky nor too slim—then there is no compelling reason for you to buy anything other than ready-made shirts. (Generally, I would suggest that the average man pay no less than $18 and no more than $42 for a mass-produced shirt.) You can buy a ready-made shirt one day and wear it the next. You do not have to buy any minimum quantity. And sometimes you can hit on a good sale.

Made-to-measure shirts are exactly that, although almost never advertised as such. The stores that sell them would like you to believe you are getting a full-custom shirt, but you are not. At these stores, a number of measurements are taken and you are given a choice of materials and collar and cuff styles. Your shirts are then made up accordingly. Usually, the minimum order is four shirts, and delivery takes about six weeks.

The major advantage of the made-to-measure is, obviously, fit. With ready-made shirts, even the better ones, you are limited to whole and half sizes for the collars and whole sizes for the sleeve lengths. And, generally, only God and the manufacturer know what the body size is. You also have to take whatever collar and cuff style you get. With semi-custom, the collars, as well as the sleeves, can be fitted as closely as quarter sizes; the shirt's body can be made to your individual requirements; and you have a wide choice of fabrics and styles.

The only problem is that they still are not full-custom

shirts. They are based on standard patterns (using the closest one to what you need), cut on automatic cutters, and made in a small selection of fabrics. Don't get me wrong! I'm not knocking them; I only want you to know what you are getting. As a matter of fact, I wear them myself, and feel they offer the best shirt available for the money.

The prices start at about $30 and go up to about $75, depending on the fabrics you choose. And unless you have one shoulder much lower than the other, or some other physical abnormality that makes full-custom shirts a necessity, I would suggest semi-customs to anyone who can afford them, can buy four or more shirts at a time, and can wait six weeks or so for delivery.

The full-custom shirt, while it offers the ultimate luxury of absolutely individual tailoring and generally the finest fabrics available, is just not realistic for most men. Prices start at about $75; fittings are time-consuming; and since everything is done by hand specifically for you, delivery is rarely fast. In addition, given the realities of the typical laundry service, the luxury is just not worth the agony. Still, if you have that kind of money to spend on clothes, there is no shirt to equal the full-custom.

* * * * * * * * * * * * * * * * * * * *

HOW TO GET A GOOD FIT

No matter what type of shirt you wear, it should fit well. A surprising number of men really don't even know what size they need, and consequently there is always something just a little bit off with their shirts. You should have your shirt sizes taken at least once a year, by someone competent enough to do it right.

Obviously, in the less expensive stores, they probably

won't even be able to find a tape measure, much less know how to use it. So find the most expensive store in your area and single out the most experienced-looking clerk. Have him take your measurements. If you can afford it, buy a shirt from him. If you cannot afford it, and feel uncomfortable at having put him to the work without making a purchase, buy the shirt anyway. Then take it back the next day for a refund; say it did not match your suit and you saw one down the street that goes perfectly.

The first area where a shirt should fit is around the waist. The shirt should be smooth all the way around, with no bagginess or bunching of material anywhere, but still loose enough to allow comfortable movement and to allow you to sit down without having the material pulling at the buttons.

The second area of fit is the length. A shirt should be long enough so that it does not pull up out of your pants during normal activity. When you buy a shirt, check the length; and when you find a comfortable one, stick with that brand and cut. Also important to the length, particularly if you are tall or chunky, is how many buttons a shirt has and where they are placed. The standard shirt has a six-button front, including the collar button. If you are tall or chunky and the bottom hits you only an inch or so below the waistband of your pants, then after only the most minimum of activity the button will slip out above the pants and the opening below it will spread apart—which looks awful.

If you have this problem, make sure the bottom button falls at least three inches below the waistband of your pants. If it doesn't, get an extra one sewn on. (Some moderately priced, and almost all expensive ready-mades, have a seven-button front, and you can always request it if you wear semi-customs.)

In another attempt to save pennies at the expense of the consumer, some manufacturers, including a few that produce very expensive designer dress shirts, are making their shirts without tails. This means that if you are above average size, or moderately active, your shirt is likely to pop out of your pants. You cannot tell if a shirt is made without tails until you take it home and open the package, but if you end up with one you should take it back and complain loudly to the management. Tell them that if you are forced to waste your time again you will take your business elsewhere—and do.

The third area of fit is the collar. This is the most crucial place, and also where most men are wearing the wrong size. They had the right size a year ago, but they've put on fifteen or so pounds, and now that size is too tight. The problem often is that it may not feel too tight, but it looks it—the collar wrinkles because of the tightness. This happens most frequently with soft collar shirts, such as oxford cloths.

Usually, middle-aged men wear their collars too tightly and men in their fifties, who are beginning to lose weight and get a few wrinkles in their necks, tend to wear them too loosely.

The best way to check to see if you are wearing the right size collar is to button it, then try to slip two fingers down the front of the collar; if you are able to move them up and down without discomfort your collar is large enough. Then repeat the same experiment using the four fingers of one hand; if they move easily, your collar is too large. In either case, have yourself remeasured.

If you do wear semi-custom or full-custom shirts and have a wide choice of collar types, you should also know that, ultimately, the height of the collar in the back should correspond to the length of your neck. A short collar on a man with a long neck emphasizes his problem, and a high collar on a man with a short neck makes him look like a turtle.

The height of the collar in the front depends almost entirely on age. If you are young, with no wrinkles, then the criterion should be how well a particular collar goes with your suit. If you are older and beginning to get wrinkles, get the collar up as high as looks decent to cover the wrinkles.

Collars should be spread in such a way as to be compatible with the lapels of your suit, and to hold the knot of your tie comfortably—with neither a lot of space showing (in which case the tie knot is too small for the collar spread) nor bulges (which means that the knot is too large for the spread).

While I'm on the subject of collars, I should point out that dress shirts no longer have to have removable plastic collar stays. Today, there are shirts with new thinner permanent stays that work beautifully; you can wash them, iron them and send them to commercial laundries without worrying about the telltale outline of a stay appearing on a collar when they are pressed. However, shirts with removable stays are still your safest choice because some dress shirts and a lot of sport shirts are still being sold with the old-fashioned thick plastic collar stays sewn in.

When you have removable stays, always take them out before sending your shirts to the laundry. If they are left in, the heat of commercial irons is so great that the stays can be fused to the collar and you can be left with a mess. Also, if you have a number of shirts with different-length collars, make sure that you use the correct stays with each shirt. If the stays are too short for the collar, then they will not do what they were designed to do, and if the collar is not stiff enough, it will flop and curl. If the stays are too long and the back end is pressed tightly against the fold of the collar, they tend to create wrinkles or bulge against the material, showing their outline.

The arm holes of a properly fitting shirt should be open enough to allow comfortable movement, but if they are too open, so much material is required for the sleeves that the sleeves are baggy (this generally is not a problem with better shirts). The shoulder seams of shirts, those seams dividing the body of the shirt from the sleeves, should fall slightly over the edge of the shoulder bone, never more than one inch.

Shirtsleeves are measured from a point midway between the shoulders down to the wrists. Most men do not know this, and therefore do not understand why putting on a few pounds necessitates longer sleeves. When you are measured for a shirt, make sure that both arms are measured, not just one. If one arm is significantly longer than the other (and it's so with a surprising percentage of men), you will have to wear semi-custom shirts to get the sleeves right.

The end of a shirtsleeve should come just a fraction below the wrist bone, and should extend about one half inch below your suit jacket sleeve. (To get this right, always have the suit jacket adjusted to your shirt, not vice versa.)

Three inches is the standard length of the cuffs on business shirts. If you wear button cuffs, two buttons make for a smoother look than one, but this is a fairly insignificant point. If you wear French cuffs and cuff links (generally considered dressier than buttons), be prepared to get your shirts back from the laundry frequently with the cuffs folded and pressed wrong.

Button cuffs should fit as closely to the wrist as they can and still allow adequate movement. While we are discussing cuff buttons, there is one button that can be very important— the one that is used to close the placket. This is the area above the cuff where the sleeve is split. This button, and its corresponding buttonhole, is normally found on better shirts and is always requested by those who know when buying a semi or full-custom model. French cuffs should be slightly looser. Although a gentleman would never wear a bulky watch for business wear, that is sometimes a factor in how a cuff fits, so you should consider it.

When you are buying a shirt, every point mentioned

above is important, because they all come together to give the correct total fit you need. And although I will not tell you to consider every aspect of a shirt before buying it—mainly because I know you probably would not take the trouble to do it—you should check those points that are most crucial to you.

· · · · · · · · · · · · · · · · · ·

PICKING PATTERNS AND COLORS

In any test, the most acceptable dress shirts—those that elicit the best responses for taste, class, credibility and effectiveness—are still, and will continue to be, white and solid colors. When properly color-coordinated or contrasted, solids go with every suit and every tie made. Of the solids, blue is the most popular, followed by the other pastels, the paler the better. A gaudy, loud yellow is not a good business shirt, but a pale, pastel yellow is.

White shirts are so effective they must be put in a separate category. In our original testing we found that men who wore white shirts were thought to be more credible, competent and honest than men who wore other colors. Our more recent tests have not only confirmed this, but given us additional positive information about white shirts. Anyone who is selling an important product (which, of course, includes themselves) or appearing before an important group, and wears anything but a white shirt is being very foolish. Even blue shirts, which are the best second choice, do not test nearly as well as white. Men in white shirts are considered by almost everyone to be more intelligent, honest, successful and powerful than men wearing any other color. When IBM first put in its white shirt rule everyone laughed at them—and IBM laughed all the way to the bank. If you are in a business where you have to sell your products and/or your ideas to other people, particularly executives, you should wear only white shirts. If you do you will substantially increase your chances of laughing on the way to the bank yourself. The only group with whom white shirts did not test well were technicians, particularly engineers. In spite of the fact that it was their favorite shirt they were much friendlier, more open and trusting when they dealt with men who wore shirts with color and/or patterns. They were definitely impressed with men who wore solid blue shirts, including end-on-end and oxford button-downs, and were much more likely to buy their high-tech products or take their advice.

If your principal business associates are over forty-five years old, or if you must deal frequently with people from the lower middle class (say you are a banker or a lawyer), never wear pink or pale lavender shirts, which have negative masculine associations. If you are black, avoid the same colors, as they have unfortunate but very real prejudicial associations. Never wear a solid red shirt, no matter who you are or what you do; it is never acceptable.

If you have a sallow complexion, you should avoid any shade of gold, green or gray, colors which generally do not enhance anyone's facial coloration.

To avoid looking like a gangster, always make sure that your shirt is lighter than your suit, and your tie darker than your shirt (with some summer exceptions). In solid shirting, generally the paler, more subtle shade is the upper-middle-class choice and the icy, shiny, darker, harsher color is the lower-middle-class symbol.

A very real practical historical basis exists for this. In earlier times, expensive shirts were made of superior-quality materials, and the materials took dye very easily, which allowed for the lighter shades. Cheaper shirts were made of harder fabrics, more resistant to dye, and were mass-produced in far greater quantities. In order to dye them evenly at all, the dyes had to be dark and strong. Now, with improved dyeing techniques and fabrics, even cheaper shirts can approximate the pale colors of their more expensive counterparts, but the psychological class associations of color still remain.

When buying solid color shirts, if you are on a budget and must buy as cheaply as possible, I suggest that you first go to the most expensive stores you can find. Look at the colors and textures of the best, most appropriate shirts, and then approximate them as closely as you can with shirts in your price range. With practice, you'll be able to do remarkably well, achieve the right look, and do so at a cost you can afford. As a matter of fact, you will also be able to take some pride in bettering your more affluent counterparts: Any fool can get the proper look for $40 a shirt, but it takes talent to do it for $16.

Shirt Materials

Oxford Cloth

End-on-End Weave

Several types of shirt are basically solid, but have a texture or pattern because the colored threads are interwoven with white threads. These are the end-on-end weave and the oxford cloth, and both are not only highly acceptable shirts, they also add a richness, texture and variety to the solid look (see drawing on page 82). In addition, end-on-end and oxford cloths, because of the white threading, are more acceptable in darker colors than is solid broadcloth.

A variation of the solid-color shirt is the pastel-colored shirt with white collar and/or cuffs. When Lee Iacocca wore one on television it became instantly acceptable even in the most conservative industries, proving once again that the name of the game is "follow the leader."

The second acceptable pattern in shirting is the simple stripe (see drawing on page 84). The stripes may range from the very thin pinstripe to as wide as one-sixteenth of an inch. Some wider stripes might be acceptable, but unless you are sure, avoid them. Generally, the thinner and closer the stripes the more acceptable the shirt. As a general rule, if you are not dealing with the best material, avoid stripes if they are more than one quarter inch apart.

The stripe can be of any color that coordinates or contrasts with the suit, as long as it is on a white background. As with solids, however, colors that are not flattering to the skin—gray, gold and green—should be avoided.

White or pastel stripes on a pastel background are acceptable for variety, but only in the most expensive shirts. They are recommended for business only if you are dealing with American or British Brahmins. It is only with this elite group that they tested well. Pastel stripes hardly ever tested positively on shirts with white backgrounds. The darker the stripe, the more acceptable it is. For instance, my tests of a deep maroon show a higher acceptance than a bright red. The same is true of a dark blue versus a light blue.

Proper Business-Shirt Stripes

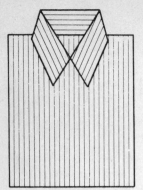

Pinstripe

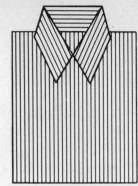

Chalk Stripe

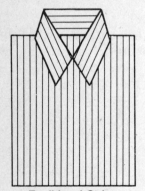

Traditional Stripe

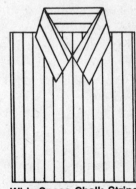

Wide-Space Chalk Stripe

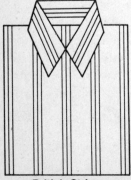

British Stripe

Simple Wide Stripe

Unless you really know what you are doing, the stripes should always be a single color, on a single color background. Some multicolored stripes are acceptable, but since there are so many variations of these, I cannot offer any hard rules. Basically, the multicolored stripe projects a lower-middle-class association in most people.

Shirt stripes should always be clearly defined and not have a washed-out look. In striped patterns, all-cotton shirts usually offer a crisper effect than the blends.

Plaid shirts are no longer acceptable in business. A simple delicate box plaid, which worked well years ago in some conservative industries, now no longer works even in the high-fashion industries. If you still have plaid shirts in your business wardrobe, I suggest that you reassign them to sportswear use and save them for your leisure time.

For business wear, unacceptable shirt patterns far outnumber the acceptable ones. Unacceptable patterns include: any wavy stripe or ribbon weave; almost every satin pattern; almost every dot pattern; almost any higher woven or intricate pattern, particularly Jacquard (including those described as the Jacquard stripe); and any pattern that tends to look washed out. As with stripes, multicolored shirts in any pattern are generally unacceptable, with the very nature of the colors tending toward lower-middle-class associations. Again, if you're not sure what you're doing, stay away from multicolored shirts.

Everything I have said about materials, colors and patterns of shirts is based on years of testing in many different ways, but always with the same goals in mind: How successfully does this shirt project taste and class, and how effective is it in giving the wearer the look he should have for success in his particular undertaking?

• • • • • • • • • • • • • • • • • • • •

HOW ABOUT SHORT SLEEVES?

If you intend to take anything I've said in this book at all seriously, note well the following: You will never, ever, as long as you live, wear a short-sleeve shirt for any business purpose, no matter whether you are the office boy or the president of the company, unless you are selling to a short-sleeve company located in the palm tree South in the summer.

In a study I conducted one summer several years ago, I used 200 executives, 100 who never wore short-sleeve shirts, and 100 who frequently wore them. The study sought to determine whether long or short sleeves had any effect on the authority of the executive over his secretary's performance in terms of the amount of time she spent on the job. I set out to measure absenteeism, late arrivals to work and lunch hours that extended beyond the officially allotted time.

The differential for absenteeism was an insignificant one percent, but it was a bad time to test for this factor, since most of the secretaries took their vacations in the summer and were less likely to stay home from work purposefully than they would have been in other periods when vacations provided no break. But the secretaries of those men who wore short-sleeve shirts were late twelve percent more often than those who wore long-sleeve shirts, and came back from lunch late 132 percent more often.

Short-sleeve shirts are symbols of the lower middle class, and therefore pack no psychological authority or power. Upper-middle-class executives, who can afford good cotton long-sleeve shirts and have air-conditioned offices, just do not wear short-sleeve shirts, as well they shouldn't.

• •

WHAT TO DO ABOUT MONOGRAMS

My favorite story about monograms concerns an executive who ran one of America's largest sales forces. He hired me regularly to dress the people who worked for him, but never in the seven years of our association did he ever ask my advice. I saw no reason why he should; he was one of the best-dressed men I've ever met. He had an extensive wardrobe of custom-made suits and shirts that were made for him by one of the best tailors on Savile Row, and he made trips to London twice a year simply to keep up his stock.

One day over lunch he asked me what I thought of his shirts, all of which had monograms on the cuffs. I said that, in my opinion, the cuff probably was not the best place for a monogram, but I was not sure. The minute I said that he became defensive. He asked if I had done any testing, and, when I said no he said, "Well, let's do it!" I tried to talk him out of doing a test aimed just at his shirts, but it was his company and his money so when he insisted, I went ahead. We took a picture of his hand showing the monogram cuff and another picture with the cuff turned around so the monogram didn't show. Both pictures showed his well-manicured hand, expensive watch and an obviously expensive suit cuff touching the shirt. We showed the pictures to a cross section of businesspeople, and asked them to guess what he did for a living. His hand and watch looked elegant so almost everyone guessed that he was a member of an upper-middle-class profession, a doctor, lawyer, executive. When we showed the picture with the monogram showing, the answers were not as positive; in fact seventeen percent of the respondents identified him as a hooker-booker.

I chose not to deliver that report personally; I sent it to

him by mail and although the next time we met he didn't say a word, I noticed his shirts were no longer monogrammed on the cuff.

I personally find monograms somewhat ostentatious, but if you have reached the middle or upper level of success, and like monograms, there is no reason not to have them. I suggest, however, that you use discreet, sophisticated lettering, no intricate scroll work, and that you have the monograms stitched on the left side about three inches above the belt line—in the European style—rather than way up on top of your nipple.

Monograms

**Simple,
Discreet Lettering
Works Best**

**Large,
Elaborate Lettering
Is in Poor Taste**

• • • • • • • • • • • • • • • • • • •

WHAT ABOUT POCKETS?

One of the little ironies of our culture is that one of the marks of a very expensive dress shirt is that it usually has no pockets, because the man who can afford that shirt usually does not want or need the pocket. Obviously, if you must wear the less expensive ready-mades and the ones you can afford have pockets, you're stuck, although this should not be a matter of any great concern. But if you are buying expensive shirts, or semi- or full-customs, do get them without pockets, since they look much better. Under no circumstances should a dress shirt have two pockets. Shirt pockets should be of the simple patch type, with no flap or button.

• • • • • • • • • • • • • • • • • • •

NO-NO DETAILS

No dress shirt should have epaulets or decorative pleats or cowboy yokes or be sewn with thread that is different in color from that of the shirt fabric. Buttons should be plain and simple and usually white.

• • • • • • • • • • • • • • • • • • •

HERE'S A BASIC SHIRT WARDROBE

One way to buy shirts will ensure that you always have what you need: Every time you buy a suit, immediately buy shirts (and ties) to wear with that suit. Too many men say to themselves, "Well, I'll get this suit, but I already have shirts and ties." When the suit comes, the existing shirts and ties usually do not go well together but are worn anyway.

The result is that the total look is inappropriate, and no

matter how careful a man has been in selecting the suit, if everything doesn't blend, the effort is wasted. Other men buy shirts on impulse, frequently guessing that they will match some suit at home—which they generally don't. The result is a bad combination and an unsuccessful look.

The number of shirts you should have for each suit depends almost entirely on how frequently you must wear the suit and how fast your laundry is. I would suggest three shirts (and two ties) as the absolute minimum for each suit. The more suits you have, the fewer shirts you will need for each one, and the more shirts you will have that will go with several different suits—but that in no way eliminates the need always to buy shirts for specific suits rather than trying to buy one shirt to go with more than one suit.

Assuming that your basic suit wardrobe is the usual mix of grays, blues and browns, I suggest the following as a basic shirt wardrobe, given that the appropriate shades of color are chosen for each suit:

4 dressy solid white broadcloth, to be worn regularly.
1 dressy solid white broadcloth, to be kept in a plastic bag, clean, ironed and always ready for emergencies. (After a year, or as needed, buy a new emergency shirt and make the old one one of your everyday white shirts.)
2 solid white oxford cloth with button-down collar.
2 dark blue pencil stripes on a white background.
3 solid blue broadcloth shirts.
2 blue end-on-end weaves.
2 blue oxford cloths with button-down collars.
2 dark blue pinstripes on white background.
1 solid pale yellow broadcloth.
2 soft solid pastels with contrasting collar and cuffs.
6 other shirts in any color or pattern (other than the forbidden ones) according to your taste and needs.

4

How to Pick Your Most Important Status Symbols: Your Ties

When I was first married, my wife and I were invited to an old friend's house for dinner. Soon after I arrived I was introduced to his son and a few of his friends. They were the most outlandish hippies I had met until that moment. It was the late sixties and I was accustomed to young men with long hair, but these were the first men I had seen wearing earrings. The rest of their outfits were just as bizarre to me. I was particularly surprised because my friend is very conservative. In fact, I often kid him when we get into political arguments about his being somewhere to the right of Genghis Khan.

When the young men learned that I was the author of *Dress for Success*, they immediately gathered around me. I expected them to be antagonistic, but to my surprise they were very interested in learning how I did my research and they asked me how I would go about dressing their rock band.

Although we never agreed on that—or almost anything else—
we had a pleasant evening and a very pleasant conversation.
One of the things that made the evening so memorable was
that at one point all of the young men got together, put their
hands on a Beatles album, and swore that they would never,
ever, ever wear a tie.

Ten years later I was invited to the wedding of my
friend's son. I had not seen him in all that time and was a
little surprised by the change. There he stood, wearing a
traditional tuxedo, with a short haircut, and looking as if he
could be working for IBM. His father proudly announced to
everyone who would listen that he had given up playing in his
rock band, finished his education, found a good job and was
doing very well.

When I looked around the room I recognized some of the
same young people I had met at that dinner many years
before. They were evenly divided into two groups: yuppies
and hippies. Some had joined the establishment; they were
wearing suits, shirts and ties and would have fit into any
corporate environment. Others hadn't; at first glance they
looked much as they did ten years earlier.

About two hours later I was greeted as "Mr. Dress for
Success" by one of the young men I had met at that dinner.
After the usual pleasantries he told me that some of the
people I had met that night had given in to the establishment—
but not him. He wasn't dressing for success. I must admit that
I took pleasure in pointing out to him that he had broken his
oath; after all, he was wearing a tie. I also said that, if he
looked around the room, he would notice that most of his
friends, including those who had not joined the establishment, were wearing ties as well. It was the one thing they had
all put on as a concession to their friend's wedding. True,
some were wearing shirts that were beyond belief, and some
of the ties were hideous, but they were wearing ties,
nevertheless.

That anecdote illustrates a point I want to make. The tie is the one thing that almost every man puts on when he is going to dress up. It is probably the single most important denominator of social status for a man in the United States today. Show me a man's ties and I'll tell you who he is or who he is trying to be.

Still, if you are like most men, you actually pay very little conscious attention to your ties. Some of you will say, "It isn't my tie that's significant, it's my car, my home, the size of my bank account, the quality of my art collection, the contents of my liquor closet, the amount of jewelry my wife has, etc., etc."

Don't you believe it—not during your working hours anyway. Those things are all fine, they'll make you very comfortable in life. But if I'm in a business meeting with you, or if you are trying to sell me something, or if I'm a juror listening to your defense of a client, I am not going to see those extraneous things. I am going to see *you*; I am going to see how you are dressed. And whether you like it or not, or believe it or not, your tie, more than any other aspect of your appearance, will determine how I and other people view your status, credibility, personality and ability.

Because I learned very early in my research that ties are so important, I have probably conducted more experiments with them and more testing of them than I have with any other article of clothing. Running through the entire litany of experiments would be impossible in this book, but a small sample is in order.

In one set of experiments, I asked a group of men to apply for jobs that were available and for which they were reasonably qualified. For some interviews, they would go properly dressed, in suit and tie. For others, I instructed them not to wear ties, but to say that they had their tie in their hand, stopped for a cup of coffee, left the tie on the counter, and did not go back to get it since they didn't want to be late for the interview.

Invariably, those men who wore their ties to interviews were offered jobs; those without them were turned down. And in one almost incredible situation, the interviewer (the president of a small corporation) was made so uncomfortable by the applicant's lack of a tie that he gave the man $6.50 (a fair price twelve years ago), told him to go out and buy a tie, put it on, and then come back to complete the interview. He still didn't get the job.

In an updated version of that experiment, I had men apply for positions for which they were reasonably qualified. Only this time I divided the job applicants into three groups. The first group went to the interviews without ties. They made the same excuses the non-tie-wearers had earlier. The second group wore ties, but they were blue-collar ties, not outlandish or silly, simply cheap or inappropriate. The third group wore conservative, traditional business neckwear.

The results were similar to that of the first experiment. The men who wore the conservative, traditional business ties were much more likely to be hired than the men in the other two groups.

What was intriguing about this experiment was the reaction of the interviewers to the men who wore lower-middle-class blue-collar neckwear. They were so put off that they really did not give them an opportunity to interview. While they usually interviewed the men without ties, they simply dismissed those who showed up with the wrong tie. They went through the motions of an interview most of the time, but you could tell it was not a real interview.

Because of this reaction, I went back and asked them to describe the different job applicants. As expected, they described the men wearing conservative ties as able, astute and capable. Most of them described the non–tie-wearers as losers. They said that no one should show up for an interview without a tie, and they couldn't accept any excuse for doing so. In their opinion, it was an unforgivable and unpardonable sin and they would never offer such a person a job. To them, it was an announcement that that person didn't really care too much for the job or the company. They made no comments about the qualifications or ability of the non–tie-wearers; they simply didn't like their attitude.

When asked to comment about the men wearing blue-collar ties, however, they usually commented about their lack of qualifications. They stated that they weren't articulate, they weren't able, and a few questioned their honesty. Three interviewers took out the man's résumé and said they really didn't believe that the person who sat before them was as qualified as this résumé indicated, and they dismissed him on that ground. Apparently, the man's tie weighed more heavily than his résumé. They looked upon the tie as the heraldic shield of the twentieth century. To these men, it identified the wearer's background, or lack of it, and in so doing gave them a reasonable way of estimating his ability. What makes this experiment so extraordinary is that most of the men making these judgments came from blue-collar backgrounds themselves.

In another set of experiments, six men were asked to have dinners in various upper-middle-class restaurants with their wives. On some occasions, they wore suits but no ties; on others, they were properly attired. On each occasion, when the check was presented, they told the restaurant manager they had left their wallet with cash and credit cards at home, and asked to pay by personal check. When they were wearing ties, their checks were graciously accepted. Without ties, they were, in many instances, refused, and the wife was forced to use the preplanned emergency solution: "Oh, wait a minute, I think I may have enough cash to cover this."

In twenty-seven restaurants in New York where ties are not mandatory attire, I asked the headwaiter or maitre d' to divide the room into two simple sections—more preferable seating areas and less preferable seating areas. Inevitably, those areas near the street door and kitchen door were considered to be the less preferable. I then spent a number of evenings observing the seating procedures at peak dinner hours of those restaurants. Invariably, there was a disproportionate number of men without ties in the less preferable areas, and almost no men without ties in the more preferable areas.

To determine how people feel about tie wearers in strictly economic terms, I took twin pictures of the same man. In one, he was wearing a nondescript gray suit and tie, in the other he wore a similar suit, but with no tie and an open-collar shirt. Over one hundred people picked at random were asked to estimate the yearly income of each "twin." Although there are obviously numerous variations in such surveys, the "twin" wearing the tie was generally awarded $3,000 to $4,000 more per year than his "brother."

We ran a second version of this experiment with men wearing appropriate ties, poor ties, or going tieless. We asked 212 people picked at random in downtown Chicago to estimate the yearly income of the men in the pictures. The respondents, as they had in the first case, assumed that the man wearing an upper-middle-class tie earned considerably more than the man with an open collar. Their range was from $4,000 to $6,000. The most extraordinary finding, however, was that they assumed that the non-tie-wearer was more successful than the men who wore blue-collar ties. Clearly, if you cannot afford a good tie, you should not wear a tie at all.

Using the same photos we questioned 112 women in a Chicago suburb. We told them we were testing a door-to-door sales organization and wanted to know which person they would let into their home to make a presentation. Although the men wearing upper-class ties were twice as likely to be allowed into the homes as the non-tie-wearers, they were not as successful as the men who wore poor ties. Apparently the upper-class look frightened the women. What our research really proved, however, is wearing any tie makes you, in the eyes of women, a respectable member of society—or at least a safe one.

Finally, in an update of my most famous experiment, the one in which I panhandled money in front of the Port Authority bus terminal with and without a tie, I hired a twenty-eight-year-old man to stop people and tell them he left his wallet home and needed $1.25 for transportation to New Jersey. He did this during the rush hour three days running for one hour a day. On the first day, wearing an upper-class tie, he collected $34.60. On the second day, when he went tieless, he collected $8.42. On the third day, wearing a blue-collar tie, he collected $9.12.

The researcher who carried on this experiment was a graduate student and a very bright one. He reported that there was a variable that we hadn't considered. He said that most of the people who gave him money when he looked like an executive looked like executives themselves, and since the Port Authority terminal was dominated by businessmen at that hour, that may be the reason he collected more money when he was dressed like a businessman.

His report so intrigued me that I immediately set up another test. I arranged for him to sell raffle tickets at a church booth located in a shopping center. The reason I was attracted to this particular church booth is that I estimated that the people shopping in the mall were just about equally divided into three groups. One third of them were obviously upper middle class, another third were obviously blue-collar, and the final third were somewhere in between, or couldn't be identified. This automatically eliminated the factor that existed at the bus station.

I arranged for our researcher to man the booth and sell tickets on three different occasions. The first time he wore a blue pinstripe suit with a white shirt and a silk foulard tie. He looked every inch the upper-middle-class businessman. In forty-five minutes he sold thirty-two tickets, twenty of them to people who obviously came from upper-middle-class backgrounds. During the second forty-five minute period he dressed in a pair of polyester slacks and a slipover jacket with a baseball emblem on it. His outfit screamed blue-collar. During this period he sold sixty-two tickets, forty-three of them to people who were obviously blue-collar, and only five to people from upper-middle-class backgrounds. The remainder went to people we couldn't identify. During the last forty-five-minute test, he wore running shoes, jeans, a blue pullover sweater and a dress shirt. You could not tell his background from what he wore. He sold fifty-three tickets, sixteen to upper-middle-class people, seventeen to men and women who were not identifiable, and the remainder to people from a blue-collar background. The sales didn't exactly break down, one-third and one-third, but they came very close.

Our findings were not revolutionary; we had known for years, because I do quite a bit of work with the fund-raising industry, that when you ask people to contribute to a cause, they are more likely to do so if you look like you come from their group.

Finally, we took a number of pictures of men in different outfits and dropped them into a larger experiment. We showed them to several hundred people who represented a fairly good cross section of the American business community. We told them the men in the pictures came from two groups. Half of them were hard-working, responsible and honest people. The others were irresponsible, lazy and, in some cases, dishonest people. We wanted to see if they could instinctively guess who was who. The executives we questioned, almost to a man, identified men wearing conservative, traditional, upper-middle-class ties as being the hard-working, reliable and honest men in the pictures. That is not surprising. What was surprising is almost everyone else questioned, including the men who were not wearing ties, picked the tie wearers as being harder working, more responsible and more able than the men with open collars.

No question, then: The tie is a symbol of respectability and responsibility; it communicates to other people who you are, or reinforces or detracts from their conception of who you should be. While the most appropriate tie, worn correctly, naturally cannot ensure your success in business or in life, it certainly can—and should—give off the right signals to keep you from being regarded as a no-class boob.

• • • • • • • • • • • • • • • • • • • •

HOW TO BUY TIES

Buying ties is relatively simple, once you know the rules and adhere to them. But it isn't as simple as telling your wife, girlfriend or secretary to pick up a few ties for you at lunch. That is the worst thing you could do. Unless the lady in question is exceptional, she is going to see you in a different light from that of your business associates, and she is probably going to brighten you up to fulfill her image of how you should dress and look. And that will, a lot more times than not, spell disaster at the office. Unless you would ask your wife, girlfriend or secretary to write your next report to the boss, do not ask her to buy your ties.

Accept the fact that buying and wearing ties correctly is a serious matter, one that requires time, effort and thought. And do it yourself; I guarantee that it will pay off.

The first thing you should do before buying ties is to determine what length they should be. There is little that looks worse on a man than a tie that is either too long or too short. When tied properly, the tip of the tie should come just to your belt buckle (see drawing on page 100). What length you will need will therefore depend on how tall you are and how you knot your tie (see drawings on pages 101–104 for the most common knotting methods.

Proper Tie Length and Proper Fitting Belt

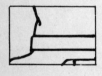

Trouser Length and Angle with Cuff

Trouser Length and Angle without Cuff

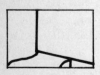

Trouser Length and Angle with High-Fashion Flare Cuff

HOW TO TIE A TIE

The Windsor Knot
Wide and triangular—for wide-spread shirt collars.

Your Left
in Mirror

Your Right
in Mirror

1
Start with wide end of tie on your right and extending a foot below narrow end.

2
Cross wide end over narrow and bring up through loop.

3
Bring wide end down, around behind narrow, and up on your right.

4
Then put down through loop and around across narrow as shown.

5
Turn and pass up through loop and...

6
Complete by slipping down through the knot in front. Tighten and draw up snug to collar.

The Half-Windsor Knot
Medium symmetrical triangle—for standard shirt collars.

1
Start with wide end of tie on your right and extending a foot below narrow end.

2
Cross wide end over narrow and turn back underneath.

3
Bring up and turn down through loop.

4
Pass wide end around front from left to right.

5
Then, up through loop...

6
And down through knot in front. Tighten carefully and draw up to collar.

The Four-in-Hand Knot
Long and straight—to complement a standard shirt collar.

1
Start with wide end of tie on your right and extending a foot below narrow end.

2
Cross wide end over narrow, and back underneath.

3
Continue around, passing wide end across front of narrow once more.

4
Pass wide end up through loop.

5
Holding front of knot loose with index finger, pass wide end down through loop in front.

6
Remove finger and tighten knot carefully. Draw up tight to collar by holding narrow end and sliding knot up snug.

The Bow Tie

1
Start with end in left hand extending 1½" below that in right hand.

2
Cross longer end over shorter and pass up through loop.

3
Form front loop of bow by doubling up shorter end (hanging) and placing across collar points.

4
Hold this front loop with thumb and forefinger of left hand. Drop long end down over front.

5
Place right forefinger, pointing up, on bottom half of hanging part. Pass up behind front loop and...

6
Poke resulting loop through knot behind front loop (see illustration). Even ends and tighten.

Today you may have a problem buying the right length tie even if you buy your tie in a good store. The standard length is 55 inches to 56 inches, but you cannot guarantee you will get that length simply by purchasing an expensive tie in a good store, even if the tie bears a designer label. Many of the best stores, for some strange reason, are selling short ties. I'm sure they pay a few dollars less for them, but I think it's hardly worth the problems it is going to cause them with their more sophisticated customers. No gentleman will ever wear a short tie. When most of us think of a fellow wearing a short tie, we think of someone with a potbelly who drives a beer truck—obviously not the image you are seeking. If the tie you bought turns out to be too short when you try it on at home, bring it back and complain loudly. It is unconscionable for a store that represents itself as a store for the businessman to sell such an item.

The width of a tie is also important, and although there is no firm and fast math that can be used to determine the proper width with a given suit, basically the width of the tie should be harmonious with the width of the suit lapels. At the present time, standard tie widths are from two and three-quarter to three and three-quarter inches at the widest end.

Next, it is important that the tie makes a good knot. To do so, it must have substance, which is provided by a lining of coarse material sewn into the tie, as well as the material from which the tie itself is made. Cheap polyesters and shiny silks slip quite badly, and light, thin silks do not offer enough substance, unless they are heavily lined. In addition to the coarse inner lining, the tie should also be fully lined or backed with a light, but good quality material.

There is a commonly held myth that you can tell the quality of a tie by counting the gold stripes on the lining. Years ago a manufacturer of tie linings decided to code his linings; he put four gold stripes on his most expensive linings and one on his least expensive. When the public got wind of this, they started looking inside ties at the number of gold stripes as a way of determining the quality of the tie. It may have worked for a short period of time, but it no longer does. Today, if you can see the lining it's probably an inexpensive tie; most good ties have backings. And if your tie lining has four, or six, or eight gold stripes, it is totally meaningless because now the people who manufacture the cheapest linings put gold stripes on them.

Since all types of tie pins or tie clasps are not at present considered in good taste, a tie should have a tab on the back of the large end, into which the smaller end may be slipped so that it does not stick out from the back of the tie.

•   •   •   •   •   •   •   •   •   •   •   •   •   •   •   •   •   •

HOW TO PICK THE MATERIALS

The best material for ties is silk. You can get away with a polyester that looks like silk, or a polyester and silk combination, which can be excellent, but you are safer if you stick with one hundred percent silk. If you have to skimp on your wardrobe, skimp on your suits or shirts before you try to save money on your ties. There is nothing that will destroy a businessman's image as certainly as a cheap tie. A gentleman will probably have a few wool and cotton ties in his closet but he will wear them to the office only on those days when he is sure that he is not going to be dealing with the men at the top. (I hesitate to give such advice since it seems that every time I dress down because I don't expect to be dealing with anyone important that day, all the really important people show up at my door.)

There are three main types of silk tie, the lightest being the foulard silk. The foulard is a fine, elegant tie, and the only problem with it, as mentioned, is that it must be substantially lined if it's going to make a good knot and keep it.

Next, there is the regular, or normal weave, silk tie. There are a lot of names for this one; I call it the solid silk. It really does not matter what you call it if you understand that it is the tie everyone immediately thinks of when you mention silk ties. It is often a solid color; it's shiny, but does not glisten; and it can be worn with almost anything, anywhere.

Last is the woven silk tie, which is not currently in vogue and is not being sold in most stores today. If it does come back in style, keep in mind that it is very difficult to get a good knot with a woven silk tie because it's so heavy. So, while you must be sure that the lining inside a foulard is heavy enough, conversely, you must be sure that the lining inside a woven silk is light enough to ensure a proper knot.

When buying a silk tie, you should expect to pay at least $14 for it, usually more (unless you're buying at a sale). Anything cheaper will look terrible after several wearings, even if it looks okay when you buy it. There is really no top limit to what silk ties can cost, but the very best ties in the best stores run well under $35. If a tie costs more, then you are paying for something other than quality.

If you are really strapped and must buy a polyester tie, there is only one rule; if it looks like a good silk, buy it. If not, don't. The only characteristic of polyester in ties to pay attention to is how well it imitates silk. The average price range for a good polyester tie is between $8 and $12. Good polyester ties tend to stand up to wear better than silks in the same price range, and can even look better after dry cleaning than expensive silk. Blends of polyester and silk are generally the best buy if you are budget conscious because they offer the rich look of silk and the durability of polyester. These are less expensive than silk, and hold up quite well.

There are three primary types of wool ties. First is the

knitted tie, which is usually a fairly sporty tie, and should be worn accordingly. All knitted ties should be wool; if they are made from an artificial fiber they should look and feel like wool.

The woven wool tie has a very bushy look to it and is made from the same types of material one would associate with the heaviest winter sports jackets.

Knitted and woven wool ties must be very carefully measured so that they will not be too short when tied; will make a neat knot; and will not be so thick that they cause the shirt collar to bulge. Usually, a simple overhand knot is the only one that will work successfully.

Because they are, at best, more bulky than other ties, knitted and woven wool ties should be generally avoided by heavy men with large necks and round faces, since the ties will call attention to the very physical characteristics that they would be wise to deemphasize. However, these are probably the most durable of ties, and will last for years, even after many dry cleanings. Some of them can even be washed in Woolite, although there is a danger that the lining (if the tie has one) might shrink disproportionately to the tie material.

The last major category of wool tie is the wool challis. It is a finer, smoother weave, and is backed and lined exactly like silk. In fact, the challis very often has almost the same look and design as silk, with the exception that it is not shiny, which makes it less formal. It is useful because it tends to wear, dry-clean and travel better than silk.

Cotton ties are worn year-round in the South, and elsewhere in the summer (but never to important business meetings). The best way to determine whether a cotton tie is good is how much you pay for it. It should be no less than $10 or more than $17.50. If you pay less than $10 you're getting a cheap cotton that will not hold up, and if you pay more than $17.50 you are being cheated, because no cotton tie is worth more.

Although cotton is such a versatile fabric that it can be woven to look like almost any other material, the predominant look in cotton ties is light in both weight and color. Because of the light colors, it is advisable to Scotchguard cotton ties by spraying them.

Linen ties are beautiful, but stay away from them unless you can afford to buy them to wear only a few times. Linen wrinkles incredibly, and the wrinkles are virtually impossible to remove.

There are some materials from which ties should never be made. The main one is acetate. Never buy an acetate tie; it's a piece of junk. Likewise, don't buy rayon, which will not hold its shape after several wearings, and even when it's new it does not yield the rich look that an acceptable tie must have.

. . . .

HOW TO SELECT PATTERNS OF TIES

There are almost as many patterns of ties as there are crystal formations in snowflakes, but only a few are suitable for the businessman who has reached the top or is trying to. This statement is not as restrictive as it sounds; there is still a tremendous variety to be found in color combinations, material and textures.

The most obvious pattern for a tie, the one that is the most useful generally, is no pattern at all. In other words, a solid. The reason is simple: A solid tie will go with any pattern in any suit or shirt. It is the perfect—and sometimes, the only—sensible complement to the very loud shirt, say a broad plaid or heavy stripe, and to any suit.

A lot of men believe they shouldn't wear a solid tie with a solid suit and solid shirt, but that is nonsense. A combination of solids is perfectly acceptable if the colors and textures are properly coordinated—say a gray suit, a light blue shirt and a maroon tie. If you wear very expensive clothes, the combination of solids tend to emphasize the qualities of the materials and tailoring by not giving the eye extraneous details to focus on. Of course, you probably would not wish to wear all solids every day; nevertheless wearing solids is the hallmark of more than one very sophisticated gentleman.

For a basic tie wardrobe, I suggest that every man have at least two solid ties, a navy and a maroon, and one other solid from the following: brown, beige, medium-range blue or gray, depending on his wardrobe, possibly all of them if affordable. The man with an extensive wardrobe should also have several light, summer, pastel solids, and maybe even a white. I don't like white solids myself—there is always the problem of keeping them clean—but it is an acceptable tie in certain situations.

There are solid color ties that have a raised pattern on them. Usually these are made from polyester but can be made from silk. The worst of these, generally the cheaper polyesters, are hideously garish even if the colors are the most conservative. If you like a raised pattern type of tie, my only suggestions are to make sure the raised patterns are subtle, and go for the most expensive you can afford, preferably silk.

The next pattern we find in ties is the evenly spaced, repeating pattern. The best known of these is, of course, the polka dot, a small round dot repeated in regular intervals against a solid background. The polka-dot tie is almost as versatile as the solid and there is, in my experience, no tie more elegant. The background color of a polka-dot tie is dominant, and should either match or contrast with the suit color. The dot should pick up the color of the shirt.

The most common polka-dot tie is dark blue with a white dot, and the reason is traditional. Years ago the de rigueur "uniform" for the upper-middle-class executive was a dark blue suit and white shirt. The tie picked up both colors perfectly, and presented a stunning, crisp, dignified look, as it still does, making it the ideal tie to take on the road. It will not only carry you through the business day but give you a very formal tie for night.

You can buy polka-dot ties with dots as big as marbles but, generally speaking, the smaller the dots, the more sophisticated and dressy the tie.

Also in the category of the evenly spaced, repeating pattern tie is the classic club tie with its small heraldic shields against a solid background—and its derivation, which I call the itty bitty fishy tie. It often features, against its mandatory solid background, some emblem of traditionally upper-class sports: a little fish with a fly in its mouth, a tennis racquet, a sailboat, a golf ball or club, a horse or polo bat, but less upper-crusty designs also work well as long as they are clean and in traditional colors. You will find these ties in all the best stores, and they sell with great consistency. This is not the tie you should take on the road, particularly if you are going abroad; in many European countries a tie of this sort is a sign of membership in a club or a professional organization and for a nonmember to wear a club tie is an unforgivable social blunder.

They go with almost any conservatively patterned shirt and certainly with every solid. Generally, it would not be advisable to wear the club tie or its derivations with any strongly patterned shirt, since the emblem on the tie will clash with the strong pattern more times than not. And even if it doesn't, it is very often inappropriate to wear a conservative tie against a wild shirt.

The next acceptable tie pattern is the rep, or regimental rep, which is the traditional tie of the American businessman. Technically, "rep" means a ribbed or corded fabric, but a rep tie is a diagonally striped tie. Originally, the regimental rep was designed to represent whatever British regiment a gentle-man served in, and each had its own distinctive stripe and coloration. There are only about forty true regimental ties, but about four hundred imitations, all of which are acceptable in this category.

The only rules for the rep tie are that the stripes must be neat, clean and generally of dark color. For summer, the stripes are pastel against a white background; this is the accepted summer rep of the upper middle class.

The next category of acceptable tie pattern is what I call the foulard, because that is the type of silk on which it is usually found. Many people refer to this as the Ivy League tie, since the pattern at one time announced that Daddy went to Yale, Granddad went to Yale, and we hope little Junior will go to Yale also. It is a tie that traditionally indicated that the wearer was not only of a certain class, but that he also belonged to an elite social group. It represented Boston and Palm Beach society, Harvard, Yale and Princeton. Although it is worn by businessmen in every section of the country today, it still has a certain cachet to it.

There are several variations of the Ivy League tie but, generally, it features a small, rounded triangle, or irregular circle, with variations inside. Because this tie is so tradi-tional, upper class and conservative, it is the business tie often found in bright new and sometimes trendy colors. Today's trendy, new foulard is bright yellow. A few years ago it was orange and I am sure it will change again. It is a very safe design as long as it is crisp, neat and repeated on fine silk.

An offshoot of the foulard is the repeating diamond pattern. As with the polka dot, the smaller the diamonds, the more sophisticated the tie. This is probably the best tie for a man in an authority position, since it says he is conservative and upper class to the members of the upper class without turning off the lower middle class with which the man might come in contact (if he is a banker or lawyer, for example). The traditional Ivy League tie, because of its prior associations, does tend to turn off the lower middle class.

The paisley tie is the sporty tie of the upper middle class. I call it the upper-middle-class amoeba run wild, since if you took an amoeba, painted it in multiple colors, expanded its size, and threw sixty of them together, you would have a paisley pattern.

Being basically a sporty tie, the paisley has certain limitations. It is not considered a serious tie, and unlike the patterns previously discussed, should not be worn to the most serious business meetings. But it is an excellent tie to wear with a dull suit. Picking up the color of a dull suit with a bright paisley tie presents a stunning effect; in fact, the basic use of the paisley tie is to blend a total look—suit, shirt and tie—together.

The paisley is one of the cleverest ties you can take with you when traveling, and is also quite good for men on strict budgets, since it contains so many colors that one tie can match several suits. And when the plane takes an unexpected bounce and you spill soup on it, no one will notice.

The paisley pattern is one that you will find mixed with almost every other acceptable tie pattern. It moves over into club tie derivations, with small colorful amoebas repeated in evenly spaced patterns against a solid background. When the amoebas are even smaller, it becomes a derivation of the Ivy League tie. When the amoebas alternate with stripes, it becomes a hybrid of the rep tie. The hybrids, particularly the club and Ivy League variations, may be worn as you would wear their slightly more conservative counterparts.

Acceptable plaid ties fall into two categories. They are either heavy woolen plaids that go extremely well with the bushy, soft flannel suit, or they are the linen or cotton plaids, usually of light pastel colors, for summer wear. Like the paisley, it is best if saved for weekends.

• • • • • • • • • • • • • • • • • • •

TIES THAT SHOULD NEVER BE WORN

The best rule for avoiding ties that may convey the wrong look and the wrong association is: Unless you are sure of what you are doing, wear nothing other than those I have recommended on the preceding pages. But I can also give you some specifics. Never wear anything gaudy, except a paisley. Never wear anything bright, except a foulard. Never wear ties with large symbols. Never wear "storybook" or "big picture" ties, no matter what the prevailing fashion is. Avoid any material that shows signs of poor dyeing, which is usually evidenced by harsh lower-middle-class colors, washed-out patterns or colors or patterns that run into each other. Avoid anything that is unusual in color, pattern, shape or size. I once saw a tie that consisted of a loose red knit enclosing a black lace background. You would not wear that one. Avoid any tie that is too short. Avoid black ties, unless you are going to a funeral. Avoid purple under all circumstances. And avoid any pattern that is hard to look at.

• • • • • • • • • • • • • • • • • • •

WHAT TO DO ABOUT BOW TIES

For business wear, bow ties create several negative impressions. You will not be taken seriously when wearing one. The only positive use comes if you are too powerful a personality, in which case they can soften your image. But otherwise you will not be thought responsible if you wear a bow tie. It is a death knell for anyone selling his services, such as a consultant or lawyer. The number of people who will trust you at all, with anything, will be cut in half.

In general, I have found that people believe that a man in a bow tie may lie. It creates the impression of being unpredictable. Thus, some experienced trial lawyers who believe they have a good case will try to keep a man wearing a bow tie off a jury. Our researchers found that there was some basis for this belief that bow tie wearers were different; when they stopped men wearing standard ties and asked them why they choose the color or pattern they were wearing they usually received a polite answer. However, when they asked bow tie wearers why they were wearing bow ties, a substantial number were rude and a few wanted to fight.

Bow ties are acceptable as sports attire, and if you do wear them for such occasions, stick to the same patterns recommended for all other ties. Do not wear them to business unless you are a clown, a college professor or a social commentator. If you insist on wearing a bow tie to business—and bow tie wearers are a stubborn lot—I suggest you wear it with the proper accessories: a red nose and a beanie cap with a propeller.

5

Putting Your Own Look Together

When I first started in image consulting years ago, I received a call from the owner of one of Connecticut's most successful and most prestigious men's clothing stores. He said he had a problem and he came right out with it: he had no taste. He had buyers who chose the clothing for the store, and even though he never attempted to wait on customers, he was seen around the premises and known as the owner and felt he needed to dress well. He had been hiring a fashion consultant to put his clothing together, but recently he had received some negative comments on how he looked.

When I met him at his home, I found a selection of clothing only slightly smaller than that in his store. But when I looked at the combinations his fashion consultant had recommended, I realized that the consultant had been dressing him directly from the pages of *GQ (Gentlemen's Quarterly)*.

The problem was that this man was six feet, four inches tall and weighed 240 pounds, hardly a size compatible with the tricky combinations and style of high-fashion clothing. Not to mention that the clothing seen in such magazines is rather atypical of the clothes worn in a suburban Connecticut town.

I suggested that the man change his wardrobe, and because he could do so from his store, he immediately began wearing the combinations I suggested. Several weeks later, when I went back to see how he was doing, the man said he felt much more comfortable and had received a number of compliments on his new look.

A year later, however, he was back to wearing high-fashion horse blankets. When I asked him why, he said I was a nice fellow and all that, but had charged him only $150 for my advice. His fashion consultant always charged him $500, and everyone knows that a $500 consultant is better than a $150 consultant. Not wishing to argue with such logic, I told the man he was absolutely correct and immediately raised my prices.

The clothing combinations I recommend for business wear do not come from the pages of men's fashion magazines. Neither are they determined by my own personal opinion. They are the result of research and testing, and they reflect the conscious and unconscious reactions of a valid cross section of the American public. They work because the American public says that these clothes, in these combinations, project a look of good taste, of credibility and of upper-middle-class success.

The fact that the colors, patterns and combinations of clothing that score the highest positive results among the largest majority of the population are all traditional and conservative should come as no great surprise. Familiarity, at least in the senses, does not breed contempt; it breeds acceptance. The most successful businessmen have for years worn conservative clothing, and will for many more years.

When I first began testing, my method was to photograph a dozen men in conservative, well-matched colors and patterns. Another dozen men were photographed in well-matched, but more modern clothing—the type generally seen in fashion magazines. When the two dozen photos were jumbled together and shown in no particular order, seventy to eighty percent of my population sample chose the men in conservative dress as more tasteful than the men in more modern garb. I recently completed an updated version of this experiment with even more startling results. This time I tested the well-coordinated fashion look with the most traditional combinations I could find. I used only outfits that were used repeatedly in the ads for the most conservative men's stores over the last ten years. Even when most of the men being questioned personally dressed in more modern colors and patterns and styles, over seventy percent picked the more traditionally dressed men as being more sophisticated. This is extraordinary since one of the main reasons the men we questioned gave for wearing a high-fashion look was a belief that it made them look sophisticated. In many men's minds tradition and familiarity, not fashion, says sophistication.

When I discovered this familiarity effect, I tested it further, using shirts and ties. I made one grouping of ten shirts and ties that were strictly traditional; and another grouping of ten shirts and ties that were nontraditional, but not gaudy. Within the two separate groups, ties were indiscriminately placed on shirts. I then asked 300 people to judge whether each combination was in good taste, poor taste or neutral. Those were the only choices.

After every ten people, I again indiscriminately combined two shirts and ties within their separate groups. Eighty-seven percent of the people chose the largest majority of the traditional combinations as in good taste. Seventy percent of the same people chose the more modern combinations as being in poor taste. (I repeated this experiment nine months ago, and there was no significant change in the results.)

With the most important business combinations my testing was far more complex. With photographs of men wearing various standard business combinations I asked a cross section of the population and specific groups of executives from different industries and different sections of the country, both men and women, to identify which men wearing which clothing were the most efficient, hardest working, the best family men and so forth. I also asked them to guess the occupation of men in various outfits; plumber, banker, whatever. If any outfit sent negative messages or identified the wearer as blue-collar to over twenty percent of the population, I discarded it.

. . . .

HOW TO TAKE THE HEADACHE OUT OF COORDINATING CLOTHES

When you coordinate clothing there are only four serious elements of concern: the colors, the lines, the textures and the styles.

In choosing color men make four mistakes. They wear colors that clash; an orange tie with a green shirt and a blue suit. They wear colors that are so muted they fade into each other; a pale blue shirt, a light blue suit and a pale blue tie. They wear colors that are not flattering; a bright red shirt worn by a man with red hair. They choose lower-middle-class colors or shades of color. There are many examples of these, electric blue or electric green—lower-class colors no matter where they are found. However, black is a lower-class color only in men's raincoats; it's perfectly acceptable in an overcoat or a top coat. These examples are obvious or should be, but I've seen otherwise astute businessmen make worse mistakes than the ones I've described.

The lines of any garment are the directions in which the pattern runs. A pinstripe suit has a vertical pattern. A plaid suit has both a vertical and a horizontal pattern. A paisley tie has a nondirectional pattern. Some club ties are nondirectional while others have diagonal patterns; rep ties have diagonal patterns. When putting clothing together, it is very important that a pattern that travels in one direction is not put next to a pattern that travels in another direction; the lines will clash.

Texture is a concern that is generally overlooked, but it can be used to match materials with very pleasing effect. A nice, heavy wool tie with a heavy flannel suit or a linen tie with a linen suit are good texture combinations. Very seldom is there a serious clash of textures, but it can happen occasionally, such as if a silk shantung tie is worn with a heavy flannel suit.

All items of clothing have a definite, identifiable style. Pinstripe suits, for example, have a conservative, businesslike style, and it would be a severe clash of styles to wear a sporty shirt with a pinstripe suit. Similarly, a traditionally patterned tie would look silly if worn with a high-fashion suit. The combination of styles must be appropriate.

The simplest, most effective and always acceptable combination of clothing is solids. The classic mistake most men make about solids is that they think they are dull, or that solids should not be combined. Both thoughts are wrong. If, in the combination of three solids—suit, shirt and tie—any one of the three is very lively, your outfit will not be dull. If you use contrast in addition, for instance, combining a dark blue suit, a white shirt and a maroon tie, you will project a sharp, fashionable look. If you see a man with three solids well put together, you can almost be sure that he is an excellent dresser, and that he accomplishes his look with the least effort. Poor dressers struggle to put patterns together and rarely succeed.

Because of its great flexibility, with patterns as well as with other solids, the solid suit should be the staple of every man's wardrobe. The most acceptable colors for solid suits are blue, gray and beige. All of these test well in almost any combination, and they are the three solids I recommend to every client.

A solid suit may be worn with a shirt of almost any pattern, and if this is followed up with a solid tie as I have shown in pictures 1 and 2 (see color inserts), it always yields a workable combination. This combination of solid-pattern-solid follows one of the first rules I offer any client who has trouble matching clothing. Never put two patterns together. If you're not sure what you're doing always separate patterns by a solid.

Pictures 1 and 2 also demonstrate another aspect of matching the solid suit with the patterned shirt. In picture 1 we have a solid blue suit with a blue striped shirt that picks up the suit, and a solid maroon tie that gives contrast and life to the ensemble. In picture 2 we have a solid blue suit, a pale blue boxed pattern shirt and a solid navy tie which picks up the suit. Over the years I've shown hundreds of pictures of different outfits to tens of thousands of people and the majority thought that outfits in which the suit color was picked up by the shirt or the tie was more tasteful. This is one of the simplest and surest methods of putting your clothing together in a pleasing fashion.

Solid suits of course can be worn with solid shirts and pattern ties. Picture 3 shows a classic example of this; a beige suit, a solid blue shirt and a striped tie. As I said earlier, you can put three solids together without great difficulty. Picture 4 is a good example of this, a beige suit, a solid blue shirt and a virtually solid tie. The reason I picked this tie is it has a pattern that is so weak and indefinite that you can treat it as if it were a solid. Another common example of a pattern that

does not count is what I refer to as the invisible plaid. In
some suits the plaid is so subtle you hardly notice it. The rule
is: If you can hardly notice a pattern, you hardly ever have to
worry about it clashing.

Pictures 3 and 4 show a beige suit, which if you know
how to wear, is one of the most useful suits any man can have
in his wardrobe. This beige suit has the slightest hint of gray
in it, is worn with an end-on-end shirt, and in picture 3 with a
traditional rep tie. If you were painting a barn or the side of a
building, you probably wouldn't combine green, bright red,
yellow, navy and beige, but this seemingly gaudy tie and this
suit work beautifully. The reason they do is they are a
traditional combination. The tie or its twin has been worn
with beige suits by gentlemen for the past forty years. In fact,
its traditional value has a greater impact than its aesthetic
value.

In picture 4 we have the same suit and shirt worn with a
nubby-textured gray tie. It is aesthetically a far more sophisticated combination. The gray of the tie picks up the hint of
gray in the suit, and the texture of the tie picks up the texture
of the shirt. Matching textures and hues is one of the secrets
of being a very good dresser. However, when I showed these
pictures to forty businessmen, thirty-eight believed that the
man with the rep tie was the better dresser. Business women,
however, responded differently. Ten of the twelve to whom we
showed these pictures thought that a man who chose a
textured gray tie for that outfit was more sophisticated and a
better dresser. This demonstrates two very interesting points.
First, there are many different ways of putting clothing together cleverly, and second, men are impressed by other men
who put their clothing together traditionally while women are
more impressed by men who put their clothing together
beautifully.

In picture 5 we have a solid upscale teal blue suit. It's the type of suit that is only found in the very best stores. It is a beautiful suit, yet if you put it with a blue shirt and a dull tie it would look terrible. However, with a pencilstripe shirt, maroon tie and maroon pocket square, the look is not only lively but elegant. The main reason for the elegant look is the pocket square. Pocket squares not only add contrast but elegance as well.

In picture 6 we have a navy suit with a blue shirt with a white contrasting collar, and a striped maroon and navy tie. Any dark suit, particularly navy blue, will look elegant with a crisp white shirt and that would be my first choice. However, I selected a shirt with contrasting collar and cuffs because it is the new executive shirt and if you do not have a few in your wardrobe you should at least consider purchasing one. I also chose it because it works. The white collar contrasts sharply with the navy suit, giving us a crisp businesslike but elegant look. The maroon in the tie adds contrast while the navy pulls the look together. Shirts with contrasting collars and cuffs are a new and welcome addition to most gentlemen's wardrobes. They are very useful. They add life to most outfits, and they go with almost everything. Shirts with contrasting collars and cuffs are almost as versatile as solids. The only suits they do not work with are strong plaids.

The main problem men have with solid suits is they think of them as being dull, and they take extraordinary steps to liven them up. As you see, extraordinary steps are not at all necessary. Solid suits are very easy to put together. There are three basic combinations that are always acceptable, a solid suit with a solid shirt and a solid tie; a solid suit with a patterned shirt and a solid tie; and a solid suit with a solid shirt and a patterned tie.

Although I don't recommend it to anyone until he has acquired a real feel for matching clothing, it is also possible to wear a solid suit with a patterned shirt and a patterned tie, particularly if the two patterns are traditional, and one of them is nondirectional or very soft and quiet. For example, if we take a solid suit and put a pinstripe shirt with it, we can use almost any tie on that shirt, since the pinstripe is usually not strong enough to create a contrast, even with a rep tie.

For an entirely different reason, we may sometimes wear a rep tie with a chalkstripe shirt and a solid suit. Although there is a strong contrast of line, it does not strike us as being negative since we have been conditioned by seeing this combination on successful businessmen so often that we accept it as an upper-middle-class combination.

Just as there is little problem in matching the solid suit, the problems with matching the pinstripe suit are almost nonexistent. The one element that goes with a solid suit but not the pinstripe is a plaid or boxed pattern shirt. The plaid or boxed pattern not only clashes with the vertical line of the stripe but also clashes in effect because the plaid or boxed pattern shirt is almost always sporty while the pinstripe suit tends to be very serious and businesslike.

The pinstripe suit will always be appropriate with a solid shirt, but the only two shirts I recommend are pale blue and white. Some other colors may work, but white and pale blue are best. They are compatible with the serious businesslike style and since acceptable pinstripe suits often have either white or blue stripes, their use of the same color shirt tends to bring out the stripe and give the suit more life. Pictures 7 and 9 are examples of this. The pale blue shirt in picture 7 picks up the blue stripe in the suit and gives the suit a crisp look. Picture 7, by the way, is a classic combination: a pinstripe suit worn with a solid shirt and a silk foulard tie. These are the three most conservative elements in a gentlemen's wardrobe, and they belong together. We showed these pictures to a cross section of the public and a group of forty executives and asked them which combination a top executive would most likely wear; the majority picked the outfit in picture 7.

It is possible to combine a pinstripe suit with a striped

shirt particularly when one of the stripes is so weak that it does not conflict with the other. However, today this once safe combination can create problems for the wearer particularly if he has to deal with women. One-fourth of the women we surveyed thought that about half of these outfits were examples of poor taste. Therefore I put only solid shirts with pinstripe suits. It is the only safe route.

Naturally, the strength of a pinstripe in a suit or in a shirt affects which other garments you can wear with it. Picture 9 is a good example of this. Here we have a rep tie with a strong diagonal stripe clashing with the pinstripe in the suit. The clash isn't objectionable because we are used to seeing gentlemen wearing this type of rep tie and this type of suit. However, the outfit in picture 9 didn't test nearly as well as the outfit in picture 10. In picture 10 we have a suit with a weak stripe combined with a tie with a strong stripe. Here the pinstripe is so weak that the clash becomes inconsequential. And even if the pinstripe were stronger, it would still work, because the tie picks up the white of the shirt and the blue in the suit. Our research showed that when suits, shirts and ties are beautifully coordinated, you can combine brighter colors and stronger patterns without anyone objecting. We surveyed conservative executives and fashion people and they reacted identically. They were far less likely to be bothered by or even notice a clash in line, color or even style if the ensembles were beautifully coordinated.

The classic pinstripe suit combination shown in picture 8 has a built-in problem. The maroon handkerchief bothered many people. It didn't exactly pick up the maroon in the tie. When you use a pocket square, unless you have a knack for putting things together, make sure it picks up either your shirt or your tie *exactly*.

Finally, there are only two combinations that are absolutely safe with a pinstripe suit: a solid shirt and a solid tie or a solid shirt and a nondirectional tie. All other combinations can create problems and unless you have a gift for putting things together I suggest you avoid them.

The most difficult suit pattern to match, as you might expect, is a plaid because of its multidirectional lines. The only shirts that can be worn with plaid suits are solids. There are no exceptions to this rule. The only tie to be worn with a plaid suit is a nondirectional one such as paislies, polka dots, solids, foulards or in some cases other plaids.

The plaid that works best is the businessmen's shadow plaid shown in picture 11. This suit is effective because it works with all groups in society. It is the suit that many clever attorneys wear when they are pleading cases before juries, and many top salesmen choose who have to deal with a cross section of the business community. I put this suit with a very conservative shirt and a solid blue tie. I did not want an elegant or even fashionable look because it might conflict with the message of the suit. That message is the wearer is a nice fellow, a regular guy and someone who can be trusted by everyone. Since many people from blue-collar backgrounds are turned off by a look that is too chic or too sharp or too crisp, I avoided it with this suit. If you own only one plaid suit, this should be your plaid.

In picture 12 we have a traditional businessman's plaid. The plaid is definite, even strong but not gaudy, and it is acceptable in most business situations. You will not see men in the most conservative Wall Street firms wearing this suit in the middle of winter, but you will see them wearing it in the spring and summer, which brings up a very important point. The acceptability of patterns and colors depends on when and where you wear them. You can get away with lighter and brighter colors or stronger patterns in suiting in the sunbelt or in the summer.

The suit in picture 13 is a boxed pattern that must be

treated like a plaid because it has multidirectional lines. With this light-colored boxed-pattern suit I put a conservative shirt and a dark traditional foulard tie. The most important element in this combination is the conservative dark tie. If you wear a light or bright suit it is advisable that you wear it with a very conservative, preferably dark, winter tie. This is true not only with this suit, but with most summer suits, including the very light cords that everyone wears with bright ties. They work much better when they are worn with dark winter ties. Our tests indicate that light summer suits worn with traditional summer ties send a too sporty nonbusiness message for the average businessman. Light or summer suits worn with winter-colored ties on the other hand send very positive messages and are recommended. The rule is summer suit, winter tie.

Picture 14 shows a bright plaid sports jacket combined with a solid shirt and a dusty rose nondirectional tie with gray designs. The reason this works well is the tie picks up the only element in the jacket it can. In most bright sports jackets it is best to pick up one of the nondominant colors. In this jacket there are only two minor colors, gold and dusty rose. Since gold wouldn't be very appealing, a nondirectional dusty rose tie is the only choice left.

There are two mistakes made by men putting shirts and ties with lively sports jackets. Some believe that sports jackets require the same conservative look as suits; they do not. Others believe the rules of good taste do not apply to sportswear; they do. Plaid sports jackets, like plaid suits, require solid shirts and nondirectional ties, preferably solids.

Although many of the men who run America still dress in blue, gray and dull plaids, there is a new upscale elegance in America's boardrooms. Many of the men at or near the top put their clothing together with care. Their object is not to be new, innovative and fashionable but traditionally elegant. Their look can be best described as upscale elegant power and they achieve it by carefully combining rich, traditional, conservative and beautifully made shirts, ties and suits. This new elegant power look has in some companies almost become a uniform for the big boys and if you want to play with them you will need to wear their uniform.

That is why, even though most businesmen spend around $350 for their suits, for the pictures in this book I selected suits from Hart, Shaffner and Marx that run around $550. Suits similar to these in quality and style are worn by most men at or near the top of corporate America. If at present you cannot afford $550 suits you should try to duplicate at your price range their style, richness and texture.

Since the suit is the most important item in any clothing combination, it should always be bought first. Whenever you buy a suit, you should, as I have urged before, ask the tailor for a small piece of the material he takes off at the cuff. Staple that piece onto a business card. Beside it, write the date you bought the suit. If it's a solid suit, the piece should be about the size of a dime. If it's a pinstripe, make sure that your swatch contains all the colors of the pinstripe, and if it's a plaid, make sure that the swatch includes all the colors of the plaid. In time, you will have samples of your entire suit wardrobe in your wallet, so you can match them with specific shirts and ties whenever necessary.

I suggest that you also write on the back of another business card a list of all the shirts you have at any given time. If you have followed the advice in this book, they will all be standard patterns and colors that will easily cross over for wear with more than one suit.

Armed with your suit swatches and shirt list, it should be a simple matter to buy ties to go with any feasible combination. You will also find it much easier to choose ties that can be worn with several combinations.

If you follow this system you will find that you are much

better able to put your clothing together and will be able to do it less expensively than before because you are buying more practical garments. One of the great advantages of traditional colors, patterns and styles—in addition to their projecting the proper image of the successful man—is that they go further in a wardrobe and will have a much longer wearable life because they are so adaptable.

As simple as my system is for any man who is willing to learn the correct styles, patterns and colors, I still have clients who want it easier. For some of them, I have set up their wardrobes as blue/gray systems with every shirt and tie matching every suit. In this way, whatever they put on works perfectly.

Others I have urged to observe two simple rules.

1. Never put two patterns next to each other.
2. Choosing only from the patterns of ties I have suggested in Chapter 4, buy ties that match or contrast with shirts and do not clash with suits.

Going along with only those two rules, a man can get up almost blind most mornings and go to work looking at least respectable, although I must admit that it limits one's wardrobe considerably.

Some readers who are both lazy and crafty will have by now discovered another way. Just take the pictures from the book that are suitable for your life-style and business and emulate the combinations with your own selection.

6

Buy it Cheap

I f you follow the system I recommend in this chapter you will find that you will be able to dress as if you are buying your clothes on Fifth Avenue, even if you do not; you will be able to dress like a success, even if you aren't; and you will be able to save a great deal of money on the clothes you buy.

The first advice I always give clients is also the most obvious: Buy your clothes on sale. But do not just look for sales at random; plan ahead for them. There are two basic sales periods in the United States. In various parts of the country, the dates may change slightly, but basically fall–winter merchandise is on sale from approximately January 10 to February 5. Spring–summer merchandise usually goes on sale immediately after the July 4th weekend, and sales last through August.

During major sales the items offered are, as I am sure you have noticed, of very mixed quality and varying desirability. So you must be carefully selective. I will give you guidelines about what to buy and when to buy.

The first priority is: Remember that you are going to buy only when sales are on. If you need a suit, wait until then if you possibly can. And when sales time comes, try to buy a few extra shirts, a few extra ties and an extra pair of shoes that you can stick in the closet for a while so you will not have to pay full price when you do need them. This requires planning, but it pays off.

My second advice is to buy from factory outlets and discount stores, if these exist in your area. Obviously, men who live in large cities have a definite advantage, since there is an abundance of such stores to choose from. But there is a warning that goes with shopping anywhere that claims to offer substantial discounts: Such outlets often offer no bargains at all. They sell shoddy goods; they mark them up by a far greater percentage than their discounts take the prices down; and they often do not mark flawed merchandise as seconds very well. I will tell you what to avoid as we go along, but remember: You must be careful.

Factory outlets and discount stores do have sales, too, at the times when they must turn over stock. And if they really carry good merchandise, some incredible buys can be made at those times.

· · · · · · · · · · · · · · · · · · · ·

HOW TO COMPUTE ANY GARMENT'S TRUE COST

Before buying any article of clothing, make sure you compute the true cost of the garment. I know very few men who do this, although it is very important. And in bad economic times, it is the only way to purchase. To compute the true cost of garments, let us assume that you see two raincoats on sale. One is marked $75 and the other $100. Both are waterproof, and should last approximately three years. The $75 raincoat must be dry-cleaned; the $100 coat is made of a wash-and-wear fabric.

If you buy the $75 raincoat, you will probably get through the first year with only one cleaning. The second year will require two cleanings. To make the coat go through the third year will require three cleanings. If it costs $15 to dry-clean and waterproof a coat, and you have had it cleaned five times, you have effectively doubled the price of the raincoat. On the other hand, the $100 raincoat, which you washed at home in your own machine, probably looked better when it was new and has cost only pennies more than its original price over a three-year period.

So it is wise to keep in mind that the cost of any article of clothing is not only the price on the tag, but the lifetime cost; and items that are wash-and-wear or permanent press frequently offer significant savings, even if their original purchase price is greater.

This is most evident in shirting. If you wish to save money, do not buy cotton shirts. A good cotton shirt costs more than polyester and cotton at the outset, and in the long run can cost three or four times as much. For example, you can purchase a decent wash-and-wear shirt for $20. You can also purchase a fairly decent cotton shirt for $32, if you shop around a bit. If you wear the wash-and-wear shirt twenty times, washing it at home, your total expenditure for cleaning probably will come to around $3, plus the time of whoever does the minimum ironing it needs. The true cost of the shirt therefore adds up to $23.

Since very few people will iron a cotton shirt at home anymore, you will probably have to send it to a commercial laundry. If so, it probably will not last twenty wearings, but closer to ten. You will have to purchase two cotton shirts to get the same wear you will get from the one wash-and-wear. This means that the true price of the cotton shirt jumps from $32 to $64, plus the cost of twenty washings. Figured at $1.50 a wash, that pushes the cost of the cotton up to $94, as opposed to $23 for the wash-and-wear. I may be overestimating durability for some wash-and-wear shirts, but the example is valid.

You must consider the expected lifespan of any garment you purchase. Many years ago, I purchased two car coats—one corduroy, one leather. The corduroy cost about $50, and the leather about $125. Three years later, the corduroy coat had cost me approximately another $25 in dry cleaning and was no longer usable. I therefore paid approximately $25 per year for my use of the corduroy coat. The leather coat had several years more wear left in it, and had cost me not a cent to clean. In the long run, the leather coat—which looked better and richer from the day of its purchase—was actually cheaper than the corduroy coat.

The advice for economizing which I have given you so far has been available for years, and although it is rarely applied, it is hardly original. The element of sophistication that I can add to this advice is to have you purchase garments that look as if you had bought them in the most expensive stores and that will last as long as the most expensive clothes available.

One of the great pluses of using my system of dress is that you will find that when you follow it, you will automatically begin buying better-quality clothing, although you will pay no more for it. To accomplish this seemingly impossible miracle, you must learn to cross-shop—not just occasionally but as a way of life.

. . . .

HOW TO MAKE CROSS-SHOPPING PAY OFF

Cross-shopping as a way of life means that at every opportunity you go into stores that cater to various socioeconomic levels, particularly on the upper levels, and look at, feel and try on the merchandise. You must develop an interest not only in clothing, but in *what* clothing makes a man look successful: which shades or colors, which patterns, which fabrics and what kind of workmanship and tailoring. At first, cross-shopping will require a conscious effort, but after a while it will become a habit.

The real trick of cross-shopping, and the one that makes it practical right from the beginning, is to cross-shop for specific items. First, look at your wardrobe and decide what needs to be replaced. Then make a priority list for replacement. Let's assume that your dark gray suit is worn out, and you have neither a dark gray nor a dark blue. You might wish to replace the worn-out suit with a dark gray, a dark blue or any other dark, conservative suit, in that order.

With your list of preferences, go to an inexpensive store. By inexpensive, I mean the store, or stores, that carry the lowest-grade clothing that is acceptable to you. Look at the suits in that store. Then proceed to the most expensive store in your area, or several of them, and look at the suits there. Take a notebook with you and attempt to identify as many differences as you can between the look of the suits in the expensive store and the look of the suits in the inexpensive store.

First, differentiate between the looks of the materials. In the expensive store, suits might have a very soft look; in the inexpensive store, a very hard, shiny look.

Then look at specific workmanship characteristics. Are the buttons bone or plastic? Is the suit fully lined? Does it have an interior cigarette pocket? Does the pattern, if it has one, match where the material is sewn together? Is the fit good? Whatever differences you spot, jot them down.

Having now compared the best-looking suits with the cheapest that would be acceptable to you, go to the store that carries suits in a range of price you wish to spend, and see which suits most closely approximate the look of the expensive suits. The reason you should always have a list of preferences is that in some cases you may come very close, while in others not at all. You may really want a gray suit, but the gray suit you can afford looks dramatically cheaper than its expensive counterpart. On the other hand, the dark blue comes closer to what is good for you. Buy the blue, or wait until you can find an acceptable gray in your price range.

Let's say you are looking for a blue shirt. Obviously, the very best blue dress shirt can be found in the expensive store. The color is pale; the fabric is soft; the buttons are bone; and the workmanship and fit are beautiful. But the same shade of blue can be found at a moderate price, and it can even be found at a really cheap price. If you are really strapped for money, you should probably go for the cheapest, as long as it has the appropriate look. It will not fit as well; it will not last as long; it will not feel as good; but under a suit jacket, and with a decent tie, only an expert could tell.

Sometimes it is impossible to duplicate the pattern, texture, quality and look of expensive, tasteful garments at low prices. But only by cross-shopping will you be able to find out. When cross-shopping, you are determining availability at various price ranges. You will see where the limits are and will be better able to judge how your money should be spent. You may be able to buy cheaper suits, but pay more for ties. But always keep in mind that the least expensive item is not always truly the cheapest in total eventual cost; and, regardless of how much you spend, the point of your efforts is that you are trying to achieve the look of success.

• • • • • • • • • • • • • • • • • • • •

HOW TO TELL GOOD LABELS
FROM BAD LABELS

For the purpose of this book, stores selling clothing can be separated into a number of categories. First come those that stock only expensive, quality merchandise. In New York, examples that come to mind are Bergdorf Goodman, Saks Fifth Avenue, Brooks Brothers, F.R. Tripler, Paul Stuart, Lord and Taylor, Bloomingdale's, and B. Altman. While I might sometimes question the appropriateness of some of their clothing for a given individual in a given situation, I would never question the quality of their merchandise, nor their integrity in making good on occasional problems. But if you are looking for bargains, there is only one time to get them in these stores—at sale time.

In many of these stores, you will find a variety of labels, and the significance of these labels is very important. First, you will find designer labels; regardless of the quality of the garments, when you buy designer-labeled apparel, you are paying extra for the famous name and you really do not get your money's worth. If you are buying at a top-level store, you have their own quality guarantee anyway. In addition, the greatest percentage of designer clothing is in the high-fashion category, and, as I have emphasized elsewhere in this book, inappropriate for most American men.

Invariably, you will also find the store's own label, and by and large it offers the best quality-for-dollar buy. The store labels of reputable stores are generally excellent, and very often are applied to merchandise identical to that of manufacturers with famous designer goods.

The third label is a combination: "So-and-so Clothing Made Specifically for (and then the name of the store)." This labeling is also a good indicator of quality in expensive stores.

It means that the store's buyer believes that the brand is good enough to put the store label on it, and that the manufacturer's name and reputation are significant enough to warrant mentioning. It may also mean that the buyer has the right of rejection of a certain percentage of that manufacturer's goods as a further guarantee of quality control. This means that, to some extent, the garments have been preselected for you, and also that you may well find the rejected goods elsewhere at significant savings.

Next in the categories of stores selling clothing comes that group of large department stores whose merchandise and prices are aimed directly at the middle class. Their quality ranges from excellent to moderate, and they also have a labeling system that offers solid value indicators to the man who is not an expert on clothing.

Some of these stores carry clothes with designer labels; again, they are to be avoided by the cost conscious. Most of the big department stores also sell their own store label, and this is an indication that the item so labeled is an excellent quality-for-dollar buy, as is the combination label featuring the name of the manufacturer as well as the store.

Department stores usually also carry two additional labels. The first is that of well-known, mass-distribution manufacturers whose merchandise is as good as their present reputation. The other is what I call the "diddledy-diddledy-boom label." This is basically a made-up name owned by the store. It is applied to merchandise with which the store does not want its own name associated, but which it believes offers good dollar value for the price. This type of label usually appears on the cheapest line of merchandise that the store carries.

If you must buy really inexpensively, neither the expensive, first-class stores nor the large department stores are the best places for you. But they do offer many advantages:

variety, quality control, customer services, generous merchandise return policies, excellent (and free) tailoring services.

If you are difficult to fit, the cost of tailoring is a very important consideration when you buy suits and estimate their true cost. If you are an exceptionally difficult fit, it is not inconceivable that tailoring could run $50 to $75 for a suit, and your money is much better spent on a higher-quality suit to begin with than on tailoring.

Whatever the good points of expensive shops or department stores, it is a fact that the vast majority of men in this country cannot afford to buy clothes in these types of stores. For these men, there are three other kinds of stores that offer decent merchandise in a lower price range.

First are the chain stores, the large chains that have stores throughout the country and put their own name on virtually all of their merchandise, or have made-up names for categories of their merchandise that are almost synonymous with the store name.

Their clothing is relatively inexpensive, and is worth just about what you pay for it. Their sales do not offer great bargains, but are generally reliable. The only suggestions I have about shopping in such chains is to read the other chapters in this book very carefully, to know what you are looking for and need, and to do considerable cross-shopping before ever buying anything. Regardless of what you can spend, you are still trying to buy clothes that create a distinct image.

• • • • • • • • • • • • • • • • • •

HOW TO WATCH YOUR STEP IN DISCOUNT STORES

Next, consider the discount stores. These generally offer the most inexpensive acceptable clothes, but these outlets also must be approached with considerable care and some knowledge of fabric and workmanship if you want to look successful. You must check for quality and for value.

Discount stores fall into only two categories: honest and dishonest. Honest discount stores can sell at their low prices because they buy merchandise that is sacrificed elsewhere. They buy manufacturers' overruns; and they take on distress merchandise from stores that are in financial trouble. Discount stores also bring in a regular supply of their own merchandise, and this is their weakest point. Their own lines are not quality goods sold at a discount, but cheap goods sold at cheap prices. So before you buy at any discount store, you should familiarize yourself with the labels that are consistently offered there and nowhere else. These are the labels owned by the discount store, and you should avoid clothing so marked, since it represents your worst buy.

You must also be extra aware of current fashion when you shop in discount stores, because they carry many articles that are so far removed from prevailing styles as to be just about worthless in trying to build your image. But sometimes you can find items that are dated but can be corrected if you pick and choose with care and know a good tailor.

Many discount stores also carry mass-distribution brand name merchandise at a discount rate, and this offers the best buys on a consistent basis. There is no better guarantee of quality, and first-line merchandise and seconds are usually carefully marked. Some discount stores cut out the brand names; and that is also usually a good indicator of quality. True, you will find some crooked merchants cutting labels out of shoddy goods, and selling them as brands that they are not, but if you do your cross-shopping, you will be able to detect these obvious frauds quickly.

Dishonest discount stores frequently reveal their true colors without your having to do any detective work. The least reputable places have one characteristic in common, and that is high-pressure salesmen. Almost invariably, they try to push certain goods on you. If they are pushing, they probably have a good reason, since the honest discounter has little trouble moving his merchandise. Salesmen who push are working on a commission basis, and their advice is going to be in their best interest rather than yours.

Do not for one second believe that the day of the huckster in clothing stores is over. On a Saturday afternoon several years ago, I went shopping the discount stores for a raincoat. After going to several stores where they very frankly told me they did not have what I wanted, I arrived at the third store and asked for my size, which happens to be 42 Long. One salesman said they did not have it, but immediately another fellow jumped up and said, "Oh, yes, we have it!" He quickly took a coat down from a rack and helped me on with it without giving me a chance to look at it. He then pulled up some of the material in the back with his hand so that from the front the coat looked as if it fit. It was actually a 46 Regular. I took it off, and my wife and I began laughing. The salesman, who thought that he just had suckered me, was busy putting the coat in a box and wrapping it, and it took him a while to realize that we were laughing at him.

Although this scene looked like something out of a 1920s cartoon, such practices are still going on. And although it seems absurd, that salesman must have gotten away with such shenanigans before. So the phrase caveat emptor very definitely prevails when you are buying clothing at a discount.

Another type of discount store is the so-called manufacturer's outlet. These fall into three categories. First is the manufacturer's outlet that isn't. This type of store does not carry standard lines and stock but merely uses the designation as a come-on. Their merchandise is purchased from odd lots, damaged goods or seconds. Another practice is to purchase goods, mark them up two hundred percent, and then discount them fifty percent.

The second type of manufacturer's outlet, which is quite legitimate and which offers excellent buys if you hit them at the right time, is the factory outlet that is actually next to the factory and owned by the manufacturer. These outlets sell their own overproduction, seconds, dated goods and odd lots.

If you do not know what odd lots are, I should explain; if you do, bear with me for a moment. You buy shirts one at a time, but retailers naturally do not. They buy an entire line and must have all sizes available. Obviously, the store must have more of the most popular sizes—15½–33 for example— than of others. At some point during the season, the manufacturer will be left with some patterns or colors or materials in which he does not have every size. If he chooses not to replenish his stock with the missing sizes, or if he can no longer obtain that specific material, he disposes of his remainders as odd lots. The man who wears unusual sizes can consequently do very well in factory outlets.

The one major flaw of shopping in such factory outlets is that they do not mark their seconds very well. Many put out seconds and overproduction and odd lots and mix them all together so that you can buy two shirts at the same counter at the same price and one will be perfect and the other will have a flaw. Until you unwrap the shirt, you never know. The practice verges on being dishonest, but it is commonly done, so examine all merchandise carefully before paying for it. Although the discounts in factory outlets are substantial— usually fifty percent or more—return policies are practically nonexistent.

The other legitimate type of factory outlet is independently owned, but sells a number of lesser-known brands. These brands are possibly just as good as those of the major manufacturers, maybe even better, but the stocks in these stores consist not only of overproduction and odd lots but also seconds and dated goods.

This type of factory outlet is a tricky place to shop, and for a very simple reason. During good times, a manufacturer can sell almost all his goods to regular retail stores at the highest possible profits. If he owns his own factory outlet, the manufacturer can keep it supplied from regular stock, and still make a maximum profit. But in such times, he is only going to supply the independent outlet when it suits him.

When times are tough and manufacturers are having a hard time moving their merchandise, independent outlets tend to stock good merchandise at excellent buys. But in good times, to keep the independent outlet operating, the owner will have to purchase goods that are frequently of secondary quality and at higher cost, and sell such goods as if they are being substantially discounted. So this type of outlet at times delivers exactly what it says it delivers, but at other times it does not. Therefore, you cannot go into one of these places and buy blindly. You must look very carefully, and you must look for labels you recognize; they are very important.

In New York one weekend, I came across items of clothing, discounted by fifty percent or more, of the following brands: Aquascutum, Arrow, Stanley Blacker, Pierre Cardin, Clubman, Countess Mara, Hammonton Park, His, Hush Puppies, Duofold, English Daks, Eagle, Jantzen, Lee, Johnston & Murphy, London Fog, MacGregor, Monte Cristo, Mr. Pants, Oleg Cassini, Palm Beach, Phoenix, Prince Ferrara, Sero, Schiaperelli and Sussex. In addition, there were many more good buys on garments with the labels removed, or carrying a store label known to New Yorkers. And I saw the labels of seven stores that sell only high-quality goods.

On that one weekend, if you had previously cross-shopped with any care at all, you could have bought half a dozen suits, several brands of shirts, ties, raincoats and shoes at half price or less, and would have wound up with the identical items being sold at the same time in elegant Fifth Avenue stores at regular price.

When one of my most successful clients availed himself of my services, he said he knew absolutely nothing about brands or labels or store names. So he developed his own system. Every time he went into a good store, he would write in an alphabetized pocket address book the brand name or label, the retail price, and a brief description of any garment he bought. After about four months, he had also compiled a listing for every article of clothing he might still need, as well as those brands that were acceptable in quality and appearance. When he went to the discount houses, he simply whipped out his little book, and bought or did not buy according to what he found.

He figured that he was saving forty percent on his clothing bill as a direct result of this record keeping, and he was able to wear exactly the same clothing he would have purchased in the more expensive stores. So the notebook method is a good one.

Discount stores and factory outlets are fine for the man who lives in a city large enough to support them, but what about the man who lives in a small town or in a city that is not a good town for buying clothing? He can shop at sales time, but then he is usually faced with a relatively limited selection.

• • • • • • • • • • • • • • • • •

GET A FREE TRIP TO NEW YORK

Many of my out-of-town clients have discovered that if they come to New York in January, they can purchase their clothes so economically that the trip is paid for by their savings. Among my clients, this custom started some years ago with eight Midwestern doctors. It has now grown to the point that there are probably 300 to 400 Molloy clients (and their wives) in New York during January, and their annual clothes-buying trips have become organized vacations.

I do not necessarily recommend that everyone in similar circumstances take this type of vacation. I do suggest that any man who finds himself in a large city try to take advantage of whatever clothing bargains may be waiting there. Whenever I'm in a new town, I always ask if the town has any famous factory outlets. Quite often local companies are proud to show off their goods, and a shopper can do very well by being a bit inquisitive and aggressive.

Saving money on clothing can also be accomplished just by buying less clothing. You can do this without sacrifices because conservative, traditional styles will go much further in your wardrobe than nontraditional styles.

The careful buyer should also consider multifunctional items. I have not bought a solid blue or camel hair sports jacket in years, but I always have one of each. Every two or three years I buy a suit that gives me that type of jacket. Usually the suits are more expensive than what I would normally pay because I want a very rich look in the jacket; but it performs a dual function, and so the money averages out. The first year I use it only as a suit. The second year I wear the jacket with contrasting pants, as well as with the suit pants.

You should also consider buying suits that are sold with an extra pair of pants. This is an excellent idea that frequently prolongs the life of a suit even though the garments are not normally of the best quality or appropriate patterns and colors. I have one friend who shops at Brooks Brothers but never buys a suit unless they tailor-make him a matching second pair of pants. This runs into money; but the true cost pays off in the long run.

The man who is truly eager to save money on his clothing should always have two lists with him. The first is a list of items he is going to need in the next year. (Purchasing any further ahead can be a waste, since you can change weight or move to another section of the country where needs are different.)

The second list should consist of items you can use at anytime. For example, anytime I see a good solid blue or solid maroon silk tie on sale, I buy it, since I know I will need it at some point in the future. Right now I have half a dozen unworn maroon silk ties, but I paid half price or less for them, and I know I'll have one when I need it, and I will not have to pay full price. Do not overstock any one item as styles do change; in fact, if you see an item on everyone's discount counter it probably is on the way out.

My next recommendation for saving money and improving the quality of your clothing is comparison living. Comparison shopping is difficult. Unless you are an expert, it is often very hard to discern quality differences when you hold up two shirts in a store. Although I owned a shirt outlet for three years and my business is clothes, I can still be fooled about the quality of one versus another. But I have developed a second system, what I call comparison living, and many of my clients and I use it.

Whenever we find a brand we like—whether it is a make of suits, shirts, ties or shoes—we keep a running record of how many wearings that brand gives us. We compare this with different brands in a comparative price range and are very often surprised to find that some of the brands we have experienced in the past as being very good are becoming shoddy.

Two developments are characteristic of inflationary times. Some well-known manufacturers maintain their quality and raise prices at the risk of losing some customers. Others cut down on quality to maintain prices and keep customers. You cannot readily notice these quality differences in the store, but you can pinpoint them after a number of wearings of a garment. That's comparative living, a continuing reevaluation of quality and price, and the only way for the intelligent clothes buyer to stay ahead of the game in hard times.

• • • • • • • • • • • • • • • • • • • •

HOW TO SPOT IMPORTED BARGAINS

Another factor that many bargain-conscious men also tend to overlook is the comparative cost and quality between imported and domestic goods. Some countries of origin produce goods of consistent high quality at fairly reasonable prices, usually thanks to low-cost, well-skilled labor.

Although any buyer should always be wary of generalities, I can offer some hints. Imported shoes from Brazil presently seem to be the best buy. There are fine shoes from Italy, beautiful ones from Greece, and good ones from England, Ireland, France and Germany, but the best buys are from Brazil.

For suits, there are three levels of imports. At the lowest, the best buys are from the large chain stores that are more and more obtaining their goods from the Orient. At the moderate level, American-made suits are the best value. At the very expensive price level, European suits offer the best quality-for-dollar ratio.

In shirts, the best polyester and cotton blends are undoubtedly American. With good cotton shirts, the point of origin does not seem to matter.

The best moderate-priced silk ties are Italian; the best polyester, American. Although there are no tremendous breakthroughs in this field, there are some good ties coming from the Orient, along with a lot of junk.

American-made socks, underwear and outerwear offer the best values.

Good buys on sweaters are available from Mexico and Yugoslavia (of the Iron Curtain countries, Yugoslavia is the only one that makes and exports fashionable items to any extent).

Gold and silver cuff links are generally very good buys when you can pick them up in many Caribbean islands and in Mexico. And although the international monetary fluctuations have made foreign shopping much more expensive in recent years, there are still some good buys for the careful tourist in Europe.

· · · · · · · · · · · · · · · · · · ·

A SYSTEM TO SAVE $32,000

When I decided to update this book, I asked a half dozen long-standing clients who I knew had used my money-saving hints when buying their clothing to prepare a record of how much time they estimated they had spent looking for clothing over a three-year period, and to make up an approximate cost analysis of how much money they had saved. Two of the men are lawyers, two are in sales and the other two are executives. All are reasonably affluent and good dressers.

These six men estimated that they saved $420 to $1,530 a year on their clothing. In an attempt to be reasonable I eliminated the top and bottom figures and still came up with a $648 average. This is a rather substantial figure, and is largely due to their living in New York with all its resources. But if we take that figure and do a bit of simple multiplication, we come to the astounding conclusion that in the buyer's lifetime of fifty years, he can save in excess of $32,000—and that's just as good as $32,000 of tax-free income.

After everything is said and done, you must spend either time or money to dress successfully. If you have the money and are willing to spend it on clothes, then all you need are the general and basic instructions found elsewhere in this book. But if you do not have the money, or want to hold on to as much as you can, you can still dress just as successfully if you are willing to spend the time, and if you know and adhere to the rules of American dress.

7

Dressing
For Success
on the Road

The first thing Tom did when he became president of his firm was to call a Chicago company he had dealt with six years earlier, and to try to resurrect an agreement that had died at that time. He knew it was a good deal and believed the only reason the agreement had fallen through was because on the day it was to be finalized, everything had gone wrong for him. He had gotten stuck in traffic on the way to the airport and had had to run for his plane; the flight attendant had spilled a cup of coffee on his tie and shirt, and, when he arrived in Chicago an hour late after circling O'Hare Airport, he discovered that his baggage had not made it with him. As a result, Tom had to attend that very important meeting wearing the crumpled suit he had worn on the plane, with the stained tie, and the only shirt he could buy in the few free minutes he had before the meeting, one with broad blue stripes.

Tom never bothered to explain to the people he was meeting why he looked the way he did. His motto was the same as that of many American executives: "Don't explain and don't complain."

The meeting lasted over two hours, and it seemed to him as if everything had gone beautifully. When he left for home, mentally he had the deal in his backpocket. However, when he went to work the next morning, the president called him into his office. He explained to Tom that in the opinion of many of the people on the board, Tom was too young to be president of the company, but he thought he could put Tom into the job, if Tom could put this deal together. Unfortunately, he had just heard from the other company; they were backing out, and that killed Tom's chances.

Now, when Tom finally got the president of the other firm on the line, he explained about the earlier negotiations and said that as president of his company, he would like to see if he could revive them. He still thought the agreement would be beneficial to all parties. The CEO in the Chicago firm had only been on the job for two years and did not know the details of the earlier negotiation, but told Tom it sounded promising to him. Four days later he called back and said to Tom, "With a few small changes, you've got a deal."

A week later, after an agreement had been reached through telephone negotiations, Tom could not resist asking the other CEO why the proposal had been turned down seven years earlier. The president of the other company told Tom that his people liked the deal now because Tom, as president of his company, was behind the deal. They had the impression the last time that the men in charge of his company were not. The man they sent to negotiate the deal, in their opinion, had no power. The CEO went on to explain that he did not know who the man was, but one look at him and the officers of the firm decided he was a loser. Before that fellow had arrived they had decided the deal was a good one, but once they saw him they decided his firm was not committed to it. He told Tom he had seen a short note on the earlier contract that said: *Man came dressed like a clown; don't do business with clowns.* Tom gulped and never said a word, but he invited the president of the Midwestern firm to San Francisco for the signing. He did not want to go to Chicago; he was afraid someone might recognize him.

The lesson of this story is very clear: no one in San Francisco thought Tom was a clown; on his home ground, in his industry and in his company, he was known as a mover and a shaker. Long before he became president of the company he was one of the people who counted. Everyone recognized he was a skilled technician, a talented manager, a powerful executive and a man on the way up. Those who knew him, knew if he stood behind an agreement, the agreement was as good as gold. But in Chicago he was an unknown quantity. The people meeting him there for the first time were forced by circumstances to make quick judgments about his ability, particularly his ability to deliver on promises. They took one look at his wrinkled suit, his gaudy shirt and his spotted tie, and decided it would not be wise to risk their company's reputation and products, and possibly their jobs, on him.

When Tom heard why the deal had been killed the first time, he felt hurt and insulted. But after he thought about what had happened, he came to the conclusion that if he had been in their position he would have probably done the same thing. What he did instead of dwelling on his mistake was to learn from it. He instituted a very strict dress code for his executives when they were on the road. I think every corporate president should do the same.

Our research indicates that Tom's experience was the rule, not the exception. The business people we surveyed on this subject, and we surveyed over 1,000 of them, agreed that before doing business with a stranger, they were forced to make a few judgment calls. They had to estimate how much ability the man had, how much power he had, and in some cases the kind of company he represented. Most of the executives and purchasing agents we spoke to said they preferred to have definite information on these subjects. That is why they preferred to deal with large local companies. If a man represents a corporate giant, you can ususaly tell something about him by his title and where he's positioned in the company; if he represents a company down the street, you can easily find out what type of person you are dealing with by checking with other people in the area or in the industry. However, when you deal with a man you have never met who represents a company from another section of the country, you have to make a number of guesses about him and his company. Therefore, before you pack your bag, you must understand that you are taking with you not only your image and your power, but your company's image and power as well, and the success of your trip to some degree depends on what you put into that bag.

There are several facts that traveling businessmen must keep in mind.

First, in different sections of this country, and in other countries, businessmen dress differently. They, like you, are conditioned by their environment whether they know they are or not; they will judge you by their standards. A region's climate and character affects the way people think about everything, including clothing, and you must adjust your wardrobe as you move from place to place.

Second, if you have never visited a business before and it is in another section of this country or in another country, your best bet is to dress conservatively. Traditional, conservative attire works best in at least eighty-five percent of American corporations and in almost all foreign companies. Executives in other parts of the world are far more conservative than American executives.

Third, the message that is most likely to get you into trouble is that you think of yourself as a superior being from a more sophisticated company, town or country, and you wear clothing that loudly announces that fact.

Fourth, your clothing must not announce that you are an inferior being without power, without prestige and without authority, and you cannot be trusted with important decisions.

Fifth, live up to expectations. If you come from Wall Street and you represent a Wall Street firm, and you are there to talk about stocks, it is important that you look like a Wall Streeter who knows something about stocks.

A truly sophisticated traveler keeps in mind all five rules, and when there is a seeming contradiction, he very subtly works his way around it. He is always aware that his image can be his greatest asset or his greatest liability.

If you live in a sophisticated area and you wish to successfully conduct business in a less sophisticated area, you must never wear items of apparel that are markedly more sophisticated than those worn by the people with whom you are going to be dealing, unless of course you are presenting yourself as an expert and the uniform of your expertise is by nature sophisticated. For example, if you go from New York to Kansas City or from Kansas City to a town 200 miles out on the prairie, or if you go from Chicago to southern Illinois, you must never look as if you are better than the people you are selling to or doing business with. If you do they will object to you and they will not want to deal with you. However, if you go to the smaller, less sophisticated town as a financial expert, and you are there to advise people on how to raise money in the New York bond market, you should look every inch the Wall Streeter you are. The same three-piece gray pinstripe suit that will offend the businesspeople in small-town America if you are there to sell them insurance or negotiate a wheat deal will reassure them if you are presenting yourself as a financial expert.

Your choice is usually not that clear-cut. It is not as simple as choosing between a white hat outfit and a black hat outfit. On most occasions you can choose outfits that will send a number of positive messages simultaneously. For example, if you are visiting a small Midwestern town as a financial expert, I suggest you wear a conservative medium-range blue two-piece pinstripe suit or a light gray two-piece pinstripe suit with a traditional white shirt and a conservative tie. That outfit will say that you are a conservative, traditional and trustworthy businessman and a financial expert without saying you are an Eastern establishment elitist. An example of the type of elitist display that might offend a small-town banker today would be one of those very expensive custom-made one hundred percent cotton soft pastel stripe shirts with contrasting white collars that are found only in the most expensive stores in New York, London and Paris and are worn almost exclusively by Northeastern establishment executives.

However, you do not have to buy your clothing in New York, London or Paris to offend people. You can achieve the same result by buying the latest fashion look in Kansas City and wearing it to Pratt, Kansas, where it is not yet available. Please notice, I said not yet. Time changes the elitist message. What is elitist in January in Pratt, Kansas, may not be elitist in February. It may become available or acceptable locally, or its design and its message may change. For example, at one time silk foulard Ivy League ties worn by North-easterners would have turned off most Southerners and Mid-westerners. Today Southern and Midwestern businessmen have adopted silk foulard small pattern Ivy League ties as their own, and anyone coming from any section of the country can wear one without fear of offending. It is no longer a

smart-ass Yankee tie or a symbol of the Northern establishment, but something that belongs to everyone.

There are also cases where the product changes. The
Gucci shoe, which identified the wearer as a Northeastern
establishment snob a few years ago, can now be worn almost
anywhere in this country because it no longer has the offensive multiple stripe that made it so identifiable. Gucci shoes
look very much like shoes made by other manufacturers, as do
many designer items that were easily identifiable as high-
fashion designer items in the early seventies. Many designers
are now putting their names on suits, shirts and ties that are
virtually indistinguishable from those produced by more traditional makers. This is both good and bad news. The good news
is you can now wear designer clothing to business and get away
with it. The bad news is that you are now being asked to pay
designer prices for traditional pinstripe suits and white shirts.
What has happened is that without ever admitting it, these
designers have taken my advice. They realize that when I said
that men did not want to look different, I was telling them the
truth and they started producing items of clothing which are
as acceptable in Kansas City as they are in New York, Los
Angeles, San Francisco or Rome.

The reverse of the "dress down" rule is equally important
not to violate. If you come from a small town and are selling
in a more sophisticated area, you must be sure not to wear
items that will identify you as a rube. It's quite common to
see Southerners in New York wearing very bright colors and
patterns. These Southerners may come from very sophisticated cities, such as Atlanta, where these patterns are perfectly
acceptable, but they simply do not work in New York. In New
York they mark the wearer as an out-of-towner or even a
hayseed and send the message that if he is not inept, he is
certainly unsophisticated. That is not the ideal message to
send to anyone with whom you wish to do business.

Many Texas businesspeople wear their ten-gallon hats and shoestring ties when they do business in other sections of the country. I once pointed this out to a group of Texas salesmen as being inappropriate and they said that anyone who did not like it should go to hell. When I pointed out to them that they would probably go without selling their product, they did not seem to care for that.

• • • • • • • • • • • • • • • • • • •

THE NORTHEAST

The most conservative area in the United States with regard to clothing is the Northeast. Its major cities are New York, Washington, Boston and, believe it or not, San Francisco. You will find Northeast clothing at the corporate headquarters of most Fortune 500 corporations, no matter where they are located. In any of these places, when you show up to do business you must be dressed in what used to be considered standard Northeast establishment attire if you wish to be as effective as possible. The men who wear this attire still run the country no matter what you have heard to the contrary, make no mistake about it.

The most acceptable clothing for dealing with these men is dark and medium-range gray suits, dark and medium-range blue suits with or without pinstripes, white or blue shirts and upper-middle-class conservative ties.

Since you are most likely to run across the American Brahmin in the Northeast cities and at corporate headquarters I thought I should make specific reference to them now. When dealing with an American Brahmin it is absolutely essential you look as affluent as possible. If you spend any less than $500 for your suits you are going to have to select them with great care. The same is true for shirts that cost less than

$35 and ties that cost less than $20. Whatever you do, when you meet an American Brahmin make certain that you are wearing a good watch and good cuff links. We showed over 200 of these American aristocrats pictures of businessmen wearing a number of different outfits, and asked them whether they liked, trusted or would consider doing business with them.

While two-thirds of them had their suits and shirts custom-made, almost ninety percent of those we questioned reacted just as well to men wearing off-the-rack suits as custom suits, as long as they were traditional, conservative and nicely tailored. Most of them said the reason they had their clothing custom-made was convenience or tradition.

Interestingly enough you can divide these very wealthy men into almost two equal groups. The first group cares a great deal about their appearance, their clothing fits beautifully, is well put together, well kept, and they wear it with a sense of style. The second group looks something like Bill Buckley; they are not disheveled, but they are certainly not fashion plates. If you ask them, most of them will tell you that clothing is not important to them. But like Mr. Buckley they have worn conservative, traditional and upper-class clothing all their lives. By the way, they are not lying to you when they answer the question that way, they are lying to themselves. When we show men from this group pictures of a number of businessmen, they had no objection to the men whose suits were a bit wrinkled, but they were totally turned off by anyone wearing a polyester suit or a lower-class tie. They are turned off, as well, by men whose shoes are not shined or whose heels are run-down. Why they have this prejudice I don't know, but the fact is they are four times more likely to comment about the quality and the upkeep of a man's shoes than their less affluent fellow executives. They were also two or three times more likely to notice the quality of a man's watch although many of them said that it was not an important factor. I believe that since so many of them commented on it, it has to be.

If you have a meeting with an American Brahmin and you can afford it, I suggest you purchase a custom-made or made-to-measure suit with functional button cuffs. The best model would be a dark gray three-piece pinstripe worsted. Wear it with a white cotton shirt and the most traditional, conservative and expensive tie you can buy. If you own a good watch, wear it. If you do not own one, borrow one. If you cannot borrow one, do not wear any watch at all. Many of these men did not wear watches themselves. It is very interesting that they were three times as likely to be without a watch as other executives, and they did not look upon non-watch-wearers as people who could not afford them, but as people who did not want to carry them around.

The conservative style that works in Boston, Philadelphia and New York is a lot more sophisticated than the clothing that works in Buffalo, Burlington, Concord, Augusta and Providence. The executives in these cities are not as fashionable or as well put together as the executives in the major metropolitan areas. They do not spend as much money on their clothing, and if you work in these cities you do not have to spend as much on yours. You will be perfectly at home if you wear a suit that runs from $300 to $325. Polyester and wool blends are common and perfectly acceptable. I call the small Northeastern cities the Middle American Northeast establishment. Their dress code is very similar to that of Cedar Rapids, Idaho, Springfield, Missouri, and Little Rock. The men in these towns dress well, but they have an anti-chic bias. Anything that strikes them as being too fashionable will turn them off. It announces to them that the wearer is probably a sharpie and cannot be trusted. This is as true in Burlington, Vermont, as it is in Little Rock, Arkansas.

The Northeast, like any other section of the country, has

a large number of small towns, and in these towns, like all small towns in America, the dress code is set by the bankers. If you want to do business in these towns, you should look carefully at how the bankers dress and copy them. Small towns can really be divided into two groups, the suit towns and the sports jacket towns. In about two-thirds of the towns in the Northeast, the top bankers in town will wear conservative two-piece suits most of the time, identical to those worn in business throughout most of America. In the other towns they wear sports jackets; the sports jackets are dramatically different from those found in most other sections of the country. They are very traditional. You will very seldom see a businessman from a small town in the Northeast wearing a jacket that is fashionable or flashy. They wear the same style jackets that were worn by their fathers and grandfathers. Their favorites are tweeds, herringbones and blue blazers. Their jackets are darker in color than those found in the South and not nearly as lively as those found on the West Coast. They wear them with traditional shirts and ties.

The people in small towns in Maine and Vermont and New York are no different from the people in small towns in Minnesota, North Dakota, Kansas and Nevada. They have an anti-big-city bias. If you visit them looking like a big-city slicker, you will turn them off and they will turn you off. In fact, their clothing bias is so strong it is almost impossible to do business with them if you are wearing a chic or fashionable or Northeast establishment look. A $600 three-piece pinstripe suit worn with an expensive white shirt and a beautiful tie and an expensive watch will identify you not only as an outsider, but as the enemy, and they will have nothing to do with you.

Since so many corporate headquarters are found in and around the three main cities in the Northeast, Philadelphia, New York and Boston, so you should be especially careful to observe the dress code of each.

• • • • • • • • • • • • • • • • • •

PHILADELPHIA

Philadelphia has a unique dress code. Even though Philadelphia is noted for being conservative, some of the bankers in that town dress even more gaudily than bankers from the West Coast—which is noted for its gaudy attire. You will see high-ranking bank officers in Philadelphia wearing sports jackets, the only major city on the East Coast where this is true. I can offer no reason for this paradox, but it does demonstrate the importance of your taking notice of clothing codes whenever you are in an unfamiliar area, and adjusting your own wardrobe accordingly.

• • • • • • • • • • • • • • • • • •

BOSTON AND SAN FRANCISCO

The reason I have put Boston and San Francisco together is because their clothing codes are almost identical. For some strange reason San Francisco has the clothing point of view of a Northeast town, and even stranger, it has a dress code which is almost identical to Boston's, perhaps because both towns have the same type of industries. In downtown San Francisco and downtown Boston, the business communities are very conservative. The Northeast establishment look is found in both. Dark three-piece pinstripe suits worn with white or blue shirts and conservative ties are de rigueur in both cities. To wear anything less conservative or less traditional when you deal in these areas is to commit business suicide. You will be relegated to the outer office and left there.

However, if you take a one-hour trip from downtown Boston or downtown San Francisco, you will find yourself either in Silicon Valley or on the Boston Loop, two of the major centers of high-tech corporate America. In both of these areas you will find an entirely different dress code. The men who run the high-tech companies along the Boston Loop, although they wear suits on occasion, generally adopt the laid-back and very traditional Northeast academic look that dominates the MIT and Harvard campuses. Their marriage with MIT has made them, in truth, as much a part of the academic community as the business community. You will find men in these offices making $100,000-a-year-plus wearing very expensive sports jackets, slacks, turtleneck sweaters, Irish knit pullovers and jeans. Outside San Francisco in Silicon Valley you have the same marriage of academia and high-tech business. Because the climate is warmer and California has a more relaxed dress code, the academic look is even more laid-back. Here you will find men wearing designer jeans and $65 cotton golf shirts.

Not only must you pay attention to the dress code in the area, you have to pay attention to the dress of the specific people with whom you are dealing. If you were to visit either of these high-tech areas for the first time, you would be very foolish if you dressed casually. You would be equally foolish however, if you wore a three-piece pinstripe suit with the rest of the Northeast establishment downtown high-authority look. Remember, if you want to deal with people it is much easier if you look like you are one of them. Research shows that the outfit that works best if you are doing business with these high-tech people is a two-piece solid blue or gray suit worn with a blue shirt and a conservative striped tie. It will announce to them that you're a conservative, traditional and most of all reliable businessman without saying you are one of those establishment types who does not like, trust or understand technicians or their technology.

Another very important reason you cannot wear a three-piece pinstripe suit when you deal with the executives in the high-tech companies is they have an egalitarian management style. Even when the men in these companies themselves wear the Eastern establishment look, and many of them have adopted it because they think it is in their best interest to do so, they are not particularly friendly to others who wear it. From their very beginnings these companies have been competing with the Japanese, and as a result have adopted some of their management practices. The most important of these is the team concept. They treat their companies as if they are teams and all the employees as if they are members of a team. The president represents himself as just another team member with a specific skill. Generally, the team uniform is what I describe as upscale blue-collar because about eighty percent of the high-tech wizards who started and often still run these companies come from blue-collar backgrounds and are most comfortable with this uniform. Because they come from blue-collar backgrounds you also have to avoid the high-fashion look. Most men who come from blue-collar backgrounds, no matter how far they have progressed, look upon males who dress fashionably as being at best effete and at worst effeminate.

• • • • • • • • • • • • • • • • • • • •

NEW YORK CITY

New York is a very important city for American businessmen, not only because there are about thirty million people in the metropolitan area, but because it is the center of America's financial community, and is the place that businessmen usually have to go to if they wish to raise big dollars. The New York metropolitan area is also the home of about one-third of the headquarters of America's largest corporations and contains the major regional headquarters of at least one-third more. As a result, New York is an extremely conservative town. Two-thirds of the businessmen in New York City go to work every day wearing traditional, conservative business attire.

The look of New York, however, is not identical to the look in Boston. New York business attire has a little more panache; ten percent to fifteen percent of the most influential men in New York City wear a high-style, conservative design-er look. They do so because the largest single industry in New York is the fashion industry, and the largest industry of any town affects the way people in that town dress. Therefore, if you visit New York you not only have to wear very conservative clothing, but it must be well tailored, expensive and put together nicely. New York executives probably spend ten percent to fifteen percent more on their clothing than executives in most other sections of the country, and the tailoring in New York is often better than will be found in small and moderate-size towns. In addition, New York executives appreciate style and quality and often recognize it in others. The biggest mistake made by executives coming to do business in the New York area is to think that dressing conservatively is enough. You must have a sense of style as well. New York is a town where looking good is very important, and looking bad can cost you a lot of money.

Here is a classic tale of how image can impact your bottom line. Ted Turner came to New York to take over CBS. Everyone knew he was rich and powerful, they knew he had built one of the greatest television stations in the nation, and that he was an astute businessman. He had come to Wall Street to convince the people there that they should risk their money and the money of their investors in his move against CBS. His basic message was trust me, I'm a winner. The success of his takeover attempt to a large degree depended on the impression he made on the Wall Street community. Ted Turner wore a slightly rumpled suit; his tie was askew; his hair was wind-blown. His look was the good-ol'-boy look. It works beautifully in Atlanta. There it says, "I am a gentleman; you can trust me." In New York the same look said, "I don't know what I'm doing, I'm not powerful, I'm not authoritative, don't take me seriously." Now, I don't for one second think the only thing that stopped Ted Turner from taking over CBS was his rumpled suit, but there is no question in my mind that if he had wanted to be identified as a mover and a shaker in New York—even with his millions of dollars and great track record—it certainly would have helped him to look the part.

Possibly being one of the movers and shakers in Atlanta made Ted Turner think the same thing Jimmy Carter's people thought when they first moved to Washington, that it was possible to take their dress code with them and make it work in another section of the country. It did not work for them and it did not work for Ted Turner, and if he and the president's assistants could not make the Southern good-ol'-boy look work outside the South, no one can.

For every executive who comes to New York and makes a mistake in how he dresses, there are ten New Yorkers who make the same mistake when they travel. The reason is simple. Many people who live in New York think of New York as the center of the world, and that they don't have to change their New York habits when they leave. As a result they get into trouble. The look that gets them into most trouble is the southern Connecticut suburbs of New York look—an upscale conservative look with a touch of American Brahmin about it. The men who wear this look will invariably pay $700 to $800 for their suits and at least $40 to $50 for their shirts. They have good hand-rolled silk handkerchiefs tucked in their breast pockets, and wear very expensive watches. They believe that their body language, verbal patterns and dress announce to the world that they are sophisticated people and superior beings. If they were truly superior— in fact, if they had the insight of the average salesman—they would never wear that style outside the Northeast, because many of the businessmen they meet resent this style and resent them if they wear it.

Another version of the same mistake is made by the people in the fashion industry. Salesmen from the garment district wear styles sold exclusively in Paris, Milan, Rome and New York when they visit Topeka. They think that because they are dealing with other people in the fashion industry their clothing is acceptable. It is not. One of the most interesting discoveries I made is that in other parts of the country men and women in the garment industry who consider themselves fashionable are annoyed by the high fashion that comes out of New York and turned off by people who wear it. Which means if you are trying to sell to them while wearing it, you are not doing yourself a favor.

Both of these groups of men have a disease I call mid-Manhattan myopia. They believe that anyone who lives west of the Hudson River is a barbarian and must be saved by them from a drab, tasteless existence. They think of themselves as superior, sophisticated beings. When, in fact, if they were truly sophisticated they would know and obey the oldest rule for the traveling man: "When in Rome do as the Romans do." This of course would include Rome, New York.

• • • • • • • • • • • • • • • • • •

THE SOUTH

If you wish to do business in the South and you are not a Southerner, there are certain rules you have to obey. A Southerner's reaction to clothing is very strong and very predictable, and the way you dress can have a major impact on your ability to do business in this area of the country. If you are not a Southerner do not wear a polka-dot tie. If you are a Southerner it's acceptable. If you are not a Southerner do not wear dark pinstripe suits or three-piece suits when doing business in the South. If you are a Southerner they are not only acceptable, they may help your executive image. They announce to your fellow Southerners that you may be more sophisticated and able than they. If you come from outside the South, medium-range solid blues and grays are far better than dark blues and grays, and white shirts work best. Outside of Atlanta and Dallas you should avoid dressing in the latest fashion. The latest fashions almost invariably are not available outside those cities. If you wear an Italian designer suit in Macon, Georgia, it will not identify you as a sophisticate, but as an outsider and possibly a kook. Although today you can wear an Ivy League tie in most sections of the South, avoid them when you are dealing with people in small towns. In fact, avoid any type of dress that could be considered exotic. Southerners are very traditional, conservative people, and you should leave anything that could be considered fashionable or foreign at home.

. . . .

ATLANTA

One of the great mistakes Northerners make about the South is they think of Southerners as rubes. The men in Atlanta spend more money on their business clothing than do men in any other city in the United States, and it shows. They are very well put together. Wearing good quality clothing in Atlanta is an absolute must. In some industries it even helps to look fashionable.

Atlanta is really two cities. The first Atlanta is Southern Atlanta. There the clothing is a little lighter and brighter and a bit more casual than in other sections of the country. This is the traditional South. It is a South where Ted Turner's rumpled suits say he is a good ol' boy, not an incompetent. If you are dealing with a firm that still has its roots deep in Dixie, you should wear lighter-colored suits with traditional shirts and ties. On the other hand, there is Northern Atlanta where many firms have a substantial percentage of employees who are transplanted Northerners. The clothing in these firms is more traditional, more conservative and slightly darker.

• •

DALLAS

While the best-dressed men in the South live in Atlanta, the most fashionable men live in Dallas. The reason men's clothing is so fashionable in Dallas is because Dallas is the home of two institutions, the Dallas Clothing Mart and Neiman Marcus. If you visit Dallas you must put your clothing together very carefully. It is still a conservative town and you must remember this. If you come from the North or the Midwest you should leave your darker suits at home. This does not mean you should not wear conservative suits, but you should wear them with shirts and ties that have as much panache as you can find in traditional attire. In Dallas, looking good is important.

• •

HOUSTON

Houston has two dress codes. Downtown Houston is dominated by the oil companies where they dress like Northern executives, very conservative and very traditional. Their suits are slightly lighter in weight and color than you will find in the Northeast, but the style is identical. The men in downtown Houston are as precise and as careful about their dress as the men in New York, Chicago and Boston.

Once you leave downtown Houston, there is a dramatic change. Men in conservative businesses will still wear suits, but they will be far more casual and less precise in their general appearance than those who work downtown. In addition, there are large industries away from the downtown area where suits are hardly ever worn. In the summer in these industries, the short-sleeve shirt, with or without a tie, is the standard uniform of the day. If you have to do business with these people and you come from another section of the country, you should wear a suit when you arrive, but the minute you get into an office, without asking permission, take off your coat and loosen your tie. If you do, you will get a far friendlier reception.

• • • • • • • • • • • • • • • • • •

JACKSONVILLE

Jacksonville, Florida, is one of the great boomtowns of America. Big buildings are shooting up like weeds. At first glance you will think of it as a cosmopolitan, conservative, almost Northern town—but don't be fooled, Jacksonville is still a very Southern town. If you are visiting Jacksonville for the first time, a mid-range blue or gray suit, worn with a blue shirt and a striped tie, would be an ideal outfit. It will let you move effectively both in the Northern companies, which are somewhat cosmopolitan in their dress, and the Southern companies, which are somewhat traditional. When you move from company to company in Jacksonville, pay very careful attention to the way the people dress. Although they may seem to be dressing the same, there are really two traditions in Jacksonville much as there are in Atlanta. The men in the Southern companies will be slightly less precise in their dress and slightly more casual in their appearance. If you wish to do business in either group, it is important that you recognize this very subtle difference and react to it. The difference between the two looks can be the angle at which you tie your tie, or whether you have your coat buttoned, or whether every hair is in place, but the difference is important. This is particularly true if you're dealing with a Southern firm. Southerners react much more positively to outsiders who adopt their dress code.

• • • • • • • • • • • • • • • • • • • •

MIAMI

Miami has a dual dress code because it is basically two populations and two cities. Miami is both an Anglo and a Cuban city. The Cubans have come to dominate the business and social life in Miami, and they have had a major effect on the way all Miamians dress. When the Cubans first arrived twenty-five years ago, Miami was basically a resort town and, although businessmen wore suits, most of the population dressed very casually. You could eat in some of the best restaurants in town without a jacket and tie. Today this is no longer true. Because they came from an upper-class background, the Cubans were suit wearers. They wore lighter and brighter suits, but they wore them not only to business, but when they went out for the evening. As a result the number of suit wearers in Miami at night increased dramatically and better restaurants started demanding that men wear jackets and ties. Several years later, when the Cubans started having a major impact on Miami business, the number of people in business who wore suits increased as well.

While the Cubans were affecting the way the natives

dressed, the natives also began affecting the Cubans. Cuban businessmen after just a few years stopped wearing what I refer to as Havana suits. They adopted the more conservative grays, blues, browns and tans of Miami natives. Today, most Cuban businessmen would fit into America's boardrooms without any problem. What has happened is that the two cultures have come together to produce an upscale conservative yet stylish dress code for both business and social life.

•   •   •   •   •   •   •   •   •   •   •   •   •   •   •   •   •

NASHVILLE

When most people think of Nashville they think of the Grand Ole Opry, cowboy boots, cowboy hats and jeans. That is certainly part of Nashville and an important part of it, but the vast majority of businessmen in Nashville are very conservative dressers. I believe that their conservatism is a reaction to the Country and Western image most people have of their town. Many of the businessmen in Nashville will tell you with some pride that they have never been to the Grand Ole Opry; to many of them, being interested in Country and Western music or dressing like a cowboy is a sign of being unsophisticated, and their clothing reflects this local prejudice. They are as conservative in Nashville as they are in any city in the South. Therefore, if you visit Nashville and you come from the North, you can wear your most conservative garments. They will look upon conservative clothing as a sign of competence and react positively to those who wear it.

• • • • • • • • • • • • • • • • • •

OTHER SOUTHERN CITIES

When you do business in any other Southern city, you can assume you are dealing in the traditional South. The gentlemen in these areas will wear traditional, conservative suits that will be slightly lighter in color than you find in most of the rest of the country. They will wear them with traditional shirts and ties, but they will not put them together with great precision. There is almost a relaxed attitude about the way they put on clothing that announces that it is not important to them. If you are visiting this area for the first time, the safest combination would be a medium-range solid blue suit, white shirt and any conservative tie other than polka dot or silk foulard. The second-best combination is a medium-range gray suit, a pale blue shirt and a maroon tie in either a solid or conservative pattern. The pattern that works best is usually a simple stripe. Both combinations will allow you to use the same shoes and socks that are acceptable in almost any section of the country. In fact, these two suits should form the backbone of the wardrobe of anyone who travels for business and spends any amount of time in the South. The third suit I would recommend, for both summer and winter, is the traditional solid beige. It is probably the single best summer suit for everyone in the South.

Although there are entire industries in sections of the South where short-sleeve shirts are not only acceptable but almost required in the summer, I suggest that if you are going to do business in these industries you wear long sleeves and perspire, unless you have been dealing with these people for years and have developed a very friendly relationship.

Suit lapel and tie widths, as well as shirt collar sizes, seem to be standardized throughout the country at present but if the styles begin to change again, be aware that it took almost two and a half years after they were standard in New York for the South to adopt the wide lapel in the seventies, and the new narrow lapel in the eighties.

• • • • • • • • • • • • • • • • • •

SOUTHERNERS GOING NORTH

Southerners who travel in the North, particularly in the Northeast, must obey several rules. Bright colors and patterns in suits that are acceptable in the South on a year-round basis do not work in the North. I strongly suggest solid or pinstripe grays or blues when you travel to the North, West or Midwest, the pinstripe being reserved for the most conservative areas and companies. Your beige suit may not travel well. Even though gentlemen in the North and Midwest wear beige suits in the summer, the shade of beige they wear is different. Northern and Midwestern beige has a touch of gray in it. Southern beige often has a touch of green, or is two or three shades lighter than Northern beige. Suits made of those shades of beige in the North announce that the wearer is from a blue-collar background and are not acceptable in business offices. Unless you are sure of what you are doing, leave your beige suit at home. Men from Texas who wear Mexican or Western attire in their home territory should not wear such clothing anywhere else, because it will be looked upon as attire for cowboys and will hurt their credibility when selling merchandise or services.

• • • • • • • • • • • • • • • • • • • •

WHAT WORKS BEST IN THE MIDWEST

The Midwest tradition for conservative attire is exaggerated and somewhat misleading, particularly in sportswear. Although the Midwesterners dress conservatively by almost any standards, wearing dark grays and dark blues themselves, they react negatively to outsiders who wear those same dark solid gray suits and dark blue suits. The best suits to wear in the Midwest are small shadow blue and gray plaids, solid dark browns, medium-range blues and very light grays. Recently, the dark brown pinstripe suit has become one of the most effective business suits to wear when you are in the larger cities of the Midwest, particularly Chicago and Minneapolis/St. Paul.

Men in the Midwest have very strong aversions to certain colors. Whether you are a native or come from the outside, never wear gold when doing business in this area. Do not wear charcoal gray except in overcoats. Wear no purple or lavender, and make certain that you wear nothing that identifies you, correctly or incorrectly, as a member of the Eastern elitist establishment. It is very difficult, if not impossible, to do business in the Midwest if you wear clothing that indicates that you are not doing well financially. Midwesterners react positively to signs of affluence and money, and it is the only section of the country where even poor taste can be effective as long as it is expensive poor taste. Businessmen, particularly salesmen in this area who are not dealing with corporate headquarters, can drive flashy cars and wear flashy wristwatches to their hearts' content. Even diamond pinky rings do not turn off people in the Midwest the way they turn off men in other sections of the country. Affluence in any form seems to work.

The most noticeable change among Midwestern executives is a new upscale elegance of the men at the top. Midwestern dowdiness, which existed ten to fifteen years ago at just about every level, has all but disappeared at this level. Today, top executives are far more elegant and put their clothing together with great care. They have a cosmopolitan look, particularly in the more sophisticated cities like Chicago, Detroit and St. Louis. However, make no mistake about it, these men, in spite of their obvious elegance, have an anti-fashion bias. They react very negatively to businessmen wearing Italian designer suits, or any similar item.

•　•　•　•　•　•　•　•　•　•　•　•　•　•　•　•　•　•

THE SOUTHWEST

For our discussion we will consider the Southwest the desert states of New Mexico, Arizona and Nevada. The large cities are Albuquerque, Phoenix, Flagstaff and Las Vegas. Their dress code makes sense only if you understand a few facts about the area. First, most of the people who live in this area come from the Northeast and Midwest. They moved to the Southwest to retire, or they were attracted by its more casual life-style. Second, like all other Western states they have a more relaxed attitude toward clothing. Third, and most important, these are desert states where the heat, particularly in the daytime, can become unbearable. It is simply not practical to wear a suit, shirt and tie if you have to spend any amount of time outdoors. And fourth, in the desert it becomes very chilly at night. Therefore jackets, although not required by custom, are often required by the climate.

If you visit this section of the country, the first thing you will notice is that there are more suit wearers than you expected. When I asked the local executives why this was, they explained that in the morning they leave their air-conditioned homes to get into their air-conditioned cars to drive to their air-conditioned offices. Air-conditioning in this section of the country is treated the way heat is treated in the North during the winter. You assume every building will have it, because every building does.

If you are making your first business trip to the Southwest, the best suits to bring along are beige, medium-range brown, light gray, medium-range blue, medium-range gray solids, and shadow plaids of blue and gray. Whatever you do, do not wear a dark suit in this section of the country. In Albuquerque, Phoenix and Flagstaff you will be looked upon as an outsider and a rather unsophisticated one. If you come dressed in a Northeast establishment look, the people will not be offended, but simply amazed. If you want to do business in the Southwest you must adopt its dress code.

However, there is one part of the dress code you cannot adopt: the Indian jewelry local businessmen often wear as part of their costume. They accentuate their conservative attire with turquoise watchbands and carvings on their belts. If an outsider adopts this, the businessmen, particularly those who were born in the Southwest, will be offended. They consider Indian jewelry local property and anyone from the outside wearing it offends them.

• •

LAS VEGAS

If you want to make money in Las Vegas instead of losing it, dress conservatively. Las Vegas is, of course, known as the gambling capital of the West and when most people think of this city they think of the brightly and gaudily lit Strip. The Las Vegas businessman's reaction to the gaudy attire seen on the strip is very similar to the reaction of the businessman in Nashville to the Country and Western scene of the Grand Ole Opry: They look upon the people who are engaged in that industry as people from a different world, and not a world with which they wish to be associated. As a result, the business community in Las Vegas is, if anything, more conservative than business communities in the rest of the Southwest. The best outfits for doing business there are light and medium-range blue and gray solids and pinstripe suits, as well as beige suits and subtle plaids worn with conservative shirts and ties. If you leave your collar open or wear anything that strikes these businessmen as being Strip-like, they will not take you very seriously. The conservative businessmen in Las Vegas are very conservative.

• • • • • • • • • • • • • • • • • • • •

THE COWBOY WEST

The cowboy West is Colorado, Utah, Nevada, Idaho, Wyoming and Montana. It is an area with few large cities and a great deal of open space. Unlike the rest of the country, the powerbrokers do not necessarily live in the metropolitan areas. Many of them live in the small towns and out on the plains, and the dress code reflects this fact. The businessmen in this area wear what I refer to as casual conservative. It is common to find businessmen wearing three-piece pinstripe suits with cowboy boots. You will find some men in an office wearing Northeastern establishment attire while others wear jeans, cowboy hats and bowler ties, and they all seem to get along just fine.

If you want to do business in the cowboy West there are several rules you must keep in mind. First, there is a real dislike for the Eastern establishment. These people feel they are manipulated by the East Coast politically and economically and they resent it. If you come in looking like a Northeast establishment slicker or a Chicago big shot, they will not treat you well. I recommend two-piece suits. The best is light gray, next is navy blue, followed by medium-range blue, dark gray or blue pinstripe, beige and conservative blue and gray shadow plaid. And without question the best shirt is a blue shirt.

· · · · · · · · · · · · · · · · · · · ·

SALT LAKE CITY

Salt Lake City is different from the rest of the cowboy West. It is very conservative because it is dominated by the Mormon Church (the Church of Jesus Christ of Latter-day Saints) and the Mormon Church is very conservative. In Salt Lake City you will find conservative businessmen dressed in a style that is not identical to the Northeast, but is similar to it. Men in that city are more likely to wear two-piece than three-piece suits but you will find men wearing three-piece pinstripe suits in almost any conservative office in Salt Lake. In addition, it is the only town in the area where white shirts give the wearer an advantage. Most of the young men from Salt Lake City spend at least a year doing missionary work for the Mormon Church. Before they are sent into the field the Church trains them and one of the elements of their training is a "Dress for Success" course. As a result I am sure these young men look upon men who are conservatively dressed, particularly those wearing white shirts, as trustworthy and reliable. If you want to do business in this section of the country you must keep this in mind.

• • • • • • • • • • • • • • • • • •

THE NORTHWEST

As you move from the East Coast to the West Coast of the United States the dress becomes less formal, and as you move from the South to the North, the dress becomes more formal. As a result, in Washington and Oregon you have a peculiar mixture of formality and informality.

There is no question that in the larger cities of the Northwest—Seattle, Spokane and Portland—the suit is worn by the vast majority of businessmen and anyone wishing to do business in this area would be wise to wear a conservative suit. Just about any conservative suit will do. All the traditional colors work—blue, gray, brown and beige—and they work in most shades (as do light cord suits in the summer). The only colors that do not work are the very light colors which are found in the Southwest and Southern California. If you wear one of these, most of the natives will think you are inept, unbusinesslike and possibly untrustworthy.

I do not want to create the impression that the Northwest is ultraconservative. It is on the West Coast and it has a West Coast casualness about it. It is the only section of the country where conservative, traditional businessmen wear sports jackets to work on a regular basis. They're conservative, traditional well-tailored classic sports jackets, but they are sports jackets. Nevertheless, if you're a visitor you must wear a suit. When we sent out-of-town businessmen wearing sports jackets into businesses where sixty percent of the executives wore sports jackets and slacks themselves, they reported that they received shabby treatment. When they wore suits they were treated just fine. So, although you will see natives wearing sports jackets, if you want to conduct business in the Northwest, leave yours at home.

• • • • • • • • • • • • • • • • • •

CALIFORNIA

California, with the exception of San Francisco and some of its suburbs, is the most casual area in the United States. Even today you can find men in traditional, conservative businesses like insurance and accounting wearing open collars. Many do it because they think it is an okay thing to do in California. Others have been taught by their experience that natives will hold at arm's length anyone wearing conservative suits or any other symbol of the Eastern establishment. A substantial portion of Southern California businesspeople do not think of the traditional, conservative dresser as an honest, competent and hard-working executive, but as an unfriendly alien from a backward, inferior culture.

I do not, however, suggest that if you work in Southern California or if you visit the area to do business that you leave your suit and tie at home. Our researchers found that in most large businesses, suit, shirt and tie wearers have an advantage over their more leisurely dressed competitors. But don't forget there are businesses in Southern California where wearing a suit is the wrong thing to do. You don't have to ask which businesses these are, you will be able to tell as soon as you walk in the door. Not only will the executives be dressed casually but they will probably ask you why you're not.

There are reasons for this Southern California attitude. The climate is salubrious. It may get chilly but it hardly ever gets cold, at least not by Northern standards. Most Californians spend eighty percent of their time in continual summer and spring. Just as important, most of the movers and the shakers in California did not make their fortunes in traditional industries. Many of the California fortunes depend on vast land holdings. The pacesetters are descendants of the old land barons who owed their wealth and power to no man, no government and no establishment. They often built their empires in the wilderness and became a law unto themselves. Their descendants reflect their life-style.

Typical and best known of this breed was William Randolph Hearst. He derived his wealth from cattle, land and mining and with it built a great newspaper chain and a home at San Simeon which surpassed all the great houses in the East and rivaled the palaces of Europe. In the style of a true Californian, Hearst called his palace "the ranch house" and served his guests, who were often kings and queens, on a table without linen and with ketchup, mustard and steak sauce set out in their original bottles.

Of course, the most publicized fortunes of Southern California are made in the movie industry. It is a world where being talented and different can bring you instant fame and fortune, and the multimillionaires who create a make-believe world by day—and to hear the gossip columnists tell it, live one by night—naturally do not take to traditional dress.

The most important reason Californians dress as they do is because they still consider themselves pioneers and innovators. The frontier may have vanished, but not for them. They can justify their pioneer spirit by pointing to Silicon Valley and to the fact that every new fad, from fast food to the hula hoop, originates in California. They think that people from other sections of the country are backward and possibly even inferior.

Nevertheless, California's dress code is becoming more conservative all the time. If you visit the major studios you will find that some of the executives are now wearing traditional suits in the land where suits were once an endangered species. Their suits are often made by Italian designers, and their ties may be unusual, but the fact that they are now wearing suits and ties is one of the great clothing revolutions of all time.

If you do business in California you should wear traditional cuts of clothing, but you must choose California colors, which are a little bit lighter than you will find in the Northeast or Midwest. Leave your navy and charcoal gray suits at home. Instead, bring with you medium-range blue and light gray. If you visit a company and find yourself the only man there with a suit, take off your jacket and tie and open your collar as if that is the way you normally do business. This will diffuse any antagonism. We ran a series of tests on the negative reaction to suit wearers in the Sunbelt in casual companies and found that the people who reacted negatively changed their minds the minute the suit wearer took off his jacket and tie. By doing so, you announced to these people that you are happy to be in their casual environment and glad to join them.

As a consultant to major corporations that are usually run by executives from the three-piece suit club I often find myself in the uncomfortable position of defending a more casual dress code for their Southern California representatives. Many of the three-piece suiters cannot imagine a serious businessman without a tie, although one-third of the serious businessmen in Southern California do not wear one. I usually convince them by telling them about a business meeting I attended in which there were seven men who all ran major multimillion-dollar corporations. All were contributing ten million dollars plus to a new venture and not one of them wore a tie. When someone noticed that I was wearing a tie, in spite of the fact that they had hired me as an image consultant, they sent out for a pair of scissors and cut it off. Then they announced to me (in a jovial manner) that I was permitted to tell their employees to wear ties, but I should not wear one when dealing with them. Everyone laughed except me; it was a $25 tie.

Please keep in mind that while many Californians do not wear suits, there are still two-thirds of California businessmen who do wear them to work every day. The difference between their suits and the suits of the rest of country is that Californians wear lighter shades. Ronald Reagan is a perfect example of Southern California dress. When he ran for the presidency unsuccessfully in 1976, he did so in light beige, light tan and light blue suits. When he wore these suits in the Northeast, he turned off his constituency. Being the most image conscious president in our history, he quickly discarded these suits for more effective darker models. He obeyed the first rule of dressing for success: Never let your clothing get in your way.

HAWAII

There are three mistakes made by businessmen who travel to Hawaii. First, many people visit Hawaii as tourists and never see the business area. They assume no one wears a suit, and that is not true. Hawaiian businessmen wear suits four days a week, Monday, Tuesday, Wednesday and Thursday. On Friday, however, in many Hawaiian businesses they wear the traditional aloha shirt. If you are doing business in Hawaii on that day, you should wear one of these shirts as well, but on all other days any suit in the California color range will be perfect.

ALASKA

I have spoken in Alaska a dozen times, and Alaska can be divided into exactly two clothing groups: those who dress conservatively and traditionally and those who never will.

Many of the businessmen I interviewed went north to escape formality and you could not get these men into a suit if you used a shotgun. Many of the natives have an attitude which is identical to that of the people in Southern California: They believe they have a right to be different because of the weather. They use snow instead of sun as an excuse, but the thinking is basically the same. You will find more men wearing beards, sports jackets and sweaters than in any other part of the United States or, as they refer to it, the lower forty-eight. Nevertheless, the standard dress for executives and professionals in most industries is not dramatically different in Alaska than it is in the rest of the country. There you will find the men at or near the top well dressed, polished, sophisticated and wearing conservative suits, shirts and ties. Unless you know ahead of time you are going to be dealing with non-suit-people, you should do the same.

DRESSING TO TRAVEL ABROAD

When I wrote the original version of this book eleven years ago, I did not include a section on dressing to travel abroad because at that time there were very strict dress codes in most parts of the world that had to be observed, and outlining them would have been impossible. Since then there has been considerable relaxation, but there are still some very important rules you must know if you are going to succeed.

1. Most sophisticated men wear the same items abroad that they wear at home. If you represent a Wall Street firm, you are expected to look like a Wall Street banker whether you are in Paris or Bangladesh. American businessmen have a very fine reputation in the world, and looking like

an American businessman is not a disadvantage—providing you look like a successful one.

2. The colors worn by the decision makers in Europe, Asia and Africa are dark gray and dark blue; not medium gray or medium blue or light gray or light blue, but dark. Although Ronald Reagan has introduced the brown suit to the United States, he has not made it an acceptable color in the rest of the world. Businessmen in most of the world will look upon brown-suit wearers as lower class, tasteless and without power.

3. You can wear solids or pinstripe suits almost anywhere in the world. Avoid plaids; in some areas they will get you into trouble. If you have a chalkstripe suit leave it home. You will see chalkstripe suits being sold on Savile Row in London, which is the mecca for the well-dressed business executive from around the world, but they're no more acceptable in New Delhi or Tokyo than they are in New York or California. Stick with pinstripes and solids only.

4. Your suits must be of good quality and fit beautifully. Custom-made suits are far more common among foreign executives than they are among Americans. Foreign executives do spend more money on their clothing, not because they like spending money, but because for them clothing is more important. In most other countries of the world what your father did for a living will determine what you do for a living. Class carries clout, and clothing is a sign of class. They pay a great deal of attention to it and because they do you should not underestimate the ability of foreign executives to accurately appraise the quality of your clothing. The ability to dress well is part of their social upbringing. Keep in mind that foreign executives, particularly Europeans, dress in the style of Savile Row not Brooks Brothers. You can get away with your boxy American suit if you only visit your clients once a

year and the cuffs of your pants break on your shoes. High waters, which for some unknown reason is the preferred style of some American executives, marks the wearer in most foreign countries as a lower-class tasteless boob. Of course if you work abroad you should have your suits tailored on Savile Row or at least in the Savile Row style, which means your pants will have pleats and be worn with braces and your jacket will have a slimmer, more stylish cut.

5. You will read in books by fashion people that you can wear conservative sports jackets abroad. It is true, but they have a very limited use. If you are going to travel extensively, leave your sports jackets at home. If you insist on bringing a sports jacket, make it a blue blazer and wear it with high quality gray slacks, white shirt and a conservative tie. But before you wear it, even in the evening, check with someone to make sure it is acceptable.

6. The only shirt any gentleman should take if he is going to travel abroad extensively is a white one. The reason is simple; white works everywhere. You can wear colored shirts at times in Italy and Spain, but you must wear white at night, so white is more practical. Your white shirts should be one hundred percent cotton, of good quality and fit perfectly because, as I have said, Europeans pay much more attention to that sort of thing.

   Whatever you do, do not wear what is referred to as a wash-and-wear shirt in Europe. They never caught on there or in Asia. Gentlemen there have always worn natural fibers. To wear anything with polyester in it when you are abroad is an invitation to social and business disaster. It will identify you in the minds of most European and Asian executives as a peasant, and they will find it very difficult to deal with you as an equal.

7. Ties are a must when you go abroad. Never enter any

office without one; to do so in many countries is an open insult and will be treated as such. In other countries, it simply identifies you as lower class or as someone who does not know what he's doing.

Remember, most foreign executives, because they can tell their countrymen's background by the way they dress, assume they can tell yours as well. Clothing is a far more significant factor in Europe and Asia than it is in the United States. Sometimes it actually tells you everything you want to know about a man. For example, in England the average gentleman probably only owns four ties and wears the same ones all his life. He wears his school tie, which will tell everyone he meets what school he attended; his regimental tie, which will tell them which regiment he belonged to; his club tie, which will tell you which club he belongs to; and his professional tie, which will tell you what he does for a living. It is always helpful, therefore, if you can talk to an American who has lived in the country for a while and ask him the rules. Anyone who has lived in England will tell you that you would never wear a rep tie unless you belong to the regiment, or an old school tie unless you've attended the school. It is the equivalent of an Englishman coming to America wearing a Harvard class ring when he has not attended Harvard. It will mark you in the eyes of the natives as a fraud and a cad.

8. A traveling businessman should wear only lace-up shoes. You can wear slip-ons in certain countries, but lace-ups are required in Italy, Spain, Portugal and parts of South America. So, if you are going to travel extensively, no other shoe should be considered.

9. You must wear an expensive watch and good cuff links if you are going to wear cuff links. You can never wear (gaudy, tasteless) inexpensive jewelry when dealing with foreign executives. They will judge you by it.

10. In most European and Asian countries a real fountain pen is a status symbol and you should carry one when you travel.

11. If you need something to carry your papers in, do not carry an attaché case. In many countries it is a sign of being a junior executive without power. You can either have someone carry your papers, or you can carry a small leather envelope. If you bring more papers to a meeting than can fit into that envelope, I suggest you have them brought by messenger or even hire an assistant for the day. You can hire the local cab driver to carry in your bags. I have seen that done, and it works well.

• • • • • • • • • • • • • • • • • • •

SOUTH AMERICA

In South America you can wear the lighter suits that are worn by the natives. Lightweight, light-colored suits are acceptable in the tropical areas of South America as long as they are worn with ties.

Since you may be asked to attend formal affairs when you travel abroad you may need a tuxedo. Before you go to a country, you should inquire at the local embassy about the country's customs. If you visit Latin America you will find that business meetings often are followed by social gatherings, and a formal attire may be required. Only a traditional conservative black tuxedo, worn with a pleated shirt, black tie and, of course, pumps, is acceptable. In South America and most European countries a tuxedo and all the proper accessories are an essential part of a gentleman's wardrobe, and you may have to bring one if you wish to do business in those areas of the world.

• • • • • • • • • • • • • •

PEOPLE'S REPUBLIC OF CHINA

All the rules about business dress are totally different in China than they are in the rest of the world.

The Chinese dress very drably. Most continue to wear Mao suits or some other type of semiuniform. It is not an accident. Chairman Mao, whose influence on the country cannot be overstated, was a student in Paris when he was a young man. Two of the most popular topics of discussion among young intellectuals at the time were social engineering or class leveling and nonverbal message sending. In my opinion, the greatest innovations in clothing did not take place in Paris in the twentieth century but in Peking. When Chairman Mao put everyone in Mao suits, his object was to wipe away all signs of class, and one of the signs of class he very well knew was clothing. He did not completely accomplish his goal, even at the height of the Cultural Revolution; Chinese army officers wore the same outfits as enlisted men but carried pens in their pockets, and if you knew how to read the code you could tell their rank by the number of pens they had. Nevertheless, in China today, obvious signs of wealth and power are still frowned upon, and people who wear them are disliked and distrusted. Forget any articles you may have read about the revolution since Mao. There have been enormous changes, but I suggest you leave home all expensive jewelry, good watches, cuff links or anything else that could be considered ostentatious. You can wear a business suit because they expect American businessmen to wear business suits, but you are far better off in blue shirts than white when you are doing business in the People's Republic. You can wear ties for the same reason; it's expected. Don't carry your papers in an expensive attaché case or sign your copy of a contract with a gold Mark Cross pen. One old China hand told me that before he goes there he always buys two dozen Bic pens. Another said he found it easier to do business wearing sports jackets with an open collar than he did wearing a suit and tie. Whether you should wear suits at all when you deal with the Chinese is a question debated: Some say yes and some say no. Generally, it is agreed that if you deal with people at or near the top, particularly people who are likely to travel to the United States, a suit is the proper garment. However, anyone who has done business in China agrees that there is one basic rule for dressing for success in China: Dress as if you have a great deal of power and very little property.

. . . .

ELSEWHERE IN THE WORLD

The most foolish mistake made by Americans when they go abroad is to try to copy the natives. In most countries it would be silly to do so, and in many Arab countries it could be insulting and possibly dangerous. Keep in mind you are an American businessman and it does not hurt to look like one.

I could spend the entire book dealing with specific local customs that must be avoided. An obvious example is not to wear religious symbols if you are going into an Arab country. Many Arab businessmen would be insulted if you came into their office wearing a cross or a Star of David. My best advice is to call the embassy and ask to be put in contact with someone in their trade delegation. Ask them very frankly to advise you how to dress. State your case quite openly; tell them you are going to do business in their country and you want to know what mistakes they have seen Americans make. Do not just ask general questions, because if you do, in the name of diplomacy and politeness they may simply skip over some very important facts.

8

How to Use Clothes to Sell Yourself

The most common form of motivation is the desire to make a sale. Selling is a process that affects everybody and in which all of us engage at many times in our lives, whether we are selling products, services, concepts or ourselves. The basic, most important point of this entire book is that any man, whether in business or in social life (and aren't the two often inseparable?), can "sell" himself far more successfully through the adroit manipulation of his clothing than he can by any other means.

I have performed tens of thousands of hours of research on nonverbal sales and run a sales training course based on this research. The course runs a full day. In the morning, I speak to the sales force and in the afternoon I meet with individual salespeople, spending from six to ten minutes with each, discussing his clothing, body language and approach. I require that each salesperson send me one week's wardrobe before the meeting. I have their outfits hung on coat racks and numbered, so that we can begin working as soon as they enter the room. After giving the course only a few times, I was able to identify most of the good and poor salesmen before they entered the room simply by looking at their wardrobes. There is no question about it; good salesmen spend more time and money on their clothing and put their outfits together more carefully than do poor salesmen.

To the great majority of men, a sale is anything but a casual, periodic occurrence. It is absolutely the most dominant force in their lives and is responsible on a crucial day-to-day basis for their businesses, their jobs, their economic well-being, their very existence and subsistence. It is primarily for these men that this chapter is written, but the information is equally valid and practical for any man. I strongly recommend that everyone read this chapter.

To cover every aspect of clothing—and of motivating your fellow man—that my research has shown to be important would require volumes, and would be of limited interest to the general reader for whom this book is written. So I will confine myself to the most crucial details.

All sales, all motivation, is a three-factor process—a seller, a buyer and a product. Starting with the seller and the buyer, the controllable elements of any sale can be broken down into simple categories. They are:

1. The appearance of the seller and the appearance of the buyer.
2. The company orientation of the seller and the company orientation of the buyer.
3. The age of the seller and the age of the buyer.
4. The socioeconomic level of the seller and the socioeconomic level of the buyer.
5. The socioeconomic background of the seller and the socioeconomic background of the buyer.

6. The race of the seller and the race of the buyer.
7. The geographic location from which the seller comes and the geographic location from which the buyer comes. (See Chapter 7, "Dressing for Success on the Road.")
8. The training, or industrial orientation, of the seller and the training, or industrial orientation, of the buyer.
9. The sex of the seller and the sex of the buyer.

All these elements have been statistically proven to exercise an effect on whether people like you, believe you—and buy from you.

I know that a great many salesmen will scoff when they read this, particularly those who are successful. In order to be good, salesmen must have enormous egos to overcome their constant defeats, because all selling is a percentage of hit and miss. And all successful salesmen, as part of their own ego propping, come to believe that they and their golden voices are responsible for sales. The mere idea that other factors play any role whatsoever will come to them as ego deflating.

I ask these men to hold their criticism for a while. By the time they have reached the middle of this chapter, if they are really good salesmen, they will begin to see that sales and nonverbal communicants are twin brothers in the business of persuasion. If they are really superb at their jobs, they will also begin to see that they have been using clothing and other nonverbal communicants for years.

For other salesmen, those who have been at it for a while but are largely unsuccessful, I suggest they pay the strictest attention. Whenever I speak before a sales force, or work with a sales force, I can virtually guarantee that I can substantially help half of the salesmen who are failures, and this group makes up about two-thirds of most sales forces. I can help them because their failure is based on the fact that they consistently project the wrong nonverbal messages.

That is why you can spend all day training a group of poor

salesmen to give wonderful sales presentations, but it won't necessarily have any effect on their sales.

Their sales are not lost because they give a poor verbal sales presentation; they would be lost no matter what they say. They lose because their appearance conveys that they are not likable, they are not honest, they are not trustworthy, that they are not even sincere. If these men will read carefully, I will show the largest percentage of them how to appear likable, honest, credible and sincere. I will show them how to sell.

• • • • • • • • • • • • • • • • • • •

NEVER UNDERESTIMATE THE POWER OF A HAIRCUT

Fifteen years ago, I was lecturing a group of young lawyers on selling themselves in the courtroom. One of the desirable influences that I mentioned was very moderate hair styles, and four or five of the young men said, "Well, we're certainly okay on that score, because that definitely describes our haircuts."

I did not really agree, but rather than contradict them outright I decided to put their haircuts to a test. We had pictures drawn of each of the young men; more precisely, we had pictures drawn of their haircuts on blank faces. Each of the young lawyers took a picture of one of the other young lawyer's haircut to work with him and queried the senior partners in his firm about the appropriateness of the haircut for court. The senior partners, who were roughly equivalent in age and temperament to the judges before whom the young lawyers worked, all made negative comments about every haircut, judging them to be too long, too effeminate, too kookie and so on.

The reactions of those young lawyers were not unique. Six years ago, after giving a speech at a Midwestern university, I was surrounded by seven young men, all of whom had their hair parted in the middle. They gathered together to collectively tell me off; they were convinced that when I told them they should part their hair on the side I was being close-minded and old-fashioned. I asked them to meet me in one hour wearing their interview outfits (each one wore a conservative suit, shirt and tie.) I had their pictures taken, first with their hair parted in the middle and then, with the help of a hairstylist, parted on the side. I instructed them to show one another's pictures to the businessmen in town and ask them to rate the young man in each picture. The businessmen thought the young men whose hair was parted on the side, like theirs, were brighter, harder working and would make better employees than the young men whose hair was parted in the middle. Since they were looking at the same young men, dressed in the same outfits, they were in reality commenting on the hair styles and not the men. In this case, as in others, when men from one generation were asked to make judgments about men from another generation, they judged them by the standards of their generation.

I am frequently asked if there are any traits common to all successful executives. There most definitely are; they always have their hair combed, and their shoes in good condition and shined. Not surprisingly they expect the same of other men, particularly subordinates. If your hair is disheveled, even if it is short, it triggers very strong negative reactions from these men. Keep it neat, and if you have hair that happens to grow in every possible direction except the right one, then you had better find something that will keep it down, or a barber who can give you a cut that minimizes the problem.

I hate to tell you this, but there is also a direct correlation between the shape of a man's face and his chances of success. The most successful face is masculine and elongated, neither too heavy nor too thin, without prominent features. In short, the perfect WASP face. Slight faces are judged as being effeminate and round faces as being ineffectual. That's the bad news. The good news is that hair can help—if you can find someone to cut it who knows what he is doing.

I have ears that stick out, and look very silly in a short haircut that makes my ears look even more prominent than they are. Hair that slightly covers my ears masks the problem entirely. A man with dark hair can make himself seem more powerful by picking up the darkness of the hair in the darkness of his suit, and by letting his hair be slightly longer than average. If a man has blond or red hair, it is a bad mistake to pick up either color in his clothing.

Older men can look much younger by affecting younger hair styles and by coloring out the gray if looking younger is a business necessity. Usually it is the opposite, and I have occasionally advised young men who are already in positions of authority and responsibility to make themselves look more distinguished by slightly, very slightly, graying their sideburns.

Changing one's hair style or hair color to make one more effective is definitely not effeminate and should not be considered as such. It is positively Machiavellian—and it works.

Blacks in the business world should never wear Afro haircuts. Men who do are less highly thought of by both whites and blacks, and are much less likely to succeed in any endeavor. (See Chapter 9, "Some Advice for Minorities.")

Most men should not wear facial hair of any kind, particularly beards. The response to facial hair is almost always negative in corporate situations, and the only men who should wear it are those men who must compensate for some other weakness in their appearance or personality. For example, if a man has no chin, a beard or mustache can make him look more powerful and more masculine-looking. Or if a man looks very young, a mustache or beard can speed up the aging process.

If a man decides he needs or wants a mustache, he needn't feel as guilty about it as he would have just a few years ago. Mustaches today do not test too badly. In fact, you can get away with them in most business situations if the rest of your appearance is conservative—providing the mustache is moderate, no handlebars and no pencilstripes. A beard, if you decide you absolutely must have one, should be full, neat and not straggly or in multiple colors, and goatees should be avoided at all costs. People do not trust or believe men in goatees; perhaps it's the devil image. I don't really know.

Very heavy beards (or long ones) look old-fashioned and out of date. All facial hair should be kept well trimmed and well shaped. If you are in any business that requires business lunches, for heaven's sake, make sure that you constantly keep your mustache or beard clean of food particles.

. . . .

HOW TO USE EYEGLASSES

Any man who must wear glasses must also recognize that they are significant factors in his total look, either contributing to it or detracting from it. The man who has good features or the man for whom any glasses are a negative influence should definitely consider contact lenses.

Wire frames are no longer considered chic. They have been around long enough so that anyone can now wear them. I suggest them for very large men or men who have large faces or a gruff appearance, as it softens you.

Heavy plastic or horn-rims are more traditional and powerful and make a man look older. I recommend them for younger men, particularly younger men who are in authority positions.

Men with heavy lower jaws and cheeks should probably wear heavier glasses, and men with lighter, thinner lower faces should probably wear lighter glasses. In both cases, the use of the glasses can help pull the upper and lower face together into a compatible unit.

Very young men, small men and men with small faces who must establish authority may find that picking up their hair color in the color of their frames is effective.

If glasses must be chosen to offset or enhance a particular facial characteristic, then trial and error is the only real way of determining what is best for any individual.

· ·

HOW TO CAMOUFLAGE LIABILITIES OF PHYSICAL APPEARANCE

The most important element in establishing a man's authority is his physical size, and most men fall into three obvious size categories—large, average and small. Unfortunately, these dimensions cannot be broken down into specific combinations of feet, inches and pounds, because size, as it applies to what clothing should be worn, is relative. But most men should have no problem in classifying themselves correctly if they carefully compare themselves to the men with whom they have the most contact.

· ·

What the Large Man Can Do

Large men, or men who have a forbidding or gruff appearance, have both an advantage and a disadvantage. The advantage is that they tend to be seen as extremely authoritative. When they speak with authority, people generally tend to believe them, even when they are extolling only the relative values of a so-so automobile or the function of an average computer. They are more likely to be believed about technical matters than average-size men or short men. Their tremendous disadvantage, however, particularly if they are very large or have a very hard look, is that they frighten people.

In one of my most interesting sales experiments, I selected six purchasing agents of very short stature and videotaped them in their daily job encounters over a three-week period. They believed I was filming the salesmen that visited them and consequently paid little attention to the camera. I discovered that when large salesmen came into their offices, the purchasing agents were often verbally rude. They were abrupt and frequently chased the salesmen from the offices. The purchasing agents seemed to be in complete command. However, when we played the film back without the sound, the purchasing agents looked as if they were defending themselves from attackers.

After some in-depth questioning, I came to the conclusion that when a man who is selling is much larger than the man who is buying, he can and often does frighten the buyer, and it is essential that he do everything in his power not to scare his client. A frightened man will immediately be turned off to you. He will escape from you, even if it means throwing you out of the office.

I told this to a sales manager once, and he said, "You've got to be crazy. My best salesman is an ex-football-player; the man's a monster. He sells twice as much as any other man in the place, and he doesn't obey your rules of dress."

I said I would like to speak with the man, and the sales manager had him come in. While most football players are stereotyped as big, dumb and insensitive, this man was anything but. When I explained my position to him, he said, "Yes, I agree."

His boss then said, "Well, how can that be? If you scare people, how the hell do you get them to buy so much?"

The salesman said, "I'll show you," and he got up, walked to the door and did a stage fall. His boss asked, "Well, what's that?" And the man replied, "When I walk into a man's office and I catch that glimmer of fear in his eyes— which I've become very sensitive to lately—I simply fall down. I pretend I've hurt my leg and have him help me. That puts me in the defensive position and enables me to make the sale."

I told that story at a sales meeting I was addressing about six months later, and afterward I was approached by another ex-football-player who told me his approach. He said, "When I walk into an office and I sense the man on the defensive, I simply drop my papers all over the floor and start groveling for them. Often the man comes around and helps me, and when he does, I usually have a sure sale."

These two very large men overcame their problems of frightening their clients in two different ways. A third way is to do it with clothing.

The large man should avoid all dark, high-authority suits, should never wear pinstripes and never wear vests. He should wear very soft colors and textures: medium-range soft gray suits, beige and brown suits and very light suits in the summer. Two combinations I found particularly effective were a medium-range soft gray suit with a medium-range blue shirt and a gray and blue tie, and a medium brown suit with a blue shirt and a brown and blue paisley tie. (I usually do not recommend paisleys for business, but this is an exception.)

The large man should avoid strong color contrasts and any articles of clothing that call attention to himself. He is the only man, in terms of size, who should wear nonauthoritative ties, and either wear those outside the recommended ones in

Chapter 4, or, if he wishes to remain within that group, stick with reps and solids only.

The large man should only wear very light shoes, and should avoid the heavier ones, such as wing tips, that are normally a staple of any businessman's attire.

The primary mistake made by most large men is not that they dress too authoritatively; somehow they have an instinct that protects them against that mistake. What they do, though, is to go into one of the so-called Big Man's shops that are now fairly widespread around the country, and take the advice of the clerks in these stores. They show the large man loud, bright, gaudy garments and tell him how wonderful it is that he can now wear such clothing, which in the past was not manufactured in large sizes. Well, if he couldn't wear them before, he shouldn't wear them now. Although they are by no means authoritative clothes, they are not right for selling, no matter what your size is.

• • • • • • • • • • • • • • • • • • • •

Here's Help for the Small Man

Along with the very large man, the man with a gruff appearance and the man with a very deep voice (or a combination of all three), I would include among problem salesman: the very short man, the man with the high-pitched voice, the man who is very thin and the man who has a round, cherubic, ineffective-looking face. These men have two problems—an authority problem and a problem of presence. The authority problem is that if they are sitting in a one-to-one business situation, they will not be believed as readily as a larger man. If they are in a group situation, their presence is not noticed and they are less effective. So they must fight both problems at once.

The authority problem is easily solved by wearing high

authority clothing: pinstripe suits, pinstripe shirts, Ivy League ties, vests. If, in addition to being very small, the man is young, he should wear only ties that are very expensive, $20 and above. I realize that this is a very expensive suggestion and the advice contradicts what I said in the tie chapter, but this man must wear ties that would not be available to a boy. One of the major problems with small men who are very young is that people still are tempted to address them as, "Hey, kid." To overcome this, they should wear only super-adult garments, the most obvious being the expensive tie.

The best shirt for the small man is the solid white; the best shoes are traditional wing tips; the best coats are heavy and luxurious, such as camel hair. They should wear only rich-looking attire, and they should be neat to the point of being precise.

Color contrast is very important for these men, and it is easily attainable with a dark suit, white shirt and dark tie. They should make sure that the contrast is equally pro-nounced in their sports clothes, particularly between any two items worn above the belt. If a golf jacket and a golf shirt are both in the same shade range, they will make the small man look even smaller.

Small men should wear attention-getting devices, includ-ing even those that I do not recommend for anyone else. A handkerchief showing from the breast pocket of the suit jacket, a diamond stickpin in this age when no one else wears them—these items have worked well for men I know. The best device of all that I have found is a unique watch that is immediately identifiable as quite expensive. Those made from gold coins, or any other equally expensive watch, work partic-ularly well in bestowing an aura of substance on a short man.

If a short or thin man wears glasses, the frames should be fairly heavy to add significance to his face. He should carry the most masculine-looking attaché case he can afford. And

under no circumstances should he carry an umbrella. Never. I
don't give a damn if it's raining cats and dogs; wear a raincoat
and get wet. An umbrella is a death knell for the small man. It
turns him into a Casper Milquetoast figure, nice but ineffective. And that is no image for a salesman of anything. Not
for a successful salesman, anyway.

* * * * * * * * * * * * * * * * * * *

Those Who Are Slightly Above or Below Average

Men who are slightly above average in weight and men
who are slightly below average in size have fewer problems
with their appearance than do very large and very short men,
but they can also improve their effectiveness through their
clothing. Men who are slightly above average can wear authoritative suits, but should avoid the most authoritative ties.
The easiest, simplest way of diminishing authority and fright
caused by size is by wearing one bright item of attire, and the
tie is the best element to use.

The slightly above average man should know that his size
is an advantage in business, giving him a definite psychological edge over smaller men, and he should use his size to his
advantage. If his superior is smaller than he is, he should
wear soft or light-colored suits and avoid strong contrasts
when dealing with him, so as not to antagonize or threaten
him.

The man who is slightly below average height may keep
his wardrobe in the same range as the average man (using the
colors and patterns recommended in previous chapters), but
he should be careful not to let his wardrobe be too drab, and
he should stay away from sporty ties (the paisley) and wear
only serious ties (Ivy League and polka dot). If the slightly

below average man is working with men who are exceptionally large, and this does happen on occasion, then he should adapt the dress code of the very short man and become extremely precise in his appearance, since size is definitely a relative matter and one must manipulate his authority quotient accordingly.

• • • • • • • • • • • • • • • • • • • •

What If You're Just Built "Sloppy"?

Some of us have a problem that, while related to size, is somewhat more difficult to define. It is simply that we are built in a sloppy way. Certain men look neat no matter what they do, and others will never look neat no matter what they do. If you are one of the unfortunates in the latter category, as I am, you must make a conscious effort always to have your hair combed, to have a very high shine on your shoes, to make sure your shirt is never disheveled and that your tie knot is always at your collar.

The best way of accomplishing all this is to set up a daily routine to check these tell-tale signs on a regular basis. The disheveled man never goes anywhere, except out for coffee. When he tries to sell, he cannot successfully sell any item that people consider serious. If you are a sales manager, never hire a disheveled salesman; if you have one, make him neaten up or move out.

• • • • • • • • • • • • • • • • • • • •

Age

In numbers as well as influence the largest group in industry to whom someone must sell today is between age thirty-four and forty-four. These men were part of the hippie generation, the antiwar generation, the drug generation, and their perceptions are markedly different from those of any other group who have held these positions in the past.

Their generation, the baby-boom generation, which trumpets its egalitarianism, does not react in an egalitarian way. They make strong judgments based on the socioeconomic level of your clothing. In fact, it is a generation of snobs. The most important rule for dealing with businesspeople from this group is to wear only upper-middle-class clothing. It's rather strange that the antiestablishment group has become so establishment, but they have.

If you are forty-four or younger, you can wear three-piece pinstripe suits. Even the older members of this group who are in business consider themselves yuppies, and they often divide the world between the antiestablishment people and themselves—and they consider themselves a superior group. If you adopt their program you announce to them that you are one of them, that you are success oriented, hard driving, someone they would like to associate with and someone they can trust and someone from whom they can buy. If you are older than forty-four, particularly if you are fifty plus, only wear two-piece suits when dealing with them. While they have outwardly adopted the establishment look, they still have a strong antiauthority bias. At one time this group trusted no one over thirty. Now it seems very difficult for them to trust anyone over fifty, particularly if that fifty or over looks like an authority figure. The men and women in this generation have no particular prejudice against patterns or colors. You can wear blue, gray, brown, beige or any other color in a solid pinstripe or plaid and they will respond positively to you as long as the colors and patterns you choose are appropriate to the environment, are upper middle class and are put together neatly. It is another irony that members of the hippie generation should be so impressed by neatness, but they are. In fact, they are usually turned off by anyone who looks disheveled.

The second most influential group of businesspeople in America are men between the ages of forty-five and sixty. They are products of the fifties and considerably more conservative than the group just described. If you want to deal with them successfully, you must wear very conservative suits, shirts and ties.

When you deal with men over sixty, you should know that they will judge your socioeconomic level and your competence based on your clothing, but they will also make moral judgments based on the way you look. Therefore, if you wish to be credible with this group, you must obey all the rules very strictly. If they are very conservative you must be conservative, if you are a stockbroker you should look like a stockbroker, and so on. When dealing with these men you will do best if you pretend that you are selling a product that has a built-in credibility problem, such as a used car. Dress and act as if you are going to church or to court. The look that works best with the over-sixty group is understated traditional. Whatever you do, do not wear anything that is even in the least fashionable unless you are sure they are likely to be dressed fashionably themselves. If you look chic, or even too carefully put together, they will not trust you or buy from you.

Men under thirty-five selling to men over forty-five should wear only the highest-authority garments—pinstripe suits, vests, wing tip shoes—and conduct themselves in a very businesslike manner.

If you are over forty-five and you wish to sell to younger men, particularly those under thirty-five, it is very important you leave your three-piece pinstripe suit and white shirt at home. You are far better off in a two-piece suit even if you're dealing with a very conservative industry. If you are dealing with an industry where the executives dress fashionably, we suggest you follow suit. Wear a contrasting collar and cuff shirt with a jazzy tie and, if possible, stay away from the darker-colored suits no matter who you are dealing with. You want to soften your appearance. Older men in high-authority garments often threaten younger men and nobody buys from people who threaten them.

. . . .

DRESS PREJUDICES OF COLLEGE STUDENTS

The prejudices of college students are violent and strong. If you turn off a college student with your clothing, you turn him off completely. There are no degrees; they either love you or hate you. College students expect you to fit the stereotyped image they have of you. If you sell rock and roll, you must look the part. College students have very strong prejudices against anyone in their own group who does not dress as they do. They react negatively to certain items for which I have no explanation, for example, pinstripe suits worn by anyone but top executives or top recruiters. They are attracted to recruiters wearing pinstripe suits because they think that a man with a pinstripe suit represents a better company and they want to work for a better company. They are also attracted to businessmen who wear Ivy League or club ties that totally turned them off just a few years ago. This group is very pro-establishment and they are looking for signs of the establishment on you if you represent the establishment.

If you are recruiting or you are selling something important (or something they identify as important) to college students, the best outfit today is the same as it was ten years ago at the height of the hippie revolution: a solid gray suit with a blue shirt and a rep tie. They also react positively to paisley ties.

There is one rule you never break when selling to college students: If you are obviously not a student, you should not attempt to emulate their dress or style; they will distrust you if you do. If you are selling anything that is not profit oriented, the slightly seedy, slightly rumpled professional look works well. But people who sell profit-oriented goods should look the part.

• • • • • • • • • • • • • • • • • • • •

WHEN BLACKS AND HISPANICS SELL TO WHITES (AND VICE VERSA)

The following paragraphs have nothing to do with racial prejudice. I use race as a sociological term. I do this because racial terms are often the best indicators of common past environment and therefore one of the best predictors of present reaction to stimuli by an identifiable group. In the same way that parents and communities pass on their tastes for certain types of food, they also pass on concepts of honesty, fair play and others. If these concepts are associated in their minds with certain types of clothing, they will also pass on these associations. Therefore, if you wish to sell to a group of people, it would be helpful to know which colors and patterns their environment has taught them to trust and which ones to distrust. That is all I have attempted to measure.

When selling to white middle America, and this includes anyone who is white and not in a ghetto or in a subgroup such as Appalachian mountainfolk, the following rules always apply:

Never wear purple or lavender.

Never wear loud colors.

Never wear bright red, even in a tie.

Pink shirts, except for end-on-end or oxford cloth, are taboo unless you know that the people you are trying to sell to are wearing them.

Do not wear jewelry.

Do not have hair that covers your ears.

If you are a black selling to white middle America, dress like a white. Wear conservative pinstripe suits, preferably with vests, accompanied by all the establishment symbols, including the Ivy League tie. This clothing conveys that you are a member of the establishment and that you are pushing no radical or other feared ideas.

Blacks selling to whites should not wear Afro hair styles or any clothing that is African in association.

If you are selling to corporate America it is very important that you dress, not as well as the white salesmen, but better than them. You have to wear suits, shirts and ties that are more expensive and more conservative than your white co-workers. It is equally important that a black salesman show signs of affluence when selling to whites. If you can afford an expensive wristwatch, buy one. If you can afford a good attaché case, buy one. Under no circumstances carry a chic or fashionable model. Alligator attaché cases and exotic wristwatches will get you into trouble.

If you are a Hispanic (Mexican, Puerto Rican, Cuban or other Latin American), you should avoid pencil-line mustaches, any articles of clothing that have Hispanic associations, and anything that is very sharp or precise. Also avoid any hair tonic that tends to give a greasy or shiny look to the hair; this also triggers a strong negative reaction.

If you are from a Hispanic background and you wish to sell to American business, the best outfit for you to wear is a medium-range or dark gray, two- or three-piece, solid or pinstripe suit with a white shirt and a very conservative tie, preferably a blue and maroon silk foulard. Men from Hispanic backgrounds also have to be very careful that their hair is very neatly trimmed and very conservative.

If you are white and selling to blacks, you will fare much better if you dress in nonestablishment patterns. Black America is essentially divided into two camps, establishment and antiestablishment, and the divisions are not dictated by income alone.

Almost all members of Northern ghettos who are in lower socioeconomic groups are understandably antiestablishment. When selling to them, you can wear nothing that carries an establishment touch. It does not matter what you are selling—cars, insurance, bonds, gold—you must not wear the traditional suit, shirt and tie uniform. (Women are much better at selling to blacks because they are considered to be outside the establishment.)

White salesmen selling to antiestablishment blacks do better if they wear mustaches, and they do even better with beards. If you must wear a suit, the best suit is a conservative two-piece model, but you should avoid a solid dark blue since it has a very negative association for blacks. Turtleneck sweaters work very well, but if you must wear a tie, it should obviously be nonauthoritative or nonestablishment.

The black establishment includes all blacks who have made it, along with almost all Southern rural blacks, no matter what their position. Southern blacks do not consider themselves disenfranchised, and their reactions to clothing are the same as the reactions of their more successful counterparts. If you are white and selling to this group, it is almost essential that you wear a shirt and tie, but it is absolutely essential that no article of your clothing represent you as a member of the establishment. Pinstripe suits, Ivy League and club ties, white shirts, all are out. Conservative gray suits are fine; beige suits are better; brown suits are out. Any color shirt but white, and any nondescript tie are acceptable. A paisley tie is most likely to elicit the greatest trust.

When selling to middle-class blacks, you cannot dress like a ghetto black, and you cannot go so far into the antiestablishment look that you begin to affect beads or the like.

The one rule that applies to blacks just as it does to the white establishment in the Midwest and the South is that poverty does not sell. Blacks will believe people who look successful, which proves that everyone has one color-love in common—green.

Blacks selling to other blacks are best served by an entirely different set of dress codes. Conservative, establishment symbols of authority and success are the rules of the day. All blacks, regardless of their own status, react positively to other blacks who have made it.

Blacks selling to people of Spanish origin and people of Spanish origin selling to blacks should each avoid wearing any items of clothing that are particularly identified with the other group.

. . . .

HOW TO SELL TO ETHNIC GROUPS

The following rules apply to anyone selling to ethnic groups.

When selling to upper-middle-class people of Spanish origin, it is essential that you dress both conservatively and nattily.

When selling to Jewish customers, do not wear brown.

When selling to the basically German populations in the Midwest, avoid a clash in the lines of clothing patterns.

When selling to Polish groups in the Midwest, avoid a clash of color. (I know there are many tasteless jokes about Poles wearing blue and red and green and yellow at the same time, but if I were you I would never put this joke to a test.)

Italians register negative reactions to clashes of color and clashes of line. The most conservative clothing sells best to Italians, and the richer-looking the better.

When selling to Orientals there are five rules. First, never wear blue; second, dress conservatively; third, avoid the Oriental shades of color (red, for example); fourth, avoid brown suits; and fifth, and most important, dress conservatively. Orientals are completely turned off by exotic dress.

Americans of Irish extraction react negatively to anyone who is too sharply dressed, too neat or put together too well. They associate such looks with being dishonest.

Mexican-Americans react negatively to anyone coming from outside the area, including other Mexicans, who wear what is best described as Mexican (bullfighters') red.

· · · · · · · · · · · · · · · · · ·

HOW TO FIT IN WITH
YOUR CUSTOMER'S OCCUPATION

To sell successfully you must also wear clothes that are compatible with the occupation and education of your customers.

People who are trained in detail work and people who derive a sense of completion from their jobs, such as druggists, accountants and engineers, may buy from you whether you are dressed in Bermuda shorts or in a suit. But they give off very negative reactions to anyone whose dress does not add up to a harmonious unit.

If you are wearing a conservative shirt and conservative suit, but have a naked lady on your tie, they will object to you, not because of the naked lady, but because your clothing is not properly unified. The same tie with an equally ridiculous jacket would be just fine.

These men have a dominant sense of fitness and completion, and if you violate it, you become less credible and less important.

Artists, architects, hairdressers, scenic designers, window dressers—anyone who is trained as an artist or who considers himself an artist—will generally have a very strong sense of line. If the lines in your clothes clash, these people will think less of your credibility and judge you severely. They think better of someone who puts his clothes together cleverly than of someone who does not, but their concept of clever is far different from that of the average man.

What the average artist considers clever is a blue suit worn with a blue and green shirt and a blue and green tie—in short, unusual, tricky combinations that work. They are much more impressed with someone who might wear three shades of blue than someone who would wear a blue suit, white shirt and blue tie.

In selling to career military men, do not wear gray suits, do not wear Ivy League ties, and do not wear business clothes at all, if you can avoid it. You will do much better in sports jackets, golf jackets and other more casual attire than in traditional business suits. Whatever you wear, military men react positively to outward signs of wealth and power.

Doctors, although they are quite conservative themselves, react well to salesmen wearing semicasual attire and up-to-date clothing. They react negatively to clothing that is out-of-date, and to people who are obviously unsuccessful.

Hospital administrators, on the other hand, generally come from lower socioeconomic backgrounds and react in much the same way as government officials.

Anyone who sells to government functionaries should know that there are two groups. The first, the older bureaucrats who have worked themselves up from the depths of the civil service, react very negatively to any sign of wealth. The best way to dress for them can only be described as shabby Brooks

Brothers—clean and neat, but well worn. These older bureau-crats, however, only make up about fifteen percent to twenty percent of the present civil service workforce. It is really dominated by a younger breed of government official who also likes a conservative look, but not necessarily shabby. These men came into the government at fairly decent salaries, have moved up the socioeconomic ladder and dress much better themselves than their older counterparts to whom frugality is a way of life.

Generally, when dealing with government officials, you should dress in Eastern establishment tradition, and avoid anything that marks you as being part of any special-interest group, whether religious, political, social or fraternal.

Men who go into high appointed positions in government usually come from high socioeconomic backgrounds, and do not take these jobs because they need the money. Many of these men are Brahmins and they react the way the Brahmins we described in earlier chapters react. However, they them-selves will not be wearing Brahmin attire in many cases. You must remember that about one-third of the members of Congress are Brahmins. They do not leave their old-money reflexes at home, but they do leave their old-money clothing at home. These men are in the public eye and because they are they dress like an average businessman—but they are not and do not kid yourself that they are. They will react negatively to anyone from an obviously lower socioeconomic background, so one must dress for these elitists not only in upper-middle-class uniforms, but in the obviously expensive versions thereof.

Most corporate purchasing agents tend to fall into two general categories. The majority of them come from lower-middle-class backgrounds (I would estimate over sixty per-cent). Today most of them have college degrees, but they are not what would be considered sophisticated people except when it comes to their own field of expertise. And because they are experts in those fields, they control considerable budgets for a large variety of business needs.

Several years ago we conducted a major study of these men and women for a corporate client. We interviewed several hundred purchasing agents away from their companies' premises and with a guarantee of confidentiality. We found their main motivation for purchasing from one company rather than another was survival—their own. To understand why they think this way, you have to understand the nature of the job. A purchasing agent very often is not going on his own initiative. A vice-president at headquarters, or a department head, both of whom probably outrank him, will give him an assignment. For example, they may order him to purchase so many widgets, have them delivered by a certain date, and get them at a good price. They are interested in a good price because the cost of the widgets goes on their department's budget, and the purchasing agent does have to get a good price, but his biggest problem is getting the widgets delivered by the date promised. An entire operation may depend on those widgets and if the widgets fail to arrive, then everything stops, and the department head or the vice-president is going to rake the purchasing agent over the coals. Therefore, he must deal with someone who, if he says he is going to deliver 15,000 widgets by the second of January, has them there. He wants someone he can trust, and someone who represents a company he can trust.

If your job is to sell to these purchasing agents, I suggest you buy a wardrobe of blue suits. You can choose any standard blue. The best are teal, navy and medium-range blue. If you wear anything other than a white shirt with a maroon tie, you should have your head examined. White shirts shout reliability, and since maroon ties help send the same message they are an essential part of the uniform. I have been researching clothing for twenty-five years and never in all that time have I discovered one look that works so well with one group as the one I have just described.

• • • • • • • • • • • • • • • • • • •

THE HIGH-TECH PURCHASING AGENT

The second group of purchasing agents makes major corporate decisions. They buy machinery, buildings, land sites, and so on. They are very definitely executive-oriented men, and the standard executive dress code will work with them. The more authority you can generate, the better off you will be.

Within this second group the most influential purchasing agents are those who buy high-tech products. They buy everything from multimillion-dollar computer systems to entire factories for large corporations and foreign governments. They are very sophisticated indeed, and do not think of themselves as purchasing agents even though they may spend most of their time purchasing equipment or supplies. In a number of cases they are professional or technical experts who are in charge of certain types of purchasing because they are the only in-house people who know enough about the high-tech products to make sensible decisions. They are scientists or technicians first, and then purchasing people.

Like most technicians these purchasing agents come from blue-collar backgrounds. But unlike the average technician, their incomes usually exceed $75,000 a year, and they live in upper-middle-class areas and have lived there for many years. When you deal with this group, two-piece gray and blue suits are best when worn with white shirts and conservative ties. The best ties are conservative, traditional stripes. Your suits must be of good quality and beautifully tailored. Shirts should fit well and your ties should be expensive.

However, remember that they still are the sons and daughters of blue-collar workers, and they will be antagonistic to you if you wear an upper-middle-class Eastern establishment look unless they themselves are wearing it. So, unless you know the people you have to deal with will be wearing three-piece pinstripe suits, leave yours at home. If you have to deal with these people in your leisure hours, buy your sportswear from the very best stores in town and buy only the most conservative and traditional items available.

• •

HOW SEX CAN HELP YOU

Since this is a book for men, I will confine my comments on sex and clothing to salesmen and female buyers. When selling to women, every other rule of dress goes right out the window. Gentlemen, note well the following:

Women react positively to any man who dresses in up-to-date fashion—and negatively to anyone who looks obviously dated. This does not mean that you can break the normal code of expectations. Say you sell stocks and bonds. Then your women customers expect you to wear a pinstripe suit. The pinstripe should be gray with a white line, worn with a white shirt and a tie that picks up both colors. The combination is conservative, but it is also up-to-date and chic.

Most women hesitate to buy from (or even believe) any man who is very short.

Women react negatively to men who wear pink shirts or to any soft pastel color in any garment other than shirts. Women react positively to power colors on men, even though they would probably choose other colors for their own husbands. They will believe a man wearing a blue suit and a white shirt much more readily than they will a man in a light gray suit and a light blue shirt. Contrast gives a man much more credibility with women.

Women tend to believe men who are very large, so large men can sell more easily to women than average-size men. They may also wear garments that make them look even larger or more powerful. Large men do not frighten women; all signs of power are received in a positive way.

Women accord greater credibility to a man who puts his colors and lines together well and with great care. When a man does not do this well, women do not think that he doesn't care; they think he doesn't know how, and they therefore minimize his ability in other areas.

Women without a business background generally dislike traditional items in clothing. Club ties and rep ties are best avoided; paisleys will work as well as almost any other nonconservative tie. White and blue solid shirts are best avoided; they will react best if you are wearing pale yellows or pastels with some sort of color in them or the new shirts with the contrasting collars and cuffs, but they must be of good quality.

All women should be treated as if they are of the upper-most socioeconomic bracket. They will respond better to Fifth Avenue clothes than to Seventh Avenue clothes, and even if you do not know the difference, you may count on this truism: Every women in America does know. This is astounding, but I tested this thesis with a group of third-grade ghetto girls and they knew the difference! I have a feeling that women are born with the knowledge.

When women are buying items they feel require any kind of comparative economic decisions—items on which they normally try to save money—the salesman selling them these items should not be dressed too expensively; if he is, women will immediately assume that he is making too much profit. With such items, lower-middle-class clothing for the salesman works much better with women in all categories except those who have absoulutely no money worries.

The most important and influential fact in a woman's judgment of clothing is her present environment. Our research indicates that women react positively to those who dress the way the poweful and successful men around them dress. This is particularly true for women in corporations that have distinctive dress codes. For example, if you are going to sell to a woman at IBM you would be a fool to wear anything but a conservative suit and white shirt. Since the most important, influential and talented men she sees every day of her life in her organization dress one way, she is going to react positively to you if you dress that way and negatively if you do not. Conversely, if you try to sell to a woman who works for Texas Instruments or any other nonsuit company where most of the men dress in upper-middle-class casual, she will react negatively if you wear a conservative three-piece pinstripe suit. Since you must wear a suit on your first visit even to a nonsuit company because they will not perceive you as a businessman unless you are wearing one, you should choose a beige, light tan, or medium range blue two-piece model and wear it with a blue shirt or a shirt with a contrasting collar and cuffs, and a lively fun tie, paisley, polka dot, etc. That look says; "Yes, I am wearing a suit, but I'm not the suit type."

• • • • • • • • • • • • • • • • • • • •

WHEN SELLING TO DIFFERENT TYPES OF PEOPLE

Frequently, salesmen tell me that they sell to too many different types of people to make my suggestions work. Generally this is not true. I suggest that any salesman who believes this make up a chart. On the chart, he should list every customer he meets in one month; the sales potential of each individual as well as the amount actually received from him; and the category of the buyer in terms of age, socioeconomic background and company orientation. This chart enables the salesman to get an overview of the people he is dealing with. It enables him to ration his time more carefully, giving more attention to those clients who could be even more important. And it also enables him to plan his days so that he sees one type of person on one day and a second type on the next.

I realize that some contradictions are built into my advice; when that happens you must use your own judgment and select the clothing recommended that best satisfies the most important factors of that individual case. In descending order of importance, these factors are occupation, age and geography. From there on, your instincts are your best guide.

DRESSING TO MATCH YOUR PRODUCT

When Gerald Ford was minority leader of the House of Representatives, he sold his product—himself—excellently. He was Jerry, the nice guy, and he dressed like Jerry, the nice guy. When he became president, he had a different product to sell—leader of the country—but he did not change his image in the beginning of his presidency and was still projecting Jerry, the nice guy. As a result a great number of people looked on him with disdain. He had to change his image—and he did, successfully. But most of the damage had already been done. The image of Gerald Ford as an ineffective bumbler hung over his presidency like a black cloud. Every time he slipped or mishit a golf ball the press jumped all over him, in spite of the fact that he was probably the best athlete ever to occupy the White House.

Ronald Reagan, on the other hand, came from a casual California show-business environment. But luckily for him, he had served first as governor of California and realized that he had to change his image when he got to Washington in the same way he had had to change it when he first arrived in Sacramento. By the time he reached the White House, he looked every inch presidential. From his first day in office everyone, including the liberal media, treated him with a great deal more respect then they had President Ford. If historians agree that Ronald Reagan was a successful president, they will also agree that one of the main reasons for his success was that he was a master of controlling image and dressed to sell his product—leadership. If you want to sell any product, you must do the same.

I was once disseminating this advice to a group of salesmen when one jumped up and said, "I sell computers. How do you dress like a computer?" I then did a very quick analysis of the audience. I first asked if there were men present who did not sell computers. Then I asked them what they knew about computers. They answered that computers are expensive, and efficient, yet they break down a lot.

I then told the salesman that he really was not selling a computer. What his client was buying when he chose between computers was the reliability and integrity of the company. If the salesman worked for IBM, his integrity was already guaranteed by the company's reputation. However, if he worked for The Small Unknown Computer Company, the only way a buyer could judge the company was by looking carefully at him. Therefore, it is more important for the salesman representing a small company to dress in a way that announces that his is a very honest, reliable company that will back up its claims and give excellent service.

• • • • • • • • • • • • • • • • • •

DO YOU KNOW WHAT YOUR TRUE PRODUCT IS?

The main problem with most salesmen dressing to suit their product is that they do not know what their true product is. They assume that the product is what it physically is. This is wrong. Salesmen must dress to suit not what they are selling, but what people are buying. The difference can be large and crucial.

I was once hired by a Cadillac dealer to help dress his sales force. He owned several dealerships throughout the country. One dealership dealt only with people who were quite rich. They were not buying Cadillacs; they were buying basic transportation. Like most upper-middle-class people, these customers trusted people who looked as if they were in the same income bracket, so we put the salesmen in good, conservative upper-middle-class attire, and their sales increased.

Several months later the owner called me and said that he had dressed his salesmen in another dealership in the same way and was having trouble. When I visited the other dealership I discovered the reason. That dealership was selling primarily to people who had considerably less money. They were not buying Cadillacs either; they were buying prestige. So we dressed up that group of salesmen with high-power-prestige apparel that conveyed that they had made it big. Sales improved.

Incidentally, I found in both dealerships that the most successful salesmen had been dressing correctly before I got there. Although we are talking about a fairly subtle difference in the appearance between the salesmen in the two agencies, that slight difference made a substantial difference in sales, because the buyer's frame of mind was substantially different.

Here then, is proof that the problem is not what is being sold; it is what is being bought.

With some products and sales methods, the point of customer attitude toward the person who sells the product is particularly significant. When working for insurance companies, I have found that salesmen who sell life insurance to people from the lower middle class had best not wear gray pinstripe suits, although they should look affluent. The very idea behind insurance (i.e., death) and the inevitable complexity and fine print of all policies scare lower-middle-class people, so if the salesman comes on as a very strong executive type, these people do not consider themselves able to hold a conversation with him. They are intimidated by his appearance and will turn him off long before he can close the sale. If he comes on as just a well-dressed neighbor, he fares much better.

• • • • • • • • • • • • • • • • • • •

HOW TO SELL DOOR-TO-DOOR

If a man is selling door-to-door, he can make one or two mistakes in trying to overcome the natural fear women have of strangers that will not let him get past the door. He can dress too much like a businessman or he can dress too little like a businessman. It may seem to be a catch-22, but it isn't. If he dresses like a high-authority businessman in a three-piece pinstripe suit, most of the women will think he is too slick, too sharp, and will be afraid of being bamboozled, so they will not let him start his presentation. If, on the other hand, he wears an open shirt without a tie, they will wonder if he is really a legitimate businessman and will worry about his real purpose, and will not let him in.

A door-to-door salesman has two products to sell and the

first product he has to sell is himself. If he does not sell himself first, he never gets a chance to sell anything else.

There are two ways of getting women to open the door to you. First, dress like a businessman but not an authority figure. Wear a beige, tan, light gray, medium-range blue or any other soft nonauthoritative suit. Wear it with a colorful shirt and a bright tie that has been carefully coordinated with the shirt and the suit. Women associate dress with decency and are much more likely to open the door to a man who is dressed nicely. The second and even more effective way to open a door is to have your company put you in a jacket with a logo on it. It will announce to the women that you are a businessman without threatening them. Either tactic will work.

Salesmen selling to offices have a different problem. If they do not wear high-authority garments, they either cannot get past receptionists and secretaries or are made to wait interminably because their importance will be judged by their clothing. Expensive power garments can cut that waiting time by one-third to one-half, so there is that much more time left for selling.

Today, IBM and its symbol-laden white shirt remain first-glance indicators of success, prestige and reliability. But when IBM first started selling computers, the world of these expensive machines was a confusing, unreliable new field. The basic idea about computers in the minds of most people was that they were unreliable. The white shirt was a brilliant tactical move because it lent the look of reliability to the salesmen even if the product was trouble-prone.

Used-car salesmen face a similar problem. People are automatically suspicious of them (perhaps with good reason), but I have found that by taking used-car salesmen out of their usually gaudy attire and putting them in blue blazers, gray pants, nondescript shirts and perhaps even a club tie with a small company logo or insignia, there is much less resistance to their sales pitch and people feel they are more credible. The look conveys a feeling of youth and innocence and it works.

When I am first invited to speak before business organizations, I know that if the men present have never met me before, they will automatically have me stereotyped as a fashion designer or consultant—someone who is frilly and flighty and unimportant. My standard wardrobe for such appearances is a pinstripe suit, usually with a vest, and a very conservative tie. This clothing immediately suggests—accurately—that I am another businessman, just as they are, that I am a man of substance, and that I am serious. This is how I am able to offset the negative connotations of my services before I even say a word.

After I have worked with an organization half a dozen times I sometimes dress less conservatively. I usually wear two-piece suits with white shirts and conservative ties, but often I open my jacket or loosen my tie as a signal to my clients that I am open and friendly; that is part of a consultant's job. When I speak before college groups, I try to wear inexpensive outfits. At the beginning of the presentation I tell the students how much my suit, shirt and tie cost, and I explain to them that if I can appear before them and talk about "Dressing for Success" with moderately priced clothing, they can use the same clothing to go for an interview. There is nothing that works as well as a personal example when selling a dress code to students or others.

Clothing can also be used to enhance further the existing positive associations of your business. If you work for a large, old corporation, and you dress very conservatively, your clothing will reconfirm the feeling in your clients that the company is still solid as a rock, reputable and doing quite nicely.

I once knew a man in Washington who sold packaged political campaigns. Since politicians are not known for giving much credence to the ideas of others, he knew he had to come on as a supreme authority figure. And he found that the best way to do it was to overwhelm them. He was a large man to begin with, but he reinforced his physique by wearing black suits and pinstripes, a white shirt and black tie. And he overwhelmed people who were not accustomed to being overwhelmed. He úsed a super-hard sell, and his clothing added to his power and prestige.

• • • • • • • • • • • • • • • • • • • •

DRESS RULES THAT ALWAYS PAY OFF

In addition to the general guidelines involving size, age, sex, race, socioeconomic background, geography, occupational orientation and product significance, there are some rules that all salesmen should adhere to, all the time. They are:

1. If you have a choice, dress affluently.
2. Always be clean; it is not always necessary to be obsessively neat, but it is always imperative to be clean.
3. If you are not sure of the circumstances of a selling situation, dress more—rather than less—conservatively than normal.
4. Never wear any item that identifies any personal association or belief, unless you are absolutely sure that the person to whom you are selling shares those beliefs. This rule includes school rings, Masonic rings, ties that are connected with a particular area, political buttons, religious symbols and other similar symbols.
5. Always dress as well as the people to whom you are selling.
6. Never wear green.
7. Never put anything on your hair that makes it look shiny or greasy.

8. Never wear sunglasses, or glasses that change tint as the light changes. People must see your eyes if they are to believe you.

9. Never wear any jewelry that is not functional, and keep that simple. Big rings, bracelets and gaudy cuff links are absolutely taboo.

10. Never wear any item that might be considered feminine.

11. Be sure to wear, do or say something that makes your name or what you are selling memorable. Clothing and accessories are a very effective ploy in the identity game. I have had clients who wore fancy watches, or have always worn the same shade of shirt, and even men who wore two different cuff links (pointing them out to people as good luck charms) to make sure that people did not forget them or their product easily.

12. If it is a part of your regalia, always carry a good attaché case or a good leather envelope.

13. Always carry a good pen and pencil, not a cheap, junky one.

14. If you have a choice, wear an expensive tie.

15. Never take off your suit jacket unless you have to; it weakens your authority. (You have to if you go to sell in a nonsuit company in the palm tree South, particularly in Southern California, and you find that no one else is wearing a suit.)

16. Whenever possible, look in the mirror before you visit a client. Although it sounds silly to be telling this to grown men, you will be surprised at how many flaws you may catch this way—hair out of place, tie slipped or badly tied, a stain on your shirt.

Make up a checklist of these admonitions, as well as any others that are important to your individual circumstances, and carry it with you at all times.

• • • • • • • • • • • • • • • • • • • •

HOW TO TEST YOUR DRESS HABITS YOURSELF

If you are really serious about improving your sales, or judging your ability, you will also do the following:

1. Have a friend take several pictures of you, wearing different outfits. Have the friend show them to people who do not know you. Ask them to judge your honesty, reliability and other such qualities. You may find that a change of wardrobe is definitely in order.

2. Never buy any article of clothing unless you believe it will help you sell. I mean it should actively help, not just be neutral or of questionable value.

3. Test every suit you presently have by keeping a record of when you wear each one and how well you fare on those days. How many doors were opened to you in your blue suit? How long do you have to wait in the outer office in your gray suit? What were people's reactions to you in your brown suit? How much did you sell in your beige suit? After six months of this, you may take a few of your suits out and give them to charity.

4. Finally, I recommend that every morning before you leave home, you station yourself in front of a full-length mirror for a minute or preferably two. You do not have to do anything else. Questions about your dress will arise in your mind and, after some thought, will answer themselves. When you do this, give yourself about ten extra minutes to get out of the house, because you will find yourself changing clothes on many mornings.

. . . .

HERE IS MY PERSONAL GUARANTEE
TO YOU

During hard times and tough sales, every salesman and every sales manager is entitled to be cynical about all the advice I have given. Let me therefore put the following formal challenge into cold print:

I will take on half the salesmen of any sizable corporation; let the corporation take on the other half. Starting with the most successful salesmen, the company gets the best man; I get the second best; the company gets the third best; I get the fourth; and this is carried out all down the line.

I guarantee that after the first year I can improve the sales of my group until its record exceeds by at least five percent the group that was previously leading. If I do not, then my services are free. All I ask is that my out-of-pocket expenses be covered, I receive a reasonable percentage of any new profits I create, and I am able to meet with at least twenty members of the sales force each day.

I can do this with no fear of loss because I know that merely by changing the physical appearance of salesmen, I can substantially increase their sales in the majority of cases.

9

Some Advice
For Minorities

A group of black executives in Chicago hired me to do a report on the best image for upwardly mobile blacks in corporate America. It was one of the most interesting studies I have ever done. We found that blacks had not only to dress more conservatively, but also more expensively than their white counterparts if they wanted to have an equal impact. We also discovered that it was important for blacks to put their clothing together well, and to choose clothing that was finely tailored, because their black skin in a society where racism still persists, aroused a prejudice that they would not be as competent and able as whites. We also found they should avoid any of the obvious signs of being chic—Italian suits, designer attaché cases and so on—because those announced that although they had the money to spend for them, they had not quite moved into the executive class. I titled my report, "Dress White."

About a week after I sent it to the committee that had hired me, one of the fellows on the committee whom I considered a friend called me and said, "John, we're printing your report, but we've changed it." I became incensed and said, "How dare you change my report, it didn't need to be changed." He tried to explain, but I said, "Before you print anything with my name on it, I want to see it," and hung up the telephone. I knew if I rushed I could catch the two o'clock flight to Chicago.

And I did catch it, just barely. When I arrived at my friend's office, he turned to his associate and said, "He actually came." I shouted, "Let me see that report," and he, with a smile, said, "There's a copy on my desk." After reading it twice, I told him that I could find no changes. He told me to read the cover. On the cover he had written one word; in red ink the title now read, "Dress *Very* White."

The man I once again considered my friend apologized for making me fly to Chicago, but explained that it was not his fault that I had jumped to conclusions. He said that the black executives who hired me knew the game, and they knew when they saw the title of my report that I had hit the nail right on the head. He was only trying to catch the attention of the young men who would be getting a copy in the mail; he was afraid that they might read the title and say, "So what else is new?"

It is an undeniable fact that the typical upper-middle-class American looks white, Anglo-Saxon and Protestant. He is of medium build, fair complexion, with almost no pronounced physical characteristics. He is the model of success; that is, if you run a test, most people of all socioeconomic, racial and ethnic backgrounds will identify him as such. Like it or not, his appearance will normally elicit a positive response from someone viewing him. Anyone not possessing his characteristics will elicit a negative response to some degree, regardless of whether that response is conscious or subconscious.

I once had a man come to me who said, "I'm a reasonably successful, honest businessman, but everyone thinks I'm a gangster."

He did have a very harsh, gruff appearance, and since gangsters, and our stereotypes of them, tend to come from a lower-middle-class background and look accordingly, I had the man dress consistently in upper-middle-class garments—pinstripe suits with vests, conservative shirts, Ivy League ties. Because his harsh features seemed to scare or intimidate people, I also tried to give him as soft a look as possible, avoiding dark colors and strong contrasts, and using instead such combinations as a pale gray pinstripe suit with a very pale blue shirt and muted tie. The look was extremely successful for him, and from then on his appearance did not detract from his position.

His problem was very similar to that of many executives who come from a Mediterranean background: They look rather harsh by American standards. The best advice I can give to men with such problems is that they stay with very soft colors and textures, wear very traditional styles, and affect the appurtenances of success.

The two groups who have the most problems with their appearance are black men and Hispanic men. It is unfortunate but true that our society has conditioned us to look upon members of both groups as belonging to the lower classes, and no matter how high a minority individual rises in status or achievement he is going to have some difficulty being identified by his success rather than by his background.

But clothing can help. For sixteen years I have been giving the following advice to my black and Hispanic clients: Dress conservatively; wear those garments that are considered upper-middle-class symbols—pinstripe suits, end-on-end blue shirts, Ivy League ties; wear and carry only those accessories that convey the same message.

In speaking before some groups of black executives, I

have been criticized for attempting to make Uncle Toms out of them. My only answer is that my black clients include officers of several of America's major corporations and representatives of foreign governments. They are hardly Uncle Toms. I stick to my advice. If you are black or Spanish in America, and if you are moving up the rungs of corporate success, you should adhere to the dress code of the corporation and of the country, even going somewhat overboard in the direction of being conservative.

This requirement of dress is not one that is imposed on you strictly because you are of a minority race; it is imposed on anyone who wishes to go up the corporate ladder. If you have to work harder at it than the white man next to you— well, so does the very short man who has a larger man at the desk next to him. Consciously manipulating your dress for success is not giving in; it is a recognition by the man who is doing it that he deserves a crack at the upper echelons of business and he's going to play the same game everyone else is playing, even if he has to play a little harder.

10

How to Get the Most Out of Accessories

There are very successful men in this country who wear expensive suits, expensive shirts, expensive ties, and who drive expensive cars. Some of these men are $200,000-a-year pimps and some are $200,000-a-year corporate executives. Without seeing them, but by merely having their major articles of clothing identified as expensive, we would find it difficult to distinguish between these two groups. By describing their accessories, we would know the difference immediately.

The word "accessories" implies items that are nonessential. But it is very often because they are nonessential that accessories are so important to the overall look of the successful man. I am sure my advice will be of little interest to pimps, but it is crucial to legitimate businessmen.

• • • • • • • • • • • • • • • • • •

WHAT TO DO ABOUT JEWELRY

The basic rule about men's jewelry is, the less the better. Too much jewelry, or the wrong jewelry, will be considered effeminate or foppish and elicit strong negative responses from most people.

Diamonds are a girl's best friend, not a man's. While diamond stickpins evoke neither a positive nor a negative reaction, I advise against them because they break the basic rule of executive dress, which is understatement. Diamond rings, particularly diamond pinky rings, shatter that rule. They scream tasteless, blue-collar, gaudy, and should never be worn by a gentleman.

Collar pins are now in style and test positively when they are worn with conservative outfits.

Tie clips are unnecessary, passé and nowadays in poor taste. They should never be worn. The same is true of stickpins, even ones without diamonds. One out of a thousand men might find a stickpin useful to call attention to himself if he has a severe presence problem, but if he does wear one, it had better be tasteful and extremely expensive.

Lapel pins and insignia rings should be worn only if you know they will send a positive and friendly message to the people with whom you wish to do business. If you are not sure, leave them at home. When we questioned executives about pins and insignia rings, we found that a sizable percentage of them felt antagonistic toward people who wore them. They assumed that if they did not recognize the pin, it was a sign of an organization they had not been invited to join and was probably an unfriendly one. Select societies are very threatening to many Americans and turn off many of them.

Several years ago I personally witnessed the reaction I'm

speaking of. I attended a meeting at which a South Carolina businessman proposed a joint venture with a man in the same business from Boston. I was part of the South Carolinian's team. The gentleman from Boston turned the deal down. Since I knew him very well, I asked him after the other man left why he had done so. He told me the other fellow was wearing a lapel pin and he didn't want to go into business with the type of person who belonged to a pompous organization. When I told him the man had won the Medal of Honor and that was the reason he wore the lapel pin, he jumped from behind his desk, ran down four flights of stairs, caught the other fellow before he reached his car, apologized and brought him back. Now, that deal went through but if I had not been there, it would not have. Lapel pins and insignia rings are very dangerous unless you know that the people you are going to be doing business with will recognize them and be friendly to them.

Some men can get away with wearing very discreet, expensive and tasteful ID bracelets. Very few men—or bracelets—fall into this category. Stay away from them.

The only completely acceptable ring is the wedding band. Period.

Cuff links should be simple and small. The most acceptable cuff link is the solid gold or solid silver ball or any variation of it. Cuff links should never be large or gaudy; if you must wear stones, wear real ones.

The only other acceptable pieces of jewelry of any kind are money clips; if they are simple, elegant and tasteful, money clips evoke positive responses.

The only item a man should wear around his neck is a tie—no beads, chains or medallions, regardless of their connotation or meaning, not even with sports clothes and not even with bathing suits. If you want to wear anything other than a tie around your neck, go into show business.

BELTS AND BELT BUCKLES

Within reason, there are no unacceptable belts; the buckle is the problem. Big, heavy or ornate buckles tend to be unacceptable; small, clean, traditional buckles with squared lines are best (see drawing below).

Belts for Business

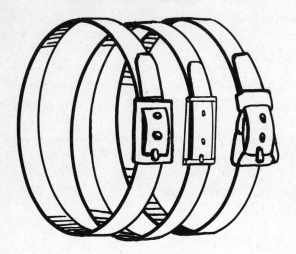

GETTING THE MOST OUT OF WALLETS

All wallets are okay and the larger pocket secretary that can be carried only in a suit jacket pocket remains an upper-middle-class symbol, but it is not as popular today as it was just a few years ago. Today most executives carry a leather tri-fold. When I asked them the reason, about half said they carried tri-folds because when they were on planes they took off their jackets and did not want to leave their wallets in them, and pocket secretaries would not fit comfortably in their pants or shirt pockets. Actually, there is only one rule for the shape of a wallet; it should be thin. Regardless of what kind of wallet you carry, it should never be crammed so full that it bulges.

In wallets, as in all other leather goods, the finer the leather, the better it will work for your overall presence. The best color for wallets is a dark, rich brown—almost cordovan. Speaking of wallets, credit cards, particularly prestigious ones such as American Express Gold and Platinum Cards, and the Gold Card of the banks, are signs of success and are regarded as such by all classes. They are essential to any businessman (you have probably noticed that it is almost impossible to rent a car without a major credit card of some sort). A man should have as many as he needs, but no more than he can afford.

. . . .

ATTACHÉ CASES CARRY A LOT OF WEIGHT

There is a story of a black minister who, every time he had to travel in the South, carried an elegant, expensive attaché case, although he had no real use for it. When he was asked why he carried it, he explained: "Without it, I'm just another black; with it, I'm a black gentleman."

Attaché cases are no longer always positive symbols of success for every group. It varies from profession to profession and from industry to industry. They are still status symbols for attorneys because they need attaché cases to carry their papers to court. Similarly, they are status symbols for engineers and architects because they are required to carry a great deal of material when they go into the field. And they are excellent for salesmen who have to carry either their products or documentation. However, today most executives at or near the top have traded in their attaché cases for simple leather envelopes; and those who carry leather envelopes carry more clout.

While only a few years ago all attaché cases were acceptable, today the only acceptable attaché cases are made of leather. The best cases are made of a dark, rich, almost cordovan tone of brown leather, but all shades of brown are acceptable. Black and gray leather models did not test well, and attaché cases made of plastic and vinyl tested very poorly. Attaché cases should have dial locks; executives do not like to carry keys. It should be plain, simple and functional with no decoration or obtrusive hardware. You can have your initials put on your attaché case only if they are small and delicate; the same is true for a company logo. Keep in mind that no executive should be forced to carry a billboard. If he does, it takes away from his prestige and his company's as well.

· · · · · · · · · · · · · · · · · · ·

MAKING THE MOST OUT OF PENS

All businessmen should carry a pen, pencil or both. There is very definitely an important look to some pens. The best is the gold Mark Cross. It has almost become an executive symbol in America, but any obviously expensive pen or even a pen that looks expensive will do. Under no circumstances should a man use a cheap pen or pencil in the presence of other men, although many do. You may think this is an insignificant point; comparatively speaking, it is. But no man who writes with a $25 pencil will ever be considered poor or a slob. If he writes with one that costs twenty-five cents, he might be.

• • • • • • • • • • • • • • • • • • • •

HOW TO HANDLE GLOVES

Every man should have several sets of gloves. Almost all gloves are appropriate, but rich, brown leather are best, followed by the wool glove. Black leather should be avoided. Gray is much better. Gloves should be thinly lined so they are not bulky. Sport gloves—suede with sheepskin lining—should not be worn with business clothes.

• • • • • • • • • • • • • • • • • • • •

WHAT UMBRELLAS WORK BEST

A man's umbrella should be black. Today most executives carry the fold-up umbrella. They carry them because they can slip them into attaché cases. Yours does not have to fold; any standard umbrella works fine as long as it is black. The multicolored golf umbrella that some men carry has a feminine overtone in certain sections of the country and should be avoided.

Remember, the best umbrella is no umbrella at all. Top executives and the American Brahmins do not carry umbrellas— their chauffeurs do. If you are visiting or dealing with a top executive, it is best you put your umbrella away as soon as you enter the building. For the same reason I advise against wearing rubbers when it rains. If you must wear some sort of foot cover in the snow, wear those lightweight black rubber boots that you can slip off, fold up and put in your attaché case before you go into an office.

• • • • • • • • • • • • • • • • •

SUNGLASSES

Sunglasses were designed to be worn in one place, in the sun, and that is the only place you should wear them. They are perfectly acceptable for leisure wear, but they are not meant for business. If you wear shades in business, people look upon you as a shady character. Most businesspeople will not trust you, believe you or like you if they cannot see your eyes.

If, for medical reasons, you must wear sunglasses indoors, buy photochromatic lenses, the type that lose their shading when you go inside. But even with these you have a problem. Your best move, if you have to wear these glasses, is to start your conversation with any stranger by apologizing for the glasses and explaining that you are wearing them for medical reasons. This will automatically eliminate the negative message that they send.

• • • • • • • • • • • • • • • • •

WHAT SCARVES ARE ACCEPTABLE

Acceptable scarves are made of silk and wool, no other materials. Some silk scarves are reversible, with wool on the other side. The predominant patterns of silk scarves are foulard and solids; plaids and solids dominate in the wool versions. Almost any pattern of color is acceptable in scarves as long as it is not gaudy. If you are not sure, leave it alone, unless it would also be an acceptable tie pattern. White scarves are generally too dressy for daytime use.

. . . .

HANDKERCHIEF DO'S AND DON'TS

Men's handkerchiefs should be cotton or linen, hand rolled and either white or maroon. Handkerchiefs worn in the breast pocket of the suit are perfectly acceptable with conservative suits. Very young men who wear pocket handkerchiefs tend to look affected. Most colored handkerchiefs, particularly the handkerchiefs that match ties, should be worn by no one.

. . . .

SHOES AT WORK

Acceptable colors for business shoes are black, brown and cordovan. Patent leather is acceptable only for men wearing tuxedos. The wing tip and other plain lace-up shoes are the traditional footwear of the American businessman. Today's slip-ons work just as well if they are dressy and obviously expensive. No business shoe should ever have metal hardware on it, and this includes designer logos. Good business shoes are conservative, dressy and made of leather.

My research found that you can often identify people's background by the shoes they wear, and this includes top executives. Most people from blue-collar backgrounds think of shoes as being functional rather than decorative. Most people from executive or upper-middle-class backgrounds think of shoes as another part of their wardrobe, and replace them when they become shabby, not when they wear out. You should ask two questions about every pair of shoes in your closet: First, do they help you maintain your executive image? Second, after you shine them, do they look fairly new for at least twenty-four hours? If the answer to either question is no, throw them out.

All-Leather Slip-on

Lace-Up

With Gucci-Type Buckle

Wingtip

Shoes may also be divided into three categories: those that will work only with business suits (conservative lace-ups, particularly wing tips), those dress shoes that work with more formal leisure wear, and footwear that is used only for leisure activities. The quickest way to announce that you come from a limited background and would not be capable of handling a sophisticated assignment is to go to the corporate outing wearing Bermuda shorts and wing tip shoes. It is as inappropriate as wearing sneakers with a suit, and yet I see about twenty-five to thirty business executives who make this mistake at corporate outings every year. If you are not certain about what leisure shoes to wear, topsiders are your safest bet. They work with almost anything.

The one exception to the conservative shoe rule exists only for short men. If you are particularly short, it can be an advantage for you to wear lifts, but you should wear them only with the most conservative shoes. The best choice for lifts are wing tips, which are rather substantial to begin with and will disguise the fact that you are wearing them.

. . . .

THE RULES ABOUT SOCKS

Business socks should be dark and over-the-calf, never only ankle length or even slightly droopy. Never.

. . . .

HATS OPTIONAL

Hats are optional. If you do wear a hat, it should be a standard style, conservative color, and nothing big, floppy or unusual.

. . . .

HOW TO WATCH YOUR WATCH

A gentleman's watch is thin, plain and gold, with either a gold or leather band. You can get away with almost any watch if it is obviously expensive, but no matter what anyone tells you, gentlemen do not wear skindiver watches or astronaut watches or Mickey Mouse watches to the office. Gentlemen do not wear cheap watches or expensive watches with cheap expansion bands; they are a symbol of the lower classes.

Good pocket watches, particularly gold antique models worn with the traditional chain and watch fob, are not only acceptable but status symbols. Naturally, you can wear them only if you wear a vest with two pockets, one for the watch and one for the fob. They are often worn by businessmen at the top and they are a favorite of the American Brahmin. It is usually the watch they inherited from Grandfather.

• •

CHOOSING UNDERWEAR

A gentleman should be able to choose his own underwear. My only suggestion is to the men who wear the same T-shirts for leisure wear and business: buy V-neck shirts—it won't matter under a shirt and tie, but your T-shirt should never show under an open-collar shirt.

• • • • • • • • • • • • • • • • • • • •

PICKING OUTERWEAR

There are three types of coats that are acceptable: overcoat, raincoat and topcoat.

The two best styles for a gentleman's overcoat are the single-breasted Chesterfield and the double-breasted British Warm. They are best because they have been around for a hundred years and they will be around for another hundred. Which means that if you buy the right overcoat it can be an investment for a lifetime. There are a number of less formal overcoat styles, but most of them have raglan sleeves and will not accommodate suits or sports jackets with padded shoulders. Since you never know what styles are going to be in fashion in a year or two, I suggest you avoid them.

An overcoat should always be made of natural fibers; long staple wool, camel hair, cashmere or alpaca and, for those with money to spare, vicuña.

A gentleman's overcoat must fit him as well as a suit, although it is not fitted in the same manner as a suit. The main area of concern when fitting an overcoat is the shoulders. You must wear the same suit jacket when you are being fitted that you are going to wear with the coat. If you have two styles of jackets in your wardrobe, wear one and carry the other and only purchase the coat if it is comfortable over both. Once you are satisfied that the shoulders of the coat fit comfortably, check the collar. It must lie flat and smooth at the neck, and the smoothness should continue right through the V in the front of the coat. An overcoat should drape smoothly around the body; it should not wrinkle. If a coat has horizontal wrinkles or the buttons pull, it is too tight and it should be rejected. If it has vertical wrinkles it is too loose in the chest area. In some cases this can be taken care of by tailoring, but in other cases it cannot. Common sense must be your rule. The sleeve length in an overcoat is just as important as it is in a suit. It should be long enough to cover not only your suit jacket, but also your shirt, with half an inch to spare. If the sleeves hang down around your thumbs, they must be shortened. And, finally, a gentleman's coat hangs two to three inches below his knee, never any longer and never any shorter.

Topcoats are not as popular as they once were, but are still worn in states where the weather never gets too cold but some kind of coat is occasionally needed. Beige and blue are the most appropriate colors but, as with overcoats, gray and brown tweeds, particularly Harris tweeds, are useful and appropriate.

The beige raincoat, as you learned in Chapter 1, is the raincoat of the upper middle class. As I said, blue is passable but not recommended and black is never acceptable.

A businessman should never wear any coat made of leather, suede or fur to work. You can get away with leather or suede coats if you deal with people in certain high-fashion industries or with American Brahmins who often wear suede coats themselves, but even with these groups they do not test well. For the average businessman they are a waste of money.

And speaking of wasting money, many otherwise very astute businessmen who dress beautifully often throw their money away by selecting inferior raincoats, topcoats or overcoats. The sophisticated businessman, who can tell at a glance the difference between a high-quality and mediocre suit, has no difficulty doing the same with an overcoat or a raincoat. Therefore, I suggest that you check the content label to see that it is made of a good material, the lining to be sure it is securely fastened, and the buttonholes to see that there are no loose threads. I also suggest you buy a coat with a label you respect from a store you can trust. It is particularly important that you buy it from a good store; not only will they stand behind an overcoat, but they will have the skilled tailors who will take the time and effort to tailor it properly.

11

The Do's and Don'ts of Sports Clothes and Formal Wear

Thirteen years ago, a major Midwestern corporation hired me to consult with them on uniforms for those of their employees who dealt with the public. While I was working at company headquarters, the president of the firm asked to see me, not because he was interested in what uniforms I was choosing, but because he wanted to discuss my clothing research for executives. After I had run through my standard fifteen-minute orientation, he said he found my ideas quite interesting because he had always used clothing as a key to help him determine what executives he would move into the home office with him.

It was his practice to bring all young up-and-comers to the home office for several months. During that period he furnished them with housing and a temporary membership in his country club. They knew they were there to be watched, but they never knew how. He said that it really was not a question of ability; these men all had plenty of it because he had many more employees with ability than he had key positions. So the way he made his choice was principally by how they dressed in their leisure hours at the country club. He contended that, if they fit in there, then they would have no trouble fitting in at the office.

For many years I believed that he was the exception to the rule, but he was not. Recently my researchers interviewed several hundred executives and over seventy percent said they often learned more about a man at social business gatherings than they did working with that person all year. The manager of one company said that he used these social business gatherings to "mine for nuggets." People were not promoted on appearance alone, he said, but those who made a positive impression were more likely to be considered for bigger and better things in the future. Several of the executives to whom my people spoke said I had created a problem that made such a procedure necessary. They explained that every young man who came to work for their company was given a copy of *Dress for Success* and, as a result, ninety-five percent of them were wearing the right suits, the right shirts and the right ties to the office and, although that was very good for the company, it made the job of picking future executives more difficult. They said before handing out my book or, as one executive put it, "before Molloy," they could guess with a certain degree of accuracy which young men were likely to have the necessary social graces that would allow them to deal effectively with executives, simply by observing the way they dressed in the office. Since this was no longer possible, they now paid very careful attention to the way the young men and new employees dressed at Christmas parties, company picnics and other social business gatherings.

• • • • • • • • • • • • • • • • • • •

HOW SPORTSWEAR HELPS BUSINESS SUCCESS

The executives we interviewed had an in-house term for these social business gatherings. They called them "dog and pony shows." It is their belief that you attend these gatherings to see the people who count and to be seen by them. In their opinion, it is often the most important time in a man's career, rather than a time to party. They explained that business is customarily conducted at country clubs, on golf courses, and at five-star restaurants, and the way a candidate for an executive position handles himself in a social setting can be as important as what he does during the day. It's obvious, therefore, that when you choose an outfit to wear to the company picnic, or to play golf with your co-workers, you should exercise as much care as when you choose your suit, shirt and tie for the office. If you do not, no matter how much you spend on the clothing you wear to work, you are not dressing for success.

The first rule of sportswear is that you should have some. The difference between men who are established in the upper middle class and those who are not is probably most noticeable in their sportswear, because men who wear suits and ties to the office every day find it impractical and boring to wear the same type of apparel when engaging in physical activity or leisure pursuits. Therefore they tend to buy apparel specifically for leisure wear.

To make the most of your sportswear, all of it should be immediately distinguishable as such. Almost any garment that may be of business use is incorrect, and so is almost any combination that is not totally composed of distinctly nonbusiness garments. To belabor the obvious: Wing tip shoes do not go with jeans; desert boots and sneakers do. Dress shirts do not go with walking shorts.

One of the distinguishing features of sportswear is color, which is often bright and sometimes even gaudy, although this does not mean that the general rules of good taste can be discarded. It is the mistaken belief of many men that once they put on sportswear they may combine garments in any helter-skelter way they choose. Not so. The basic business rule of not putting patterns against patterns is equally sound for sportswear, and colors that clash are colors that clash, regardless of their use. Poorly matching patterns and colors in sportswear, or even mixed styles of sportswear, can be as detrimental to a man's career as the same faux pas in business wear.

· · · · · · · · · · · · · · · · · · ·

COLORS TO AVOID

There are certain colors in sportswear that tend never to look right. Surprisingly, one of the colors that usually looks cheap, and therefore inappropriate, is light blue. Anything that falls into the category of light or sky blue tends to have negative connotations, while anything that falls into the category of baby blue tends to evoke good vibrations. If you are not sure which is which, avoid the lighter shades of blue.

Harsh or bright yellow should also be avoided; if you wish to wear yellow in sportswear, it should be pale and soft.

Maroon is better than red; the darker the red, the better it tends to work. Purple is a poor idea, regardless of the shade. Orange is almost impossible to match, except with another orange and white. Green and gold are not always bad, but they are negative ninety percent of the time, for a variety of reasons, and therefore make bad color choices.

The best colors in sportswear—the ones that are always safe—are navy blue, white, maroon, khaki and beige. If you use them, you will have to try very hard to go wrong. The brighter colors are acceptable, sometimes even preferable (in ski wear, for example), as long as you understand that they must be properly coordinated and in good taste.

Materials and textures have a very definite effect on sportswear. You should always avoid silk, velvet and velour (although velour shirts are acceptable in winter). Any material that is so sheer that it can be seen through registers strongly negative. The best looks in material and texture are denim and real cotton and real wool. Sportswear made of synthetics in blends is recommended over one hundred percent synthetics and must be of the best quality, because anything less looks cheap and awful. As a general rule, synthetic sports garments should have the look of cotton or wool, with the exception of ski clothing, which because of its nature and purpose must be and look synthetic.

• • • • • • • • • • • • • • • • • • • •

SPORTSWEAR PATTERNS: GOOD AND BAD

The best patterns in sportswear are solids and plaids. Circles, dots and stripes are generally bad. Any pattern that is busy, wild or moves in multiple directions is bad. Any pattern that looks as if it should be on a rug rather than on a garment is bad.

Good leather works very well for sportswear. Cheap leather is good for nothing. Other than belts, shoes and, occasionally, gloves, no leather garment should be black. Leather jackets that cut in and stop at the waist—the Eisenhower style, for example—tend to trigger a strong negative response.

The two basic mistakes that most men make with leisure

wear concern quality and fit. Cheap sportswear is lower-middle-class sportswear and looks it. It is inappropriate when it is new; it bags and sags and fades and doesn't last and, in the end, is more expensive than if you had bought good quality to begin with. Every man should spend comparatively as much for his sportswear as he does for his business wear.

• • • • • • • • • • • • • • • • • • • •

WHY FIT IS EXTRA IMPORTANT

Sports clothing should fit as well as, if not in some cases better than, business clothing because of the bright colors and patterns and sharp contrasts that are hallmarks of most sports clothing. If a garment does not fit, have it carefully fitted by a tailor. If the jacket of a conservatively colored and patterned suit is slightly too long, that is often unnoticeable because the jacket and pants tend to blend into each other. But with a boldly patterned sports jacket, worn with sharply contrasting slacks, the slightest flaw is immediately noticeable. Shirts and slacks, especially, must often fit better because no jacket goes over them to hide any imperfections. One of the most obvious fit problems with sports clothes involves very tall or very short men wearing walking shorts. With the short man, the shorts are very often too long and must be tailored up. The tall man will usually have to buy his walking shorts in special tall man shops so that they are long enough.

If a man knows absolutely nothing about sports clothing, and does not wish to learn, then the most important advice I can give him is to always buy the best garments in the best, most established and traditional stores. Granted, that is expensive advice, but it works. Line up ten men in various sports outfits from Sears, Brooks Brothers and Saks, and I will tell you which is which. It is not that the clothing from Sears will always be wrong, but the clothing from Brooks, Saks and other upper-class stores will almost never be, provided you avoid anything that is trendy or fashionable and you choose the correct type of clothing for the appropriate occasion.

Since all acceptable sports clothing must have the upper-middle-class touch, the most acceptable looks are those that are traditional to the leisure pursuits of that class. Since leisure pursuits and looks are basically seasonal, I will describe the acceptable looks in seasonal order, beginning with winter.

• • • • • • • • • • • • • • • • • • • •

GO FOR THE BRITISH LOOK

On any winter day, if you stand on Fifth Avenue in New York, you can spot any number of men wearing clothing that would be much more at home on grouse hunts in the British Isles than on Fifth Avenue. There have not been many grouse on Fifth Avenue recently, and most of the men in those clothes would not know which end of the gun to fire if there were. But this is beside the point. The point is that we are basically Anglophiles in our attitudes toward clothing, particularly in sportswear, and so the look is absolutely acceptable.

The look has many variations, but it is basically beefy or tweedy, heavy and British. Jackets are of heavy tweed or widewale corduroy, frequently with leather or suede patches, or they are reversed sheepskin. Slacks are of heavy wool, in either tweeds or subdued plaids. Shirts are heavy wool in Scottish plaids, and look like lumberjack shirts, except no lumberjack could afford one. Socks are heavy wool, and scarves are very tweedy or feature tartan plaids. Gloves are sheepskin lined. Shoes are generally neutral suede, and are very often high-topped. Fisherman's knit or Irish knit sweaters in off-white or light beige are part of the look, as are other very heavy sweaters in either navy or maroon.

Combined with this look are leather coats, rich, expensive cotton velour shirts (never, ever buy cheap velour), heavy worsted or herringbone suits, good turtleneck sweaters and Russian fur or Swiss mountain climbing hats. Now you have the basic staples of a gentleman's winter sports wardrobe.

• • • • • • • • • • • • • • • • • • • •

THE SKI LOOK

The other specific winter look that is acceptable is the ski look. Almost all ski garments are bright nylon, and while some of the garments tend to look a bit out of place for street wear, skiing is a very in sport and the garments are quite acceptable as sports attire. Although no negative connotations are set off by older men wearing ski clothing, the look is basically young, and one rarely sees it on men over sixty.

• • • • • • • • • • • • • • • • • • • •

DENIM

The one acceptable sports look that bridges all seasons, even though it it not really allied with any specific leisure activity, is denim. Almost every type of garment imaginable is made from it, and almost all of them are acceptable.

When most of us think of denim we think of jeans. A gentleman's jeans always are tailored to fit him—not everyone near his size—which means, if you wear yours off the rack with a standard waist and length, the chances are nine out of ten that you do not have the right look. And you will never have the right look if you wear jeans right out of the dryer; you must have your jeans pressed and dry-cleaned when necessary. A gentleman always makes it a point to look neater and crisper than "Joe Average," especially when he is wearing the same things that "Joe Average" wears.

• • • • • • • • • • • • • • • • • • • •

THE EQUESTRIAN LOOK

The next acceptable sports look is the one associated with horseback riding. If there is an aristocratic tradition in America, horsemanship is part of it. Because of their easier accessibility to the masses, most other traditional upper-class sports have been appropriated by the lower classes, but horseback riding largely remains the province of the rich or landed gentry, particularly in large cities and suburbs. Equestrian garments, therefore, tend to be upper-class symbols and are perfectly acceptable sportswear—on the way to the stable and back. If you do not know what appropriate riding garments look like, then you have no business buying them.

• • • • • • • • • • • • • • • • • • • •

THE SPORTS CAR LOOK

A hybrid between riding clothes and the British country gentleman look is the combination affected by sports car enthusiasts. Composed generally of a well-fitting tweed jacket, cavalry twill pants, a hand-knit, rustic-looking sweater, jodhpur boots, a tweed cap and open-backed racing gloves, this "look" really exists more in fiction than in fact, although it is seen occasionally in the Hamptons, worn by the owners of $70,000 sports cars. Like equestrian gear, it really says that the wearer has a higher-class mode of transportation than the rest of us. Owners of Toyotas and other fundamental means of transportation should avoid it.

Although no longer the exclusive property of the upper middle class, golf, tennis and boating (from sailing to yachting) are still associated with some degree of success, and the right attire naturally has to be acceptable for spring, summer and fall.

• • • • • • • • • • • • • • • • • • •

THE TENNIS LOOK

The easiest sports look is the classic tennis look, composed of white short shorts, a white knit shirt with collar, a white sweater if necessary, white socks and white tennis sneakers. The only acceptable colors are maroon and navy stripes, usually only one of each, on each garment. Off the court, the shorts are exchanged for white duck pants. Today, in most country clubs including the most conservative ones, upper-middle-class variations of this all-white look are acceptable probably because all the pros are wearing and selling colored outfits. However if you're going to go to a club for the first time and you do not know their dress code, stick with white.

• • • • • • • • • • • • • • • • • • •

GOLF? OF COURSE!

Since golf is still pretty much the one game played by most upper-middle-class men and most industry executives, the right look for it is most important for any man trying to achieve success. As a matter of fact, this is the one game I would advise every young man on his way up to make an effort to learn. It can easily take years to impress your superiors in the formal setting of the office, but much less time in the camaraderie of the golf course. I daresay that almost as many important corporate decisions in this country are made on the golf course as in the office, and if you cannot be there because you cannot play, then you cannot be a part of the decision-making process.

Needless to say, the proper golf look is definitely upper middle class, although there are tremendous variations from location to location, from old money to new money, and from clique to clique. The only way to learn what is acceptable to the group you are interested in joining is to observe carefully and assimilate quickly.

The mistake made by most golf enthusiasts is that they tend to overdo in amassing the equipment, gadgets and doodads associated with the game. The only essential pieces of equipment are clubs, balls and shoes. Everything beyond that tends to be nonfunctional. Such semifunctional items as the golf hat and golf glove are acceptable. The clothing worn on the golf course tends to be a man's everyday leisure clothing.

Old-money golfers seem to be just as happy in their well-worn Brooks Brothers chinos or corduroys and knit shirts as in anything else. With their golf shoes off, they look just as they might look while puttering around the garden or paying a Saturday visit to their favorite dispenser of spirits. New-money golfers tend to go more for the better, newer golf pants and golf shirts that are immediately identifiable as such because of their brighter colors, inevitable golf logos, or endorsement from everyone's favorite pro. The look carries over into the lightweight throwover golf jacket with crossed-club insignia, and hats with the same. In addition, you can buy everything from club ties with crossed-club insignias to pen and pencil sets with golf balls on the tops. As long as such items are expensive and in good taste, they are proper and acceptable, although they should never be overdone.

If you are still not exactly sure how to go about it, buy your golf outfits in the most conservative men's store in town. Choose a clerk who has been there for a while. Tell him the name of the club where you intend to play and he will probably be able to tell you what is appropriate, or at least what is worn by the other club members. At some clubs you will find all the men wearing chinos and in others you will find them in the brightest golf pants in town. If you are going for the first time you cannot get into trouble with a good pair of chinos, one hundred percent cotton golf shirt and accessories that you bought at the pro shop, but look around carefully and follow the lead of the people who have been there for a while.

• • • • • • • • • • • • • • • • • •

THE YACHTING LOOK

Yachting sportswear—the white pants and navy jacket with brass buttons and ascot or scarf—is dying, along with the old rich who so dearly loved it. Occasionally, it is still seen around Palm Beach, sometimes in the Caribbean and about twenty times a day along the plushest ports of the Mediterranean. But unless you travel in those circles, on your own yacht and not someone else's, or you are practicing to become a seafaring gigolo, this is a look that is best left to your betters and to the geriatric set.

For the rest of us less-privileged salts, the best boating or sailing look is made up of sneakers or topsiders, cotton pants and shirts of good cotton in light, pastel colors and denims.

There is very little to say about beachwear, since it is

worn by every class in just about every style. The only thing that distinguishes the upper-class beach lounger from his less fortunate brothers is that when he comes to the beach his torso and his feet are covered. This is because most good resort hotels will not allow you to walk through the lobby unless you are wearing something on your torso and something on your feet. If you do not want to carry sandals, I suggest you bring topsiders. You can wear them with all but the most formal leisure wear and without socks to the beach. There are bathing suit sets and about seventy-five percent of the men at good resorts will wear them, but it is not necessary. You will find men wearing expensive navy golf shirts with blue bathing suits. Most gentlemen try to match the top with the bottom, but you don't even have to do that. I have seen more than one president of a Fortune 500 corporation, including several Brahmins, wear a golf shirt that he just happened to have in his bag with his bathing suit and sneakers or topsiders. The only advice on beachwear is to buy good beachwear from the most traditional store in town and you will hardly ever go wrong.

. . . .

SEASONAL LEISURE WEAR

Some clothing is basically sportswear with no specific use or look, except whatever is dictated by the season. This includes suits that are a bit too bright, or too wildly patterned, or of unacceptable material (corduroy in most occupations) to be worn for business wear. In the colder months, or in the colder areas of the country, this clothing is not too difficult to choose: The right looks are basically woodsy, outdoorsy in comparatively mild patterns and colors.

Solid navy or camel hair blazers are as conservative and as

elegant as one can get in sports clothing, but they are still sports garments, and should seldom, if ever, be worn to the office with contrasting slacks. They are no longer acceptable if worn with matching slacks. Today, blazer suits are only worn on weekends and even then usually not by sophisticated men. If you own one I would suggest you wear the pants and the jacket separately.

In the South, and in the summer in other areas, a much more varied range of warm weather attire is acceptable. The most formal components are the many suits that can be worn to the office and then double as sportswear depending on the shirts, shoes, ties and accessories. I have illustrated this in Chapter 5, by showing a traditional summer pinstripe suit with a vest and a conservative tie, which is perfectly accept- able for business in any but the most formal offices. Changing the shirt to a plaid and the tie to a bow tie, it becomes a very sporty outfit. It can be turned even sportier with dark brown pants, or, if you use the suit pants, white shoes and a white belt.

Most seersucker and cord summer suits give you this adaptability.

The second variation of the summer look is the sports jacket with contrasting pants. Here we run into a great deal of difficulty, and here is where most men go wrong. Some men choose a sports jacket that is too conservative and looks as if it might be part of a suit. This should be strenuously avoided. Let me say it again: Sports clothing should look like sports clothing, and for the summer this means it should be quite lively with a bit of color in it.

Other men go too far in the other direction, and choose clothing that is too gaudy. In fact, many patterns and colors in summer sportswear are acceptable, but the best are solids and plaids. The plaids may be quite wild and even gaudy, as long as they are worn with calm, solid pants and as long as they are traditional in shape, detail and color.

The same rule that applies to putting business clothing together applies to combining items of sports clothing, only more so. Put solids next to patterns, and only wear one wild pattern in any outfit. Do not buy any patterns in any garment that are almost solid—no invisible-plaid jackets and no raised-weave ties.

In any season, with any sportswear, make sure that what you are wearing is a harmonious, acceptable unit. This means no dress shirts with walking shorts, no ski pants with British hacking jackets, no ties with knit shirts, no black, executive-length hose with white sailing pants.

· · · · · · · · · · · · · · · · · · · ·

THE USES OF LEISURE SUITS

I had three pages in the earlier edition of this book explaining why you should not wear a leisure suit. I described it as a "loser suit," and apparently everyone listened since nobody with any sense wears them anymore. If you still have one in your wardrobe, take it out and bury it. I would suggest you burn it—but it is probably made of polyester and won't burn.

· · · · · · · · · · · · · · · · · · · ·

HOW TO PICK THE RIGHT FORMAL WEAR

Formal wear is a lot more important to most businessmen than they realize. Invitations to company affairs that read "black tie optional" should be read as, "black tie for all those who are sophisticated enough to own a tuxedo." Obviously the people running the affair would not have a black tie optional affair unless they themselves were going to wear tuxedos, and since the name of the game in business is follow the leader, you should wear one as well.

For a sophisticated businessman, a black tie invitation, whether it is to a purely social affair or a social business affair, means only one thing: Wear a tuxedo. For the last one hundred years a tuxedo has been the uniform of a gentleman after sundown and, like most uniforms, wearing it properly requires that you obey a very strict code.

A gentleman's tuxedo is black and only black. You may wear a white dinner jacket in the summer or in the tropics, but since today's black dinner jackets are made in lightweight fabrics, they are not only appropriate but considered superior by many, even in the tropics. If you have a dinner jacket in your closet with nonuniform color, or with piping, or even worse, one of those damask-patterned fabrics, take it out and bury it, because if you don't bury it, it will bury your career.

There are a lot of variations in the design of tuxedos. You can choose one with side vents or no vents, but as with all uniforms, the safest choice is always the most conservative, and that is the center vent. For the same reason I suggest you pick one with notch lapels because that is the model worn by most executives today. However, if you own a tuxedo with peak lapels, which are a little bit more fashionable, or a shawl collar, which is a little bit old-fashioned, they are perfectly acceptable and you can continue to wear them.

Formal shirts should be elegant, simple and white. You will occasionally see a gentleman wear a blue shirt, but I suggest you avoid it. All other colors are absolutely taboo. Formal shirts can be pleated or tucked. Ruffled shirts are only appropriate on MCs in strip joints.

Tuxedos require black bow ties. The tie should be satin, velvet or a grosgrain and should match the facing of your lapel. While black bow ties do not go out of style, you should not wear one of those very tiny ones that were popular twenty-five years ago or one of those big ones that were popular ten years ago. Your tie should look as if you bought it within the last five years. If you can tie a bow tie, get one that ties: if you cannot, purchase a model that detaches in the back. Whatever you do, avoid clip-ons.

Formal wear requires that you wear black patent leather pumps with black bows, or black leather lace-ups. If you do not have a pair of black leather shoes with you when you are on the road, you can wear well-polished, very plain shoes. Whatever you do, do not wear wing tips. It is the one setting where that executive slipper does not announce that you are a member of the club, but that you're an outsider and a clod. Your socks always should be black, over the calf and made of silk or some similar lightweight black material.

The traditional formal shirt demands that you wear studs instead of buttons, with matching cuff links. Traditional studs and cuff links are made of onyx, but they can be made of anything; gold, diamonds, pearls, rubies, sapphires—almost any precious or semiprecious stone. If you buy a set of cuff links and studs specifically designed for tuxedos, they are almost invariably tasteful and, if you buy them in a good store, you can guarantee they will be acceptable. Every gentleman should own a good, and usually expensive, set of cuff links and studs whether he rents his tuxedos or owns one.

Whether you rent or own depends entirely on you. If you go to three or more formal affairs a year, you should own a tuxedo. In fact, many of the executives we spoke to said that a tuxedo is an essential part of a gentleman's wardrobe. If you agree and decide to purchase one, you should purchase a good quality tuxedo from a reputable store in a lightweight worsted.

If you own a tuxedo, there still will be times when you are going to have to rent; when you are out of town or when your tuxedo is in the cleaners. On those occasions there are several things you must keep in mind. First, make sure the rental outlet is reputable. Second, if possible visit the rental store one or two weeks before you need the tuxedo. Try to get there on a Wednesday or a Thursday because those are the days when they have a larger selection. Most people return rented tuxedos on Monday or Tuesday, then they are dry-cleaned overnight and put back in stock.

Since the tailoring done by a rental outlet is often inadequate, you should pick up your tuxedo at least two or three days before you need it, making sure that the tailor is available. And remember, whether you buy or rent, the look has to be crisp and classic, because that is the entire point of putting on a tuxedo in the first place.

12

How to
Dress For Success
With Women

I f you have read and started to follow the preceding advice in this book, you are definitely on the way to improving your business image and, hopefully, your change is for upward mobility.

But how is your sex life?

If you are counting for help on the clothes and combinations I have thus far recommended, it could probably stand improvement.

I wish I could report that a man's sexual image tagged right along with his business image, that the look of success after five o'clock is the same as the look of success before five o'clock. Unfortunately, the facts belie this. In American business, most people who make the important decisions in the lives of most men are other men. In American romance, the people who make the important decisions in the lives of most men are women. And most women's views of men's fashions

269

are, as I've emphasized before, diametrically opposed to most men's views of men's fashions.

Unfortunately for the man who wants to dress for both business and romantic success, this dichotomy of taste requires two distinctly separate wardrobes, one for the office and one for after work. Hopefully, you can afford to cater to this double standard.

For the purposes of this discussion, when I refer to "most women," I mean most single women between the ages of eighteen and thirty-five. When referring to other types of women, I will so specify.

Since clothing is directly related to physical characteristics, I must first describe the type of man most women prefer. He is neither the Charles Atlas type nor the skinny fellow who always gets sand kicked in his face. He is young, well muscled, relatively slim and relatively tall, with a thin waist, well-rounded buttocks, masculine hands and a masculine neck. The backs of the hands and neck are especially attractive to most women.

If you luckily possess these characteristics, it is to your advantage to show them off as best you can. If you are different, and most of us are, the trick is to camouflage your negative points.

For example, most women prefer a man with thin hips over a man with wider hips. If you take photographs of three men—one with thin hips dressed in tight clothing, one with wide hips dressed in loose clothing, and one with wide hips dressed in tight clothing—most women will prefer the man with the thin hips. But some women will prefer the man with wide hips who wears loose clothing. Virtually none will prefer the man with wide hips in tight clothing.

The reason is that most women have a great sense of appropriateness about clothes (even if that sense is largely misguided when it is applied to the business world) and they look upon a man with wide hips who wears tight clothing as too ignorant to cover up his problem. When they dress themselves, women have been taking it from where it is and putting it where it ain't for years, and they expect (and have respect) for the man who does the same.

So display your sexy characteristics and cover your lack of them.

• • • • • • • • • • • • • • • • • • •

WHEN TO BARE YOUR CHEST

Most women like men in open shirts, but they expect this display of masculine chest to be confined to appropriate locations; at a bar, on the beach, at a sporting event, at his apartment or hers, but not on Fifth Avenue. There, women find it tasteless and not very sexy.

Men who wear polo shirts as part of their casual attire should know that most women consider these shirts sexier if they are of darker colors than the pants or shorts they are worn with. When the shirt is not darker than the pants, it should be a solid color. For some reason, in casual shirting, women find solids sexier than patterns.

Most women do not find Bermuda or walking shorts sexy. In fact, they find them markedly unsexy, and much prefer the shorter tennis shorts.

• • • • • • • • • • • • • • • • • • •

HOW SLACKS SHOULD FIT TO PLEASE WOMEN

Slacks can fit a man in several different ways. The style that elicits the most favorable response from women is the hip hugger, particularly if it is tight and worn by a man who has the figure to support it. Another type of pants that is attractive to women are those with high wasitbands, which also tend to show off a man's hips and figure. Although women like a man's pants to be tight in the hips and on the upper legs, they are also attracted to pants that flare at the bottom even though they are no longer in fashion, probably because the flare increases the illusion of thin hips.

When I showed women a number of "costume" looks for men, the two they found sexually most attractive and stimulating are the costume of the male flamenco dancer, and the tight jeans, open shirt and rough masculine look of the American cowboy. Obviously, no sane man is going to go into his neighborhood singles bar wearing a flamenco costume, but he can adopt the cut of such clothing to his more standard garb.

High-heel shoes and boots make men stand differently, which throws their hips into a different angle, and women find this attractive. If you have the choice, high-heel boots have a better connotation than high-heel shoes, which to women imply femininity when worn by a man.

• • • • • • • • • • • • • • • • • • • •

HOW SHIRTS AND SUITS SHOULD FIT

In standard dress shirts, women prefer tapered shirts on any man whose figure can support this style.

Some tapered shirts are sewn in such a way that the seams add even more emphasis to the tapered look. If you do not have the figure for tapered shirts, again, do not wear them. Wear shirts that are loose, but not baggy or sloppy.

Most women prefer suits that are tapered at the waist and that emphasize a man's shape. In addition, since women

Suits

European-Cut Suit

Standard American-Cut Suit

find the backs of men's hands and necks so attractive, high-fashion collars and the tendency to show more cuff add emphasis to these attributes. Women dislike any garment that bags or sags, and this includes overcoats, which should have the same tapered look as suits.

Although I have already warned you that excessive jewelry should never be worn to the office, women do find it attractive on men, so if you wish to wear it after-hours, it is a sexual plus. But it is a minus unless it is tasteful. What's tasteful? Small and discreet and expensive is tasteful; large and gaudy and cheap is not.

. . . .

WHAT WOMEN INFER FROM A MAN'S CLOTHES

When a women sees a man who is not dressed well, she does not think that he is not dressed well; she says to herself that he does not know how to dress well. And she then correlates his ability in dress with his other abilities, or lack thereof. She assumes that any man who knows how to put together tricky combinations is clever, and women like tricky combinations. As you will have gathered, I do not generally recommend putting patterns together; it is too difficult for most men to master well. But to attract women, it can work nicely.

With a plaid suit, it is possible to wear a wide-stripe shirt or an open-neck shirt or a box-pattern shirt so long as the shirt pattern is smaller than the suit pattern and preferably in the same color. A muted paisley or small, neat pattern or tone-on-tone tie will complement the look. Again, you must be adept at doing this, and knowing how to do it well is a gift.

With any of the striped suits I have recommended, you

can wear a plaid or checked shirt with a club tie or plaid or
paisley or bold print. If you can do it well, you will improve
your attractiveness to women, but if you cannot do it well,
don't try. The best way to learn how to do it is to look at
enough store windows. Whenever you see patterns on patterns that are effective, go in and buy both the shirt and tie
together. Never take one without the other.

* * * * * * * * * * * * * * * * * *

ATTRACTING THE WOMAN EXECUTIVE

There is one group of women for whom the above
research has a limited value. They are women executives,
particularly those who work in conservative companies. When
we showed them the same pictures we showed other women
their answers were different from any of the other women we
questioned. They were attracted to the same physical type of
man—tall, well muscled and slim—and they were attracted to
men who wore their clothing well fitted, but they were, in
addition, attracted to men who wore conservative, traditional
power clothing. They described men in conservative suits as
being sexy and alluring. If you are trying to attract a woman
executive, it would help if you wore a well-tailored, obviously
expensive and carefully coordinated three-piece pinstripe suit,
conservative shirt and power tie. Several of these woman said
they found men in such outfits almost irresistible. Keep in
mind, that if anything, they are more sensitive to good
tailoring than their less affluent sisters, and therefore your
suits must fit perfectly. They were very impressed by men
who wore custom suits, even when they had no idea that they
were looking at a custom suit.

• • • • • • • • • • • • • • • • • •

THE COLORS THAT ATTRACT WOMEN

In researching what colors women are attracted to in men's clothing, I found that they like dark, authoritative colors, even in sportswear, on the upper torso. Women are always attracted to with-it or in colors and to certain combinations, navy and maroon being the most prominent. Men who wear bright shirts with dark suits, and bright contrasting colors are considered clever. The only significance I found to be connected with the color red is that women feel that men wearing bright red ties are quite sexy.

Women definitely and always prefer men who are up-to-date; and in women's clothing, there are always in and out colors. If you keep abreast of women's in colors and adopt these for your own outfit, with discretion, most women will consider this quite clever.

• • • • • • • • • • • • • • • • • •

HAIR STYLING AND COLOGNES HELP

Women are attracted to men who have their hair styled in the latest fashion. Today that is a lot shorter than it was only a few years ago. They find men who wear the most modern types of glasses most appealing. Today, that's a toss-up between wire frame glasses and thin boned or plastic glasses. Although they are turned on too by men who wear mustaches, they are turned off by most men who wear beards, and today they are turned off by men whose hair is dirty, disheveled or greasy looking; in spite of the fact that that is the look of some of today's sex symbol rock stars. The same young women who said that long hair was attractive on their favorite rock star said they would not go out with a man whose hair was as long.

Women are attracted to certain smells; most of them say they like a man who "smells good." The men's colognes that women found to be most appealing are Perry Ellis, Halston, Polo, Paco Rabanne, Aramis, and Old Spice. The more masculine smells that most men would think are the most appealing are not thought to be very sexy. In addition to wanting a man to smell good, most women are also attracted to men who smell like men after physical activity. If any cologne manufacturer can ever come up with a combination of both, he will have it made.

. . . .

WHAT SELF-CONFIDENCE REALLY MEANS TO WOMEN

Most women will say that they are attracted to men who exude what they call self-confidence, but what my follow-up research has shown is that what they are talking about is really more akin to arrogance.

In testing in singles bars on New York's Upper East Side, I used two men who had tested equally sexy in the eyes of most women. When I asked the men to act in a self-confident or assured manner, the relationship between their demeanor and the way any women were attracted to them was practically zero. Yet when I told the men to act arrogantly, they were far more successful in being judged sexy and attractive. I do not know the meaning of this, and am not sure I want to find out, but take it for what it is worth.

Women who are older than forty react to just about the same stimulants as the younger women, with the exception that they are more attracted to slightly heavier men. They also tend to be less impressed with the European-cut suit, preferring men who wear more traditional, conservative suits, which is what they were brought up seeing at home. Generally, the older a woman is, the more apt she is to dislike men whose hair is styled.

When Don Juan was on his death bed, he was giving advice to a young man who wished to follow in his rather-to-be-envied footsteps. When it came to the discussion of the clothing the young man should wear to attract women, Don Juan told him simply to attract one woman and let her pick out his clothing. Thus clothed, the young man could then pick out all the other women he desired.

The advice is still quite sound. There is not a woman in the world who would not be flattered if asked to help choose a man's clothing, and almost all of them will choose garments that are sexually attractive on you. So let them. My only word of caution is to make sure they pick out garments that are not going to be worn to the office, but only those you are buying specifically to make yourself attractive to women. Remember that the two definitely do not mix.

• • • • • • • • • • • • • • • • • • •

HOW TO DRESS FOR THE WOMEN IN YOUR OFFICE

Some men must dress for women in the office, but usually in order to be more authoritative rather than to be sexy. Most women who work in offices say that they like their bosses to dress with-it, in nice colors and clever combinations. They will say that they work harder for such men, but in every study I have ever done, I have found that the traditional look in clothing is far more effective for men in authority, if only one or several women work under his supervision. If a man has a large group of women working for him, then it is essential that he dress up-to-date, that he keep the cut of clothes neat and sharp.

This does not mean that he should wear the latest Italian suits or the more outlandish designer ties, but that he put his clothing together with some obvious care and that he make sure he knows at least what is going on in men's fashions and adhere to them somewhat. Women will have much more respect for him.

The man who has a great number of women working under him should wear dark, authoritative suits, dark blues, gray pinstripes, and his suits should be very well tailored. He should make a particular effort to wear shirts and ties that are coordinated with his suits, and he should keep his personal appearance as neat as possible. If the man is much younger than the woman under him, he should dress even more conservatively than I have suggested. The one element of dress that every woman insists upon is executive-length socks, never ankle socks, which they find quite unattractive. As do most men.

The same rules apply to the man who has a large number of women as colleagues. If he is neat and precise in his dress, his female co-workers will think more of him and be willing to help him more. Women do to men what they do to women. Fairly or unfairly they apply the standards of their own sex to the other sex, and since being neat and well coordinated is a sign of being a decent, responsible woman to other women, they carry this attitude over to men.

Men who have women as bosses—and there are a great many today—must adhere to a completely different set of rules. If a woman is going to make the major decisions about your career, then you must dress to please that woman.

Eleven years ago we reported that most women in positions of authority responded negatively to men who wore

three-piece pinstripe suits and other authority garments, because they found the men wearing them threatening. This is
no longer true. Women in management positions today are
not threatened by men who wear high-authority garments. In
fact, they tend to be attracted to them, they think of them as
more competent subordinates and are more likely to promote
them, particularly if they work for conservative companies.

Women pay a great deal more attention to what their
subordinates wear than do men. Not only must you dress
conservatively and traditionally for them, you must have a
more extensive wardrobe if you work for a woman than if you
work for a man. Most male bosses will not pay much attention
to what you wear as long as you do not stray from the
company dress code or come to work looking disheveled. In a
premanagement or professional position you can get away
with as few as five or six suits if you work for a man, while if
you work for a woman in a similar capacity you will need a
minimum of nine suits—and you would be better off if you
owned a dozen. The average woman will look upon you as less
sophisticated if you wear any one outfit too often. For the
same reason, you will need more, and more varied, shirts along
with a large selection of ties. Remember, your clothing must
be put together with great care because these women, like
other women, judge you according to feminine standards. If
you do not put your clothing together well, they perceive that
you are not as clever as you should be because all clever
women put their clothing together well.

If you work in a conservative company, you should not
dress in a jazzy way. Many of the women we spoke to thought
that some of the men working for them took liberties with
their dress that they would not take if they were working for a
man. They looked upon variations from the dress code as a
personal affront, particularly if the men under them dressed
too casually. They were equally enraged when male subordi-

nates were disheveled. I suggest that you check your personal appearance at least twice a day, particularly if you tend to be a little bit sloppy. Women administrators we spoke to said they were enraged when male subordinates did not look their best. They consider it a man's duty as well as a woman's always to be put together neatly. Many of the women managers said they never bothered to tell men under them they were dressing improperly because they did not consider it their job to do so, but they certainly held it against them.

Finally, if you have a woman boss do not take too seriously any compliment you receive. Compliments are fine but they will not get you promoted. However, if she makes a negative comment pay very careful attention. You can be sure of one thing, if she makes a negative comment, it is not an idle remark. The women executives we spoke to said that it was their way of giving advice and they were positively impressed with men who took their advice and unimpressed and annoyed with men who ignored it.

This insistence by woman managers that their male employees dress better is undoubtedly one reason for the new upscale elegance in business today.

13

How to Dress Up Your Office For Success

Obviously, professional qualifications are important for lawyers, doctors, architects and others—including wardrobe consultants—who are in business for themselves. But so are appearances, and the only appearance that will help such men is the appearance of success, prestige and power. I hope that I have by now established how importantly clothing contributes to this look of success. Another significant element in this look of success that can be controlled is the physical setup of your office.

Unfortunately, most corporate executives have little control over the look of their offices because the office arrangement, furniture and decor are usually controlled by the companies for which they work, at least to a considerable extent. Such control, however, is absolutely crucial to any man who must bring in business, who must bring in clients or patients from the outside, and especially professionals in business for themselves. Corporate executives would be well advised to follow as many of my research-based tips as their management will permit.

The impression that anyone from the outside will have of any man will depend in no small measure on the setting in which he sees that man functioning—his office. Men have realized for years that offices are important. But most have not sought to systematize their concern, to make their offices yield the ultimate benefits possible.

The people who sell office furniture are much more concerned with selling the products they have been given to sell than with selling power. They are more interested in selling something new rather than something useful. There are some decorators who are wizards at office arrangement, furnishing and decor, but they are few and very expensive.

• • • • • • • • • • • • • • • • • • • •

HOW TO MAKE IT BIG

Like successful clothing, the successful office exudes the qualities of the upper middle class. It is (or looks) spacious and uncrowded. It is rich. It is well kept. It is tasteful. It is impressive. It is comfortable. It is private.

The most important aspect of any office is size; it should be as large as possible. Obviously there are financial limitations attached to this advice, but if you have a section consisting of several offices, as most professional men do, and you must skimp, be sure to skimp somewhere other than on your personal office.

About as important as your office's size and richness is its address. The best addresses are generally the most expensive, and no matter what city you work in, you should have the most prestigious address you can afford. This is even more important if some of your clients come from a distance. For years, most of my clients have been from New York, and I maintained an office on West 55th Street, right off Fifth Avenue. Knowledgeable New Yorkers know that this is a highly respectable location, but to the executive from Kansas City or the banker from Amarillo who may be considering my services, West 55th Street might at first suggest West 55th Street off Eighth Avenue where his best friend was mugged returning from the theater last year. So now, since more and more of my clients and prospective clients are from areas away from New York, I am moving to a Fifth Avenue office. To any man I want as a client, Fifth Avenue suggests prestige and substance. Any man to whom it doesn't say that, I can't help much anyway.

An office with a window or windows is better than an office without. An office with a window and a beautiful view is the best you can come by. If the view through your window is of an air shaft or similar atrocity, be very sure to keep your window covered.

The ideal office has two well-defined and separate areas: one in which the central object is your desk; and the other an informal conversation area, with a couch and/or chairs in a comfortable grouping. The best office for such an arrangement is L-shaped, but that is quite difficult to come by unless you have the money and ability to rearrange walls.

• •

THE PRIORITY: THE DESK

After you have chosen your office, the most essential piece of furniture—and it should be chosen first—is your desk. The desk should be as large as possible without crowding or dwarfing the office. A desk that overpowers the space into which it is put creates a strongly negative impression. Regardless of its style, a desk should be functional for your needs and work habits. It should be wood or have the look of wood and should be as expensive as you can afford. All types of metal desks should be generally avoided; they do not look as if they belong to a man of substance and power.

The next item to acquire is your desk chair. In most cases, the best chair is a large one that comes up to the back of the head. It should be a standard office chair, various styles of which will blend with any decor from antique to ultramodern. The only man who should avoid the large chair is the very small man. He should choose a chair proportional to his size because a large chair will make him look even smaller.

In front of your desk should be two comfortable chairs for visitors. They should be of good quality, in either leather or Naugahyde, preferably matching your desk chair. The most acceptable colors for desk and visitors' chairs are deep maroon, deep green, dark, rich brown or tan. At present, the most common and sought-after color is black, but it is not as effective as the above colors because they give off a much richer look.

• • • • • • • • • • • • • • • • • • • •

WHERE VISITORS SHOULD SIT

Always place visitors' chairs in front of your desk, never at the side. Somehow, when a visitor moves up to the side of your desk, he invades your area of privacy and cuts down on your authority in dealing with him. Sitting on the side is not as psychologically comfortable for him nor as effective for you. Keep the chairs in front of the desk.

Depending on the space available for your second area, you should at least have a couch (it can be small if necessary) and a coffee-type table that fits in with the rest of the room's decor. If you have an exceptionally large office, and if your work requires it, you might also add a third area in which you would place a small work or conference table with chairs around it. The best example I've ever seen of this was an antique table with matching antique chairs; it gave the powerful impression of a small boardroom in the office.

The only other items of furniture that are completely acceptable in most offices are bookcases, credenzas and filing cabinets. But if at all possible, you should keep your filing cabinets in your secretary's office or in some other area. Important men just do not have obtrusive filing cabinets in their offices.

• • • • • • • • • • • • • • • • • • • •

HOW TO HIDE PAPERS

If you are in a type of business that requires you to have a lot of papers in your office, I suggest that you keep them on top of a credenza behind your desk rather than on your desk. A clean, neat, uncluttered desk is absolutely essential to a spacious, uncrowded-looking office, and to any man of prestige and power.

Bookcases are both useful and impressive, so long as they contain useful or relevant or impressive items—business or reference books, leather-bound first editions, small art works, perhaps antique items related to your business, a stereo set if you are in the music business, small personal collections such as scrimshaw. But don't go overboard with these items. I have been in offices filled with globes, which is fine for men in worldwide businesses, but somewhat excessive for accountants. The one item of furniture that should never be present or visible in any office is a bar; many men will object to it.

Before buying any item of furniture for an office, make a scale drawing of the room and of the furniture you want. If it looks spacious and uncrowded, fine; if anything makes the office look crowded, do not buy it. If you already have it, throw it out. It is far more important that an office look open than that it contain any particular item.

• • • • • • • • • • • • • • • • • • • •

HOW TO GET THE MOST OUT OF FLOOR COVERING

After acquiring the necessary and appropriate furniture, choose a floor covering. The best flooring is parquet covered with several area rugs delineating and separating the different areas of the office. The next best, particularly if your office is too small to handle several rugs, is parquet flooring covered with a room-size rug that leaves about a twelve-inch border of wood showing around the room. The wood must be finished properly, and the quality of the rugs is quite important. Unless your office is ultramodern, choose the richest, most expensive Oriental rugs you can afford. They are warm, colorful and distinguished.

If you do not have or cannot install good wooden flooring, then choose wall-to-wall carpeting. There is really no other solution in the offices of important men. Tile or inlaid linoleum are strong negatives and should never be used. If you do have wood, never leave it bare; bare wood is too cold and makes sounds echo too loudly.

Whatever type of carpeting you have, keep it clean. Most decorators choose pale rugs, and most executives never see to keeping them clean or replacing them when necessary. Dirty or shabby rugs are not proper symbols for the offices of successful men.

• • • • • • • • • • • • • • • • • • •

BEST WALLS, CEILINGS AND COLORS

Having purchased your furniture and covered your floors, you are ready to cover your walls. If your office is small, white walls will make it look more spacious. If the ceiling is low, the lighter the color it is painted, the higher it will look. If the ceiling is too high for the size of the office, you might make the walls white and the ceiling pale blue, which will seem to bring it down. If any one wall of the office seems too distant from the rest of the office, painting it a darker color than the other walls will help; adding paintings or bookcases to such a wall will also help.

Assuming that the office is of a suitable size, off-white or eggshell or very light beige—which are all the same color, really, but paint manufacturers have their own names—is the best wall coloring for a man's office. The only other completely suitable color is pale blue. All others will tend to get you into varying kinds of psychological trouble.

If you are going to use wallpaper, the textured types are best for a man's office. There are excellent grasscloths and woven bamboos that offer richness, depth and substance to an office.

Some men, because of their businesses, must keep bulletin boards, charts, graphs or plans on their walls. If you must, try to keep them in as unobtrusive a place as possible, preferably on the wall with the entrance into the office, never behind you.

. . . .

HOW TO "FRAME" YOURSELF FOR MAXIMUM AUTHORITY

In the ideal office, the desk acts like a throne, giving you power over those who come in. They should be impressed with your importance and authority. The best way to create this impression by instant visual impact is to position your desk and yourself within a frame that automatically turns you into its central element. The best elements to create such a frame are either a window or pictures directly behind the desk. The best frame is an open window with a beautiful view. If you have such a view, use it as the central frame behind your desk. Although most decorations ignore such considerations, if one has a view of constant colors (not seasonal ones such as green trees), and these colors are followed through in the office, the dimensions of the office will seem to be extended.

If you do not have a window, or are unable to position your desk in front of the window, paintings will accomplish the same effect. You must decide what painting, how large and how many, but regardless of these decisions the painting or paintings should be symmetrically positioned directly behind the desk, and not appear off-center or askew.

. . . .

HOW TO SPOIL A WELL-DESIGNED OFFICE

Many men hire decorators to do their offices, and the decorators do magnificent jobs with all the major items. But after the decorator is gone, many a man then decides to personalize the office with a clutter of paraphernalia on his desk and knickknacks around the room. Don't make those mistakes. Keep on your desk only what you absolutely need there, nothing else. And don't clutter the room with extraneous doodads or junk. When the office is finished, and ready for you to work in it, to see clients or patients in it, it should be clean, clear, spacious and sparsely decorated with only tasteful elements, if you wish it to be effective.

Some decorators and some men might disagree with my advice, but just keep in mind one thing. I am not interested that a man have a beautiful office (although there is no reason why he can't and still adhere to my rules); I am interested that a man choose and furnish and decorate his office as a functional tool, as a symbol of power and importance so that he may better perform his job and increase his income.

The best general look and feel of an office is the look of wood and leather. A wooden desk, wooden bookcases, wooden paneling, wooden arms on chairs all look rich and luxurious and impressive. The modern look of chrome and steel and glass is also acceptable, but the man who chooses such a look must make up his mind that the office decor and furniture must be changed every few years. Modern offices, because of their stark lines and sharp contrasts, tend to become boring very quickly, both to the inhabitant and his frequent visitors, and modern furniture tends to date very quickly.

The man whose business absolutely requires the keeping of files in his personal office should consider using a modern office, if only because modern filing cabinets tend to be rather attractive, while old-fashioned ones look terrible. The man with money and an imaginative decorator can also come up with some creative and unobtrusive places and furniture in which to keep files, but this gets quite expensive. For most men, the modern look is far easier on the wallet.

• • • • • • • • • • • • • • • • • • • •

HOW TO TEST THE EFFECTIVENESS OF YOUR OFFICE

A very simple way to test the effectiveness of your office is to photograph it from the entrance door and also to photograph (from the same perspective) the offices of several friends who work in the same profession. Then show the pictures to strangers and ask them to rate the importance of the men, only in terms of their offices. You'll get a pretty good idea of where your office stands comparatively.

In addition to your own personal office, you must also be concerned with your secretary's office or area. Four general rules apply for a secretary's office.

1. It should be tied into the boss's office in some way, usually by proximity, so that there is no confusion as to whose secretary she is.
2. Although it should be tied in, it should be distinctly different from that of the boss. If it is a miniature copy of his office, this would cut down on his authority. The best way to achieve this distinction is to change the color of the carpet or the type of floor covering as you move from one area to the other.
3. The secretary's office should be a separate, defined area, not just a space that is encroached upon by general office traffic. It must be arranged so that the secretary has a sense of territorial domain. This increases her sense of power and authority, and greatly boosts her effectiveness.
4. A secretary should face so as to look parallel to her boss's door, never away from it or into it.

. . . .

AND HOW DOES YOUR SECRETARY DRESS?

Very definitely related to the authoritative look of any office is the dress of a man's secretary. This is an element that is very delicate and often impossible to control—particularly since most secretaries work for less than munificent salaries and don't like their tastes and private lives encroached upon. Still, the more ladylike, dignified, prestigious and efficient she looks, the better the impression she will make on all visitors, and the better they will think of you.

. . . .

HOW TO MAKE THE WAITING ROOM HELP YOU

If you're in any business that must attract clients, never forget that they are your most precious assets, that without them, you're out of business. You must make them comfortable and make them believe you are important at all times, and this includes the time they spend in your waiting room. It's the first part of your offices that they see, and will leave a distinct impression on them. Your chairs or couches should be comfortable and substantial; they should be clean and pleasantly arranged.

The waiting room, like all the rest of your office, must immediately spell upper middle class to every visitor. Good wood, good leather or good upholstered furniture will always accomplish this; modern furniture sometimes will not, and you must be careful in its use. Good rugs or good carpeting will help. A decorator look will help, although this is not a foolproof concept because not all decorators can produce a decorator look.

Tasteful art work, whether paintings, prints or sculpture, gives an upper-middle-class impression. The easiest (and one of the most effective) ways to create an upper-middle-class look in a waiting room is the right choice of magazines. Any combination of the *New York Times, Newsweek, U.S. News and World Report* and the major business magazines—*Fortune, Forbes, Business Week, Barron's, Dun's Review*—plus whatever prestigious specialty or general-interest magazines are relevant to you or your clients all make a good and lasting impression, provided they are always the latest issues and not torn and tattered.

14

For Lawyers: How to Dress Up Your Case and Win Judges and Juries

When I became America's first wardrobe engineer, my initial clients were courtroom lawyers. Because of their diverse and important clothing needs and because they face constant and crucial problems concerning appearance—their own, their clients' and that of the juries before whom they must work—I have continued to advise a growing number of individual attorneys and law firms over the years.

Good courtroom lawyers are super salesmen and consummate actors, and they well realize that nonverbal forms of communication are frequently just as important (and sometimes more so) as the facts of a case. Clothing and appearance are hardly the only important nonverbal communicants, but they are the only ones within my province.

The rules for lawyers are much the same as for salesmen, but they must be broken down further and must be stated somewhat differently.

295

According to all my research, there are only two kinds of judges in America. Both come out of clubs. In the large urban areas, judges generally come from lower-middle-class backgrounds but have moved into the upper middle class by virtue of their positions. Basically they come out of political clubs. In the case of rural or small-town judges, the judges' daddies were usually judges and often their granddaddies were judges, too. They come out of the country club. The manner of dress should be almost the same before both groups, but some slight differences must be observed.

Before both groups, you should wear upper-middle-class clothing when you can. I say "when you can," because in some cases the attitude and makeup of the jury will be more important than the attitude of the judge; if so—and only each individual attorney can decide—clothing compensations must be made.

Before the urban judge, you should avoid the Ivy League tie. You should avoid any sign of ostentation. You should avoid any look that is with-it, chic or in. Urban judges tend to be quite ticklish about their newfound socioeconomic positions, even if they've held them for some time, and often look upon anyone coming into their courtroom as a potential threat to them personally. Anyone who doesn't treat their courtrooms with respect, and that means anyone who dresses in a manner that *they* think is unbecoming, will be dealt with harshly. Their reactions may well be subconscious; no judge will ever tell you that he's ruling against you because of your smart-ass tie, but believe me, many of them will.

Although your clothing should be conservative in the urban courtroom, it should also be up-to-date. If four-and-a-half-inch ties are the predominant style in that locality, wear them, as long as they are in conservative and acceptable patterns and colors.

Rural or small-town judges unconsciously observe much

the same rules. The only difference is that you should never dress up-to-date before them. Rather, well-worn Brooks Brothers is the rule of the day, or whatever style is predominant with the local gentry.

Dressing for juries requires considerable acumen and practice because their makeup rarely fits textbook models. Once a jury has been chosen every lawyer should make a list of every person on that jury, according to those of the following factors that are most important. He should choose his clothing accordingly, just as he directs his case presentation accordingly.

The rarest jury in America today is the old-money jury, composed only or predominantly of the power or hereditary elite. With such juries, one should dress in basically the same clothing that one wears before the aforementioned judges. If the jury is in a rural area or small town, your clothing should be ultraconservative; if the jury is in or close to a large city, you can wear more up-to-date apparel, but every item and every detail of your clothing and your client's clothing must be immediately identifiable as upper middle class if you expect to be accorded credibility.

Before grand juries in large cities, you are dealing with a slightly different social group. These tend to be self-made men and women without very well established backgrounds who have made it by virtue of intelligence and hard work. They consider themselves the backbone of the community and expect anyone appearing before them to affect a similar appearance if they are to be believed. With these jurors, the conservative dark blue suit is the most effective, either solid or with pinstripes, and the Ivy League tie must be avoided. The rep tie and solid shirt, which are staples of the male members' own wardrobes, are also effective.

In most suburban societies, you will find a varied but white population, and will therefore generally face a white jury with mixed socioeconomic backgrounds. In this area, I suggest dark blue suits, white shirts, rep ties and very structured appearances. This is the uniform that the lower-middle-class members of the jury expect. When dealing with lower-middle-class whites on a suburban jury, never wear a gray suit. I know this is the suit that most lawyers wear, but that's because they don't know not to.

According to a Burlington House study, most lower-middle-class whites buy suits for one social function: a funeral. Men at the lower socioeconomic levels are very unsure of themselves socially, even within their own group, and they have strict rules they live by. The dark blue suit is a symbol of important occasions and important people, and it is the one "good" suit that most lower-middle-class men have. If a lawyer comes into a courtroom wearing a gray suit and says to a jury made up of such men (or their wives) that he is their neighbor, their friend, one of them and that they should therefore believe him, his verbal approach may be perfect, but his visual approach is a lie.

They know that their friends do not wear gray suits on important occasions. If the lawyer wants to tell them, "I am in a position of authority, I am an expert, I know more than you and you should listen to me for that reason," then he may wear the gray suit, even with pinstripes and a vest, but he is taking a very serious risk because he may offend the jury by asserting his superiority.

Before the suburban black jury the lawyer basically faces middle-class blacks who have worked themselves up out of the ghetto. They have made it in American society, and they expect to be treated as if they've made it. You should not wear the dark blue suit because to them it represents the old-line, antiblack establishment, which they neither like nor trust. Yet they display the typical, general middle-class prejudice of trusting only older members of the middle class.

The best suit to wear is a medium-range solid gray.

If you have an equal number of lower-middle-class whites and middle-class blacks on a suburban jury, dress for the blacks. The prejudice of the whites against gray will be less than the prejudice of the blacks against blue.

The white lawyer working before a black suburban jury is foolhardy if he attempts a "Hey, buddy, I'm one of you fellows" approach. It can't work. Therefore, he is much better off if he presents his case as an expert, and the gray suit is best, preferably combined with a light blue solid shirt and rep tie. Middle-class suburban blacks are quite status conscious, and they are offended by anyone who does not dress as they think he should.

All small-town and rural juries have one major prejudice in common: They detest the smart-ass big city slicker. The one essential rule before such juries is to wear nothing that indicates you are more sophisticated than they, nothing that indicates you are better than they, and absolutely nothing that they associate with big-city clothing. Whenever one of the richest and most successful lawyers in Chicago must try a case in southern Illinois, he drives down in a pickup truck and dresses very much as if he is more familiar with the truck than with a courtroom. I know a lawyer in New York who makes in excess of $300,000 a year, but whenever he must work on Long Island or an upstate farming area, he takes off his jacket, rolls up his sleeves, puts on the sloppiest tie he owns, and drives to court in his sons' car.

The color prejudices of rural juries are exactly the same as the color prejudices detailed in Chapter 7, and the same geographic breakdown prevails.

Before rural juries, wearing dated clothing is an effective idea, as is a lawyer taking off his jacket, rolling up his sleeves and loosening his tie in the courtroom. Rural juries react negatively even to local lawyers who "put on airs." Anything one can do within reason to be as informal as possible and become regarded as one of the people is a positive move.

Because of their varied makeup, urban juries are by far the most difficult to dress for, but here are some basic rules.

If the jury is predominantly white and upper middle class, you must wear upper-middle-class garments that are up-to-date and conservatively fashionable. If the jury is predominantly white and lower middle class, their reactions will be virtually the same as those of the lower-middle-class suburban jury. So you should wear a dark blue suit, white shirt and very conservative tie. With an urban jury that is predominantly black but middle class, a medium-range gray suit, light blue solid shirt and rep tie work best.

Urban ghetto blacks on a jury change all the rules dramatically. Since most of these blacks can be classified as antiestablishment, or leaning toward antiestablishment in their attitudes, you cannot wear standard courtroom garb successfully before them. (Women lawyers have much more innate credibility with ghetto blacks because women are not considered part of the establishment.) White male lawyers do better before ghetto black juries if they wear beards, if they are not too neat, if they display items that identify them as standing apart from the establishment and if they avoid any item of apparel that is authoritative. Young lawyers will do better before ghetto black juries; age in a white lawyer is an automatic negative with most blacks.

The real problem with urban juries is that the judge is almost always white and upper middle class while the jury seldom is, and is mixed at best. The lawyer in such cases must decide where his most critical problems are and dress to meet them. If he decides to dress for the jury, though, he should at least make a conscious attempt not to turn off the judge.

Minority lawyers working before judges should follow the same rules recommended for white lawyers. Minority lawyers working before minority juries should wear establishment clothing that exudes success. The best garb for the minority lawyer in a courtroom, assuming that he knows nothing about the judge or jury, is a dark pinstripe suit with vest, a white shirt and a conservative tie. The look communicates to whites that the lawyer is no threat, and it says to blacks, "Look at me, I have made it," which is the most positive possible message.

In general, all lawyers should advise their clients to dress in ways similar to the lawyer's own garb in the above situations. Some subtleties can offer additional help. The most innocent look is the young look, and the younger a client can look, the better off he is. Close-cropped hair, closely shaven— any detail of appearance that Hollywood has conditioned people to equate with angelic qualities works wonders.

If you have a client with a beard or mustache, no matter who is on the jury or who the judge is, make him cut them off. Have him dress as conservatively as possible, in a dark suit, white shirt and conservative tie. As strange as it may seem, the look of innocence crosses all racial, age, socioeconomic and sex lines.

Carefully planned clothing can provide an effective boost for any client. For example, when your client is on the stand and *you* are examining him to get your version of the story across, put him in a very soft gray suit (authoritative but not offensive), a solid white or pale blue shirt and a light gray and blue tie, something with large patterns or perhaps a solid color. Your goal is to have the client look calm and to have the jury remember what he says. Dressed in such an easy-to-look-at combination, the jury can look at him for a full day and remember a great deal of what he says.

When the prosecutor or attorney for the other side is questioning him, if possible, put him in a very dark blue suit, a crisp white shirt and a bright red tie, preferably with a difficult-to-look-at but still elegant pattern. Put a bright red handkerchief in his breast pocket. This combination will make it quite difficult for the jury to look at him, and the less they look at him the less they will remember of what he says.

If he's being questioned by your side and wears glasses, have him remove them before taking the stand; if being questioned by the other side, have him wear them.

A week and a half later, when the jury is deliberating, they will remember far more of what he said in his easy-to-look-at appearance than in his difficult-to-look-at appearance.

If you are representing a client who is accused of having power and misusing it in any kind of so-called white-collar crime, diminish his look of authority by having him wear a pale beige suit, a pale shirt (not light blue) and a pale tie. This combination suggests to a jury that this is not really a man of authority and raises the question of how he could have misused what he obviously doesn't have.

If you are defending one of the men in a mass trial, it is very often to your advantage to dissociate him from the other defendants. If this is the case, you should dress differently from all the other lawyers, even if it means appearing somewhat outlandish, and the client should dress differently from the other defendants. The visual separation will definitely help.

In a case on which I was consulted, involving three men accused of corporate shenanigans, my client took my advice and dressed much differently from the other two. He was found innocent while the others were found guilty. On the facts presented, one of the other two was clearly innocent, but he looked so much like the third man who was clearly guilty that the jury lumped them together in their verdict. Any experienced lawyer can cite many cases when clients were found guilty simply because they dressed incorrectly.

In addition to using clothing as a courtroom tool for

themselves, clothes-conscious lawyers can tell much about prospective jurors merely from their appearance. When I was researching this aspect of trial work, I placed all potential jurors into three categories: strongly antiestablishment; neutral, but tending toward prejudice against large organizations; and proestablishment. About twenty-eight percent of the population is composed of strongly antiestablishment people; approximately twelve percent is composed of strongly proestablishment people; and approximately sixty percent is neutral. But if the neutral people are sitting on a case involving a corporation against an individual, no matter what the nature of the case is, they will tend automatically to favor the individual.

In any jury selection, approximately sixty percent of the people, regardless of their category, will *attempt* to be fair, while the remaining forty percent will vote, to a certain extent, based on preconceived prejudices. Any lawyer must decide, based on any individual case, which groups are in his best interest to sit on the jury, and which are in his worst interests, and strike them accordingly. (Obviously, in all my advice to lawyers, I am well aware that there are many factors in addition to clothing that affect decisions, but my advice is limited to appearance since that is what I know.)

People who are openly antiestablishment generally identify themselves quite readily. Any woman who is disheveled, wears hippie or bohemian attire, has an austere look with her hair tied back in a tight bun, affects mannish dress or rather unfeminine dress components, goes braless, or who either verbally or by dress identifies herself as a proponent of women's liberation should definitely be regarded as an antiestablishment type. Women over thirty who wear dark glasses in a courtroom would fall into the same category, although women who are younger than thirty usually do this only because they think it's in.

Obviously, an antiestablishment look varies from community to community, which individual lawyers must take into consideration. In New York City, for example, there are many more acceptable establishment looks than there are in Kansas City.

Any man anywhere who wears shoulder-length hair or beads or bracelets is antiestablishment. Afros on blacks tend to indicate the same attitude. Men who wear unusual color combinations tend to be antiestablishment. Normally, this would mean bright color combinations or bright colors in individual garments—orange shirts, red jackets, green and yellow and purple ties—but unusual combinations can also be mixed into a normally conservative look. For example, if a man wears a pair of black pants, a dark blue jacket, a green pinstripe shirt and a black tie, he does give off a conservative impression, but the combination is unusual enough to assume that the man is probably antiestablishment.

Another typically antiestablishment person is the one who dresses down for jury duty, someone who dresses obviously poorer than he would in everyday life. These people treat jury duty as a lark, and act and dress as if they're going to work in the yard or rake leaves. They may be top executives who wear scruffy pants and unshined shoes. One must be careful to determine a prospective juror's occupation because an executive who dresses this way is dressing down, but a cab driver does it out of necessity and habit and is not dressing down.

Men whose educational levels are equivalent to those of most executives—college level or above—but whose appearances would exclude them from executive ranks, tend to be antiestablishment. This group includes college graduates with beards, who wear only lower-middle-class clothing, or whose hair length would be unacceptable in a corporate job.

White middle-class men who wear either orange or purple in any obtrusive way and men who wear shirts or ties with wild patterns tend to be antiestablishment. This is not true of many blacks and men of Spanish origin, who may wear wilder patterns and colors as a matter of custom.

The strongest proestablishment types are executives who look the part in the courtroom. They come to court dressed in the same clothes they would wear to work, standard business suits, acceptable shirts and ties. Next comes lower-middle-class men who do not wear shirts and ties in their daily lives—bartenders, truck drivers, cab drivers—but who do dress up for jury duty. They do so because they believe jury service is an important obligation.

Men who are extremely precise—with every hair in place, a perfectly knotted tie, impeccably fitting clothes—also tend to be proestablishment, as do men who seem to look old-fashioned. By this I do not mean that their clothing is dated, only that it is extremely conservative. Such men wear narrow-lapeled suits, narrow ties, button-down shirts and lace-up shoes. Also tending to be proestablishment are men who dress for jury duty just as they dress for work, regardless of their occupations, and men who wear traditional patterns, even if these patterns are on rather casual clothes.

Because of the extreme variety of acceptable women's clothing, it is quite difficult to identify proestablishment women by appearance alone. Women who dress conservatively tend to be proestablishment, and even though this is the only reasonable indicator I have been able to isolate, it is not always accurate.

Once a potential juror has been placed in one of the above categories by the lawyer, it is time to begin more extensive questioning of the individual to determine his propensity to either help or hurt a particular case. Veteran trial lawyers are well aware that some potential jurors will lie in answer to questions, some to get on cases, some to get off them, and some for countless other reasons.

Although I do not pretend I can spot any liar in a

courtroom merely by appearance, in my many years of advising and consulting with lawyers I have come up with several identifiable types who tend to lie and should be questioned and challenged far more attentively than most other poeple.

The first type, and the easiest to spot, are people—both men and women—who have no self-image, no self-esteem. They wear clothes that obviously do not fit, that are mismatched; their hair is not combed; their shoes may be scuffed and unshined—not because of economic necessity, but because they do not care. In questioning anyone who falls into this pattern, it is often wise to ask questions already asked by the opposing attorney to check for discrepancies. This type of person tends to tell each attorney what he thinks that attorney wants to hear, and although he's not telling a deliberate lie—he's lying to himself as much as to the lawyer—the end result remains the same: He is a liar.

The second type is the habitual liar, the person who lies all the time and to whom lying is just as natural as wearing a coat in winter. This type of person uses lying as part of his everyday weaponry in dealing with the world and generally lies visually as well as verbally. Men or women who dress as if they are in an age group other than their own—a forty-five-year-old woman dressed like a teenybopper, a twenty-five-year-old man who dresses as if he were sixty—definitely fit into this category. People who dress in contrast to their socioeconomic status—professional men who dress as if they are not, plumbers who dress like stockbrokers (not the plumber who dresses up for court, putting on a shirt and tie, but the plumber who is wearing all the correct upper-middle-class symbols)—these people are lying to themselves about who they are, and they are very likely to lie to you.

The only exception to this rule is young people. Whether they are or are not, many of them look at themselves as being outside the establishment and they dress accordingly. They are generally not lying to themselves, but really are trying to be honest with themselves, and they will generally be honest with you.

The easiest visually detectable liar is the job-description liar. If a man is earning his living as an accountant, he is a part of the establishment whether he knows it or not and whether he admits it or not. If he dresses or acts or has his hair cut in any way that says he is not an accountant, then he is putting on the world and putting on himself. Either way, he is more likely to be untruthful than the accountant who looks, acts and dresses like an accountant. The same is true of truck drivers, doctors, of almost any group.

All of the preceding guidelines are no more than that. Every lawyer must take into consideration the tremendous variations that can occur, the amount of personal judgment that is required on the spot, and use the guidelines accordingly.

15

A Special Word
For the
Professional Man

Once you master upper-middle-class dress, the differences in your effectiveness are only a matter of
degree. But here are some specific rules for those
men who are in business for themselves and must attract and
keep clients or patients in order to stay in business.

Upper-middle-class clothing attracts upper-middle-class
clients, and neutral clothing attracts neutral clients (those who
may belong to any class but need and can afford your services). Typically, neutral clothing consists of a solid dark blue
suit, white shirt and any conservative tie, preferably the rep.
Acceptable upper-middle-class garments are those described
in the rest of the book.

If your job requires that you represent yourself as an
expert, even to the lower middle class, you should wear
upper-middle-class garments. If you must sell yourself to
industry as an expert, you must dress to look relevant to your

field. An artist should not look like a stockbrocker and a stockbroker should not look like an accountant.

Once you have achieved the look of your field, you must look as if you are successful at it. If you're a stockbroker, you will do much better wearing a $600 suit and a $30 tie than you will if you wear anything less. The artist or creative type may dress either in a conservative or casual style. If he opts for a casual look, jeans and sweaters for example, he should select only those that are well tailored, obviously expensive and in excellent taste. If he chooses a more traditional outfit, say a suit, it must be stylish and carefully accessorized.

If every man who must attract clients were to dress every day so he looks at least as successful, as conservative and as well turned out as any client he is ever likely to meet, he will dramatically improve his success. (I have done this for consulting firms who have reimbursed their staff consultants for the clothing I chose for them, and these investments proved to be extremely profitable for the companies.)

Medical men fall into a very unusual category, and although most medical men are not concerned with their appearance, they should be. There are five basic uniforms that medical men wear; let me start with the worst. The upper-middle-class suit is absolutely taboo; most people object to a doctor looking like a successful businessman. If a doctor insists on dressing in this style many of his patients will look upon him not as a healer with whom they have a special relationship but as a businessman with whom they have a deal, and if the deal goes bad they sue. Next comes the neutral suit—dark blue or medium brown solid. The neutral suit is basically classless, and a doctor can wear it, but I advise against it. Many doctors wear conservative sports jackets and slacks as a matter of course, and of all street clothing, this is probably the best combination, acceptable for all purposes other than extremely serious consultations.

The doctor's hospital all-whites, worn without a shirt and tie, are the next-best thing he can wear while working. It is a high-authority outfit. But the best outfit, and the one that is the easiest to affect, is slacks worn with an upper-middle-class shirt and an upper-middle-class tie and white doctor's jacket. This look conveys that the doctor is a member of an elite group. It definitely identifies him as a doctor and, as much as appearance can accomplish this, makes whatever he says and does seem all but infallible.

For men on the periphery of medicine—chiropractors, podiatrists, optometrists and so forth, whose specialties are often misunderstood and sometimes held in low esteem—the shirt, tie and white jacket can improve their credibility tremendously and should become their standard wardrobe.

The only medical professionals for whom I do not recommend white is dentists; they tested best wearing pale blue and beige medical blouses with a good pair of slacks.

16

Corporate Image

During the last twenty-five years I have been retained as an image consultant by several thousand American companies, including over 300 of the Fortune 500 corporations. Most of the time I was brought in to dress their salespeople because personal experience had taught their sales executives that better-dressed salesmen were likely to be better salesmen. The second reason I was hired by American companies was to package their executives. Most of the men at the top of large corporations believe, as I do, that the way in which an executive dresses affects his ability to function both inside and outside the company. The final reason I was brought in by American companies was to help choose or design uniforms for their employees who had public contact. These are the people who, in the eyes of many executives, represent the company to the public; so the impression they make is very important.

During the same period I was retained by a dozen Japanese firms and, although two of them were interested in my packaging their salespeople, the rest hired me to help design uniforms for their employees. Whether the employees had public contact or not was not a factor in determining whether they should wear a uniform because there is a difference in management philosophy between Japanese and Americans. While most American executives believe that their company's success depends primarily on their ability to sell their products and their company to their clients, most Japanese executives believe that the success of their companies depends primarily on their ability to sell their own employees on the company and its products. They are convinced that if they can do so their employees will put forth greater effort, which will help them produce better and sell more products than their competitors.

Over the years I noticed the difference in the type of assignments I was receiving from Japanese and American companies, but I never thought much about it until four years ago when I was visiting my wife's relatives in western Pennsylvania. I stopped to have lunch at a local bar that I had been told did not look very appetizing but served great homemade kielbasa. The conversation of the people at the bar so fascinated me that, instead of staying for half an hour as I had planned, I stayed for three hours.

I had read in the local paper that the employees who worked at a plant in town were on strike. It was not a traditional strike where employees ask for more money and greater benefits, it was a survival strike. The management of the company had informed the employees that, unless they made major concessions in wages and benefits, the plant would be closed. After listening to the conversation at the bar for a while, it became clear to me that the men at the bar did not believe the ultimatum given by their company's executives although it was evident that they were aware that the company had closed a half dozen similar operations around the country. It was apparent that they considered the executives in the company to be the enemy and they did not trust them or believe anything they said.

After an hour, one of the fellows in the group put on a suit jacket that he borrowed from one of the customers, pretended to have a large cigar in his mouth, and began imitating one of the executives. He had the executive calling on him and his fellow workers to join the team and make sacrifices to save the company. It was obvious what the men at the bar thought of that suggestion; the minute our friend got into his role they started to laugh and heckle him. One man stood up and said, "Excuse me, sir, but are all you decent fellows, in your five-hundred-dollar suits and your beautiful offices going to come down on the floor and work with us?" The man playing the part of the executive immediately said, "Of course not; that's not *our* job, that's not what *we* do on the team. We have to keep our white shirts white and our new suits pressed. That's what *we're* paid for." The men at the bar started howling and one chimed in, "And that's *all* you do."

It was apparent that these workers were sensitive about the fact that the executives wore suits, shirts and ties and they did not. It was also apparent that they considered the suit, shirt and tie to be a uniform that announced that the executives were to be considered superior beings, and that they, by implication, were to be considered inferior. Not surprisingly, they found that message insulting and degrading and they objected to it. I am certain that back at corporate headquarters, the executives believed that the outcome of the strike depended entirely on whether the men would be willing to take big cuts in pay and benefits. As a matter of fact, several of the men at the bar mentioned during that three-hour afternoon that, while they would find it difficult to give up the money and benefits they were being asked to give up, they probably would go along if they thought those executives were being honest with them. But they did not. Two of the men used an identical phrase: "If we give in to them on this today, they'll crap on us tomorrow." In the minds of these workers, their manhood, their dignity and their self-worth demanded that they say no to the offer. I learned later that that was exactly what they did—and the plant closed.

The reason I had found that afternoon so fascinating was that I had spoken to the executives of that company four years earlier and, quite frankly, I felt guilty. Sitting there, it was easy to see that one of the reasons these employees were not going to take those pay cuts was because they thought the suits, shirts and ties which I had encouraged the executives of that company to wear identified those executives as the enemy. In fact, several times during the afternoon they did not refer to them as the executives or the bosses, but as "the suits."

Now, there is no question but that the advice I originally gave the executives of that company was valid. I had told them that, if they wore conservative suits, shirts and ties to work they would be more likely to move up in the company, and that they would find it easier to communicate with, and work with, other executives. What I had not realized was that, while I was dressing them for their personal success, I was dressing their company for failure.

Although I was upset, I was not ready to throw my research out the window. I had hard data to prove that subordinates worked harder and longer for bosses who dressed in upper-middle-class authority garments (conservative suits, shirts and ties). I also had rather substantial data that indicated that if an employee believed his company was big and powerful and was capable of looking out for him, he was more likely to give that company his loyalty. Based on that, I assumed that men who worked for giant corporations would be more likely to be loyal to their companies than men who worked for small corporations. During that afternoon in Pennsylvania I learned that was not true. Those men at the bar felt little or no loyalty to the company. They had repeated over and over that the company "stunk," and that it was run by a bunch of dirty blankety-blanks who had used them for years and who now were going to throw them into a garbage can because they were no longer needed. They did not even consider the possibility that the men running the company could be telling the truth, that foreign competition *was* forcing them to produce products at a lower price and that, if they could not cut costs in this plant, they were going to have to close the plant and move elsewhere.

I had worked on the company loyalty research personally, and now I went back and reread most of it. When I finished I was convinced it was valid—but that three-hour session in that bar still bothered me. I had a feeling I had missed something and so, during the next three years, anytime I visited a town where I had a client, I surveyed their employees in my spare time.

I did not conduct these surveys at the local plants. Instead, I visited the local watering holes next to the plants. I found if I could get employees talking in that setting, the answers they gave were far different from those they gave when the surveys were conducted on company grounds. My procedure was to go to the local bar, find an empty space close to the middle of the bar about fifteen minutes before quitting time, and wait for the employees to arrive. After the bar started filling up, I would turn to the person next to me and ask him if he worked for the company. If he said yes, I asked if he would mind telling me something about working there. At first most of the men were hesitant, but when I told them that the reason I was asking was I had been offered a job with the company several years earlier, had turned it down, and often wondered if I had made a mistake, they usually opened up and talked freely. (Of course, I never reported what these people said during these interviews to their companies or to anyone else.)

After running about forty of these informal surveys, I came to the conclusion that the Japanese were making the right decision when they worried more about what their employees thought of the company than what their customers thought of it.

The reason my earlier research had not applied to the men at the bar was because most of my corporate clients, even though many of them had very large blue-collar work forces, had assigned me to do image and opinion surveys only of their white-collar workers. I think a great problem is the assumption on the part of many executives that the blue-collar work force belongs not to them, but to the union; they do all their negotiating with the blue-collar work force through the union. As a result, any animosity felt by many blue-collar workers toward executives—wearing traditional suits—is not known to those same executives.

Interestingly, the women who worked in blue-collar jobs had a different reaction to both men and women in suits. They recognized it as an executive uniform but they were not offended by it. The blue-collar jobs they held were usually traditionally male jobs and often paid better than the other jobs held by women in the same company. They looked upon their blue-collar uniform as a sign of status. One woman said, "If you see a woman wearing a hard hat, you know one thing—she's got a brain under it." When she said that, two other women wearing hard hats clapped. Obviously, if you can create a blue-collar uniform that men would be as proud to wear, it would solve much of the problem of low employee morale.

In making that claim I am not underestimating the amount of antagonism felt by blue-collar workers toward the management in most factories. I am simply identifying one of the causes of the problem. I'm saying that we have learned that if you eliminate that cause the problem will be less severe. It is my opinion that the best union organizers in America are not men with plaques and union buttons who work for the AFL-CIO, but men wearing $450 suits who work for USX and General Motors.

True, some executives in charge of blue-collar workers know they can be effective when they dress like the workers. That is why, before they go to the floor, they take off their suit jackets, roll up their sleeves, loosen their ties or put on smocks. But there is an even better way of going about sending a team message. Recently, two companies, at my prodding, had their executives who worked in factories wear uniforms that were identical to those worn by the men on the line (in the style of the Japanese). In both companies we had an independent third party research employee attitude before and after the uniform dress code was adopted. In both cases they reported a dramatic positive shift. Most of the blue-collar workers were far more comfortable with executives who dressed in the same uniform as they did. The blue-collar workers believed that it changed the attitude of the executives, and the executives believed that it changed the attitude of the blue-collar workers. They were both right.

In one company the plant manager was so happy with the effect the uniform had upon the workers that on those days when he had to wear a suit because he had a meeting outside the plant, he carried it to the office in a garment bag, and only put it on when he left for the meeting.

A number of the executives in both plants said the most positive effect of the uniform was that it opened the lines of communication. Even those who were not quite sure it built a team spirit agreed it broke down barriers.

The manager in the second plant took this approach a step further and ordered his managers and foreman to eat lunch with the men. He ate with them as well. He told my researchers that he could not have done that in the past, he just hadn't fit in. True, the workers were suspicious of him at first, but now he is an accepted member of the lunch group. He thinks he can ask his employees anything and he is convinced they will give him an honest answer.

Some executives reported that one result of the more open lines of communication that resulted from wearing uniforms was that for the first time they had become friendly with the people who worked for them. One man said that he had been surprised to learn that some of those fellows on the line were very bright and quite articulate. He said he had never listened to his employees before—but, of course, he had never really talked to them before. Another manager reported that for the first time in his life he had been invited to an employee's home, and that he had been delighted to go.

We found that the minute we put the American executives into uniforms which broke down the barriers between them and their blue-collar employees the entire workplace atmosphere changed.

. . . .

EIGHT RULES FOR CHOOSING UNIFORMS

Choosing uniforms is a complicated business, and some unfortunate executives get stuck with the job even though they are really not qualified. Here are some rules if you ever find yourself in that position:

1. Buy only from a well-established uniform company. Even then you must be careful; your interests are not necessarily theirs.

2. If you have a choice between stock uniforms and uniforms you design yourself, choose stock uniforms. You cannot predict how the details for custom-made garments will come off unless you are an expert. And unless you are an expert, you are going to make mistakes.

3. If you have a uniform designed specifically for your company, do not leave the message your company sends to the world in the hands of a designer with no background in business, and no background in motivational research. If you are not going to hire an expert to control the message your uniform sends, choose beige and/or blue uniforms. Generally, they will be the safest.

4. Get a guarantee that the uniform fabric is being manufactured by a major mill. Get an airtight guarantee that the material will be produced continually for years to come, so you can get the same uniform five years from now if you are happy with it. Remember, if it sends a positive message, you are not going to want to let it go.

5. Hire an outside firm to have the standard wear research done on the uniforms before buying. They should be comparative statistics so you can evaluate the research.

6. Be sure that the uniform company has a tailoring service in your area, not just a local tailor they hired to get your contract.

7. Insist on speaking to executives at other companies who have purchased identical or similar uniforms. Ask your contacts about their experience with the tailoring service and ask them what happens when an employee does not fit into a stock uniform or damages a uniform.

8. Do your own testing. Before you make a major commitment to buying uniforms in quantity, buy one or two, put them on your employees and take pictures of them. Then take pictures of your employees wearing the clothing they normally wear to work.

Show those pictures to as many people as possible from the same socioeconomic and educational background as your customers and/or employees. Ask them what the people in the pictures do for a living; how well they perform; if they're good workers; if they get along with their fellow workers; if they are nice; if they're friendly; if they're efficient; if they would want to be waited on by one of these people; if they would trust them with their money; and so on. If you ask these questions and other questions designed to test your uniform's message, you will very quickly find out whether the uniform will have a positive or negative impact. I suggest that, if practical, you test several designs, one against the other, and choose the one that tests best.

With only those rules in mind, anyone should be able to buy a uniform for a corporation and not get buried too badly.

If you are buying a uniform for public-contact people, the function of that uniform is to add authority, credibility and status to the person wearing it. Of all the businesses in the country, the airlines understand this best. Their flight attendants, who, regardless of training and expertise in airline safety, spend most of their time as waiters and waitresses in the sky, wear uniforms. Although bowing to fashion is part of the job, most of these uniforms are reasonably authoritative, and immediately identify the wearer as an authority figure in times of emergency.

The uniforms of the pilot, copilot and navigator are never fashionable, but their black or navy uniforms, white shirts and black or navy ties are supreme authority uniforms. They exude power and competence. They also reassure passengers by conveying the subtle message: *We will take care of you*.

The separation of these two distinct looks is important. It would be quite simple to have the flight attendants wear uniforms that are copies of the pilots' uniforms, but, while this would increase their authority, it would decrease that of the pilot through association. In practice, the uniform of each crew member today perfectly defines his image and establishes his function.

A guard cannot look like a nobody. The function of a uniform must also mesh with expectations of the people whom the wearer of that uniform must deal with. Several years ago, I was dressing the sales forces for an Oregon manufacturer who owned two plants. While talking in the office one day he asked if I could do anything to help him stop employee thievery. He said that his guards wore uniforms because he knew that this added to their authority, but he must still be doing something wrong because the volume of theft was so high. I asked him to let me see the uniform and he said, "Oh, a guard will be here in a minute. I sent one of them out for our sandwiches."

A few minutes later a guard wearing a baggy uniform came in bearing sandwiches and coffee.

When the guard left I said, "That's your problem."

He did not know what I meant, and I went on to explain. "You dress your guards to look like nobodies, and you compound the problem by sending them on errands. That guard could not protect anything because of his image; to your employees he's not a guard, but a gofer."

After spending several days around the plant I came up with the following approach: We changed the guards' title to "Security Officer," we took away the poorly shaped uniforms and gave them well-tailored upper-middle-class conservative suits, shirts and ties, and we prohibited them from running errands. Within six months employee thievery was cut in half.

By solving one problem, however, I created another. Since the guards were now wearing suits and ties they were not identifiable to outsiders, and burglaries increased at night. Therefore, we had to establish two distinctively different uniforms. We left the day men in their suits but changed the night men into uniforms that were as close as we could come to those of the local police. (Since the two factories were separated by several hundred miles and the uniforms of the police in each locality differed, we had to have separate uniforms for the night guards in each factory.) Once the changes were completed, thievery in the two plants from both inside and outside was significantly diminished. So the function of the uniform depends as much upon the people the wearer must deal with (or influence) as his actual job.

For example, if the largest percentage of people a uniformed person must deal with and influence are upper middle class, then the uniform absolutely must be made of only upper-middle-class colors, as outlined in the previous chapters of this book.

The geography and ethnic background of your customers or your clientele can further be instrumental in the success of any uniform. In banking, for example, while one particular shade of green indicates to the greatest percentage of the population in Detroit that the wearer is a thief, and discourages depositors, dark blue jackets evoked a negative response in a ghetto of New York City because they reminded the clients of a police uniform. If you had a bank in either of those areas, those colors in your uniforms would not enhance the bank's image and could conceivably hurt it. Unfortunately these local prejudices—which could wreak havoc with the uniforms in national and multinational corporations—cannot be determined without specific research.

• • • • • • • • • • • • • • • • • • •

WHO SHOULD WEAR A UNIFORM AND WHO SHOULD NOT

In deciding on uniforms, you are always faced with the problem of how far they should be extended into the company and who should wear them. That depends entirely on the nature of the company. I recommend that everyone in factories, including the top people, wear the same uniform. I would not make the same recommendation for a bank. Banks almost always deal with the general public, and must always maintain the highest reputation; and therefore, it is usually a good idea to put tellers in uniforms.

Once you dress your tellers in uniforms, most uniform companies will try to persuade you to do the same with your bank officers. This is not normally a good idea. While a uniform will usually increase the authority of a teller, it will decrease the authority of any man whom the public is conditioned to seeing in a standard business suit, shirt and tie.

When a bank buys uniforms, they would not buy them for every branch at once, but test several types at different locations until they have settled on the right uniforms. This would be a good example for you to follow.

One thing you must be very careful about when you are buying uniforms is to choose the right uniform for your women. Most uniforms on the market today are sexist. They destroy the effectiveness of the women who wear them. Many uniform companies, if you allow them to design your uniforms, will give you a far more authoritative, traditional and conservative uniform for the men than they do for the women. They will usually put women in something fashionable and feminine. The women will at first react positively to such an outfit, but that outfit has several built-in drawbacks. Our experience has taught us that women will wear a conservative uniform far longer than one that is fashionable. If it is fashionable or, even worse, trendy, they will want to trade it in before you have paid for it.

A major problem is that most of these uniforms destroy the wearer's authority and credibility. This is particularly destructive since one of the main problems women face in business is being taken seriously. Wearing feminine uniforms, your employees will have a great deal of difficulty handling customers, particularly in an emergency situation, or if the customer is upset. The customer will undoubtedly ask to speak to someone "important." The wrong uniform can destroy a woman's effectiveness and the effectiveness of the entire organization.

A classic example of fashionable uniforms destroying the wearer's authority involved the stewardesses of an airline crew in the late seventies. While attempting to evacuate their plane after an emergency landing they were themselves forced to leave the plane by male passengers who were convinced that the stewardesses in their "adorable" costumes were helpless women who needed saving. When those macho passengers threw out the only people who knew what to do, they endangered the lives of all the other passengers. You will notice that all the airline companies have returned to very conservative, traditional uniforms for their flight attendants because they found that only while wearing those uniforms can the attendants act effectively in emergency situations.

The least expensive uniform is not always the best, although many of the highly competitive uniform companies will try to convince you that they can do the same thing for you cheaper than the next fellow. They will back up their word by showing you how, using exactly the same material as a more expensive competitor, they can do it for less. What they will not show you is that their dyes may be harsher, and their seamstresses sloppier. Ultimately, that several dollars' difference in the cost of a uniform may well be the difference between a lower-middle-class uniform and an upper-middle-class uniform.

• • • • • • • • • • • • • • • • • • •

DRESS CODES

In addition to conducting employee surveys, I continued to run the image surveys that I have been running for corporations for years, following the same procedure: I arrange to have a professional photographer take pictures of employees at two or three in the afternoon on two days chosen at random. If we are dealing with a department where the people do not work in an office, I arrange to have their pictures taken when they are leaving the office to go into the field. In addition, I visit the headquarters and as many branch offices as I can during a six-month period. On those visits I walk through the offices as unobtrusively as possible, taking notes about the way people in various offices dress and how I think their dress impacts their performance and the image of the company. The visits I make to these offices—including the president's—are always unannounced. If I'm going to be useful to the company, I must see the clothing that their people normally wear to work.

After visiting at least one-fourth of the major offices of a client company, I arrange to meet with the corporate officers in the largest room they have, usually the boardroom. Before they come in, my assistants arrange the photographs that we have collected, either directly on the walls or on bulletin boards we hang on the walls. On the top level we put the pictures of all the executives. We divide them according to office and location. On the second level we put the pictures of the professionals and managers of various departments—legal, engineering and so on—and we put them directly underneath the executives for whom they work. On the third level, we put the pictures of all the people who work in these departments: the accountants, the engineers, the lawyers, the managers, the underwriter. On the fourth level we put the pictures of the clerical people who work in these offices, and on the fifth level we put pictures of blue-collar people who work at those locations. On the sixth level we put the people who work in uniforms in various sections of the country. In the sixth set of pictures we always have two groups: the pictures that the uniform company originally used when they were selling the uniform, and pictures of the people in the field actually wearing the uniform—which often looks very different. Naturally, as soon as the executives walk into the room they look at the pictures. Many of them, particularly those who have worked at corporate headquarters for many years, find this a very enlightening and sometimes sobering experience.

It can also be a very dangerous experience because of what I call the "Going to dress those slobs" reflex. Ninety percent of the time, when the executives walk into a room wearing their $600-plus suits, whether they learned to dress at their daddy's pinstripe knee, or learned the rules in the school of hard knocks, they immediately want to get everyone out there to dress as they do. Unless I restrain them, they pick up the phone and start screaming at the man in charge of the San Jose office, telling him he had better whip his people into shape. I am so certain of their response that as they come into the room, I have them promise that before they do anything we will sit down and discuss the problem calmly.

I explain to them that America's most successful companies have dress codes that match their management philosophy. For example, IBM was founded by Mr. Watson, who came out of a marketing and sales background. His experience taught him that dressing conservatively opened doors and announced to the world that he was a serious businessperson. That is probably the main reason it is not surprising that when Watson established a dress code for his entire company it was a dress code that worked best for salesmen. The conservative suits, white shirt and shined shoes worn by IBMers say that they are serious professionals and that they represent a reliable company. That is important today, but it was even more important in the early days of IBM when computers were less reliable and IBM had financial problems that hurt the credibility of their salespeople. By putting his men into conservative outfits Watson announced that IBM was a dependable, conservative company that would stand behind the large, delicate machines they sold. Undoubtedly, sending that message succesfully was one of the reasons IBM succeeded. It has become one of the world's great companies because its dress code has always matched its philosophy and its management style.

When Pat Haggerty helped found Texas Instruments he set up an entirely different dress code in that company. As an ex-naval officer he avoided anything that struck him as a uniform. He and the other founders of the company came to work with open collars and no ties. Mr. Haggerty believed that uniforms inhibited creativity, and would turn off the very people he wanted to attract.

Haggerty not only had a very casual dress code, he designed very casual corporate offices. In fact, his corporate offices looked more like college campuses than industrial sites. He sent a series of nonverbal signals to the academic whiz kids and the technical geniuses that they would be welcomed, respected and cherished at Texas Instruments. No question about it, his message worked. Texas Instruments attracted a surprising number of those technical wizards and became one of the world's best engineering companies.

As you can see, both of the above dress codes fit the management style, the philosophy, and the aims of the companies for which they were designed and, because they did they helped those companies succeed.

I go on to explain to them that their companies or the Fortune 500 companies whose dress codes they have copied were formed either in the late nineteenth or early twentieth century. They did not grow up overnight. They are products of pre–World War II thinking and management style.

Before World War II, education, at least a college education, was generally limited to the upper class in America.

Harvard was not filled with the best and the brightest, but the richest and the best-connected, and they ran America. There was a real gap between the socioeconomic and educational backgrounds of the workers and the bosses. Most blue-collar workers recognized this gap and accepted it as normal. The clothing worn by the men in corporate America at the time reflected the truth that existed in society and in the company. Society at the turn of the century consisted of two classes: people in charge and the people they were in charge of, the bosses and the workers.

Today, the distance between the classes has lessened. The rich are not as rich or powerful as they once were. They still live very comfortable lives, but modest by comparison with the rich of just fifty or sixty years ago. And, although the poor are still poor and comparatively powerless, they are not as poor or as powerless as they once were. What is more, the sons and daughters of an average American today, or even a poor American today, have a much better chance of acquiring money and power than did their grandparents. Conversely, the sons and daughters of the rich have much less chance of achieving power than did their grandparents. It is not that they do not have an advantage and are not more likely to be influential in our society, it is that they are not the only ones who are going to be influential. Things have changed and for the better. However, the dress codes based on the autocratic social system that long ago disappeared still exists in most corporations and, in most, they are counterproductive.

I do not want to give the impression that if every company in America developed a laid-back casual dress code as did Texas Instruments, they would improve their profit margin. They would not. The biggest problem in America is not good dress codes or bad dress codes, it is umbrella dress codes. Dress codes which put everyone in the company in the same uniform. Even when umbrella dress codes are successful you pay a price for them. If you look at America's best-known and most successful dress code company, IBM, you can see this. IBM, in spite of its reputation as a technical company, has never been considered by most technical people as an innovative company. They build good products and have the ability to market those products successfully, but their motto never really has been, "think"; it has been "sell and then think."

The problem with this is that in the long run the salvation of IBM and every other high-tech company in America will depend on innovation in the creation of new products, not just on selling them. In order to do this successfully IBM is going to have to attract and hold creative people. I believe that IBM will have limited success in this area unless they change their image.

I speak at about thirty colleges a year and in the past two years, whenever possible, I have interviewed the top engineering students in the schools where I spoke. These are the brilliant and innovative people, mainly young men, that every high-tech company—including IBM—would like to have working for them. Eight of the twenty students I interviewed told me they would not even consider interviewing with IBM. Seven others said that IBM was not their first choice and in most cases it was not even their second. Among the remaining five students, only two expressed any real desire to work for IBM. The reason most of these creative student engineers said they did not want to work for IBM was they believed that IBM did not encourage creative people. Whether IBM does or does not is not really the question. The fact is, the students hold this belief and it affects IBM's ability to recruit them. It is not going to be easy for them to win these young people over. When I told the students that the experimental engineers at IBM that I interviewed said that they were as free at IBM to experiment as they were at any other company, and possibly freer, I do not think they believed me. Only one student openly challenged me, but the others I think were just polite enough to dance around the topic.

I am not suggesting that the executives or salespeople at IBM throw out their conservative suits and white shirts; that would be silly. I think that they should continue to dress the way they do. IBM is a very successful marketing company and to change the way their salesmen or executives dress would be counterproductive. However, instead of denying they have a dress code, IBM should admit that one exists for their salespeople and executives and then announce loudly and clearly that the other people at IBM have the freedom to dress in any way they want. They should make this announcement where the young engineers are likely to hear it. If I were IBM I would make it a point of running ads containing pictures of bearded and tieless experimental engineers wearing colored shirts. Instead of showing one face to the world, IBM should show several faces. They should make a major effort to convince the talented engineers of this world that there is a place for them at IBM.

Texas Instruments has a similar problem. Their umbrella dress code sends a message that engineers, and only engineers are really going to be influential at Texas Instruments. After interviewing several dozen people in marketing and sales, I came to the conclusion that most of them really did not believe that they were ever going to have a major say in how that company was run. Which means Texas Instruments must have a very difficult time attracting and keeping ambitious sales and marketing people—the people Texas Instruments needs most.

A company's dress code and its resulting image can have an effect not only on its ability to recruit and hold talented people and to develop specific areas in the company, it can have a direct effect on its sales. Apple Computer is a classic example of a company with a public image problem. Several years ago a friend of mine was hired to research why people bought various brands of personal computers. Since the two biggest personal computers on the market were IBM and Apple, he asked a number of people who purchased either one why they made their choice. The people who bought Apple generally chose it because they thought it was simpler and easier to operate. Those who chose IBM chose it usually because they thought IBM was a large company and would stand behind its product. They had faith in the company. In ninety percent of the cases the people who bought personal computers did not have enough information to make a technical decision and they really were not making one. Several of those questioned in focus groups said they actually would have preferred purchasing the Apple Computer because they thought it was simpler, but were not sure that Apple was going to be around in a couple of years and therefore chose IBM.

When asked to describe IBM as a company and Apple Computer as a company, these people had two dramatically different pictures. IBM, in their mind, was a great giant who was too large to disappear. Apple, on the other hand, was a company run by whiz kid engineers who had been producing computers in the backs of garages just a few years ago. They knew it was bigger than that now, but they were not quite sure how big it was. When asked to estimate the comparable size of IBM and Apple, they accurately estimated IBM's size and vastly underestimated Apple's.

In the middle of this research IBM announced it was pulling its PC Junior off the market. My friend wondered if people would no longer think of IBM as the company that always stood behind its products; after all they had just given up on one. But the fact is that the numbers changed very little. Most of the people who had to choose between IBM and Apple still chose IBM when they were looking at the same price range, and still chose it for the same reasons.

Their perception of the company had more effect on what they purchased than the reality of how the company acted in the marketplace.

During my meetings with the heads of large corporations, I am always surprised to learn that they have given such little thought to the fact that their company should show the world not one face, but several. They should be interested in showing a different face to their employees than they do to their customers, and a different face to their customers than they do to their competitors. They should also realize that the way their employees dress has a major impact on their corporate image.

But the executives I talk with usually admit that when it comes to *looking* at corporate dress, most of them simply ignore it. These same men who spend millions of dollars in developing logos and packaging their products don't spend a dime packaging their people. They say they have not done it because they do not think it has to be done. Most of them are happy with the way their people dress. When I ask them how they decide if their dress code is satisfactory, they tell me they rely on instinct, on what they feel good about. When I ask them if they would package their products or pick a logo based on the same instinct, the response is always no. They say those factors are too important to guess about—and usually, as soon as they make that statement, realize they have made a mistake.

Every major company should have at least one person on staff who is responsible for the company's dress code. That person should not be a minor assistant to the president, but someone with real power on his own. It should be someone with a good overview of the company's philosophy and goals. That person should look at the company as a series of operating units, each with a different function and different clothing needs. His object should be to have the men in accounting dress like accountants and the men in marketing dress like marketing people. The employees who meet with the public, if they wear uniforms, should wear a different uniform than the employees on a production line. The executives who work in corporate headquarters should have one dress code, while executives who work in a manufacturing plant should have another. Their dress should be determined by their jobs and the people with whom they work. Their clothing should be designed to help them perform their jobs more effectively.

Once a dress code has been decided upon—and that decision should be made at the highest level—then the people who obey the dress code should be rewarded and those who do not should be punished; this is particularly true of executives.

There are a few general rules to keep in mind when planning a company's dress code.

First: Executives at corporate headquarters, sales and marketing people and the men who represent the public in the company eye should dress conservatively. This conservative, traditional image will announce to your white-collar workers, the general public and your customer that yours is a reliable, conservative company and can be trusted.

Second: Although there should be a general dress code, each branch, each division and each office in each section of the country should be able to argue that they should be exempted from part or all of the dress code, and, if their arguments are valid, they should be listened to. I am not suggesting that the dress code be optional, but I do think you should get feedback from the people who are directly affected by it. You will find that most men in marketing, as well as executives in corporate headquarters, would be uncomfortable wearing other than a traditional attire. Men who are good at their jobs usually have an instinct for what works. Everyone should not be allowed to follow his instincts, of course, but, if the majority of the men in a job disagree violently with the company dress code, you should at least seriously review it.

Third: Executives in charge of blue-collar workers should dress like the workers.

Fourth: If your company sells several products or services to a number of customers in different businesses and in different sections of the country, you will probably need a flexible dress code for your salespeople—but a dress code nevertheless. So much of sales is nonverbal that a sales force without a dress code must be considered an amateur operation.

Fifth: Never let unqualified people choose your company's uniforms. This includes the head of human resources who knows no more about clothing than any other executive, any woman just because she likes clothing and dresses well (including the wife of the president), the uniform companies who are experts at creating uniforms, not images and, finally, committees of employees, who because of their blue-collar backgrounds, will pick uniforms that send the wrong message almost every time. There is only one way of getting a less effective uniform than the ones chosen by employee committees, and that is to insist that the uniform include the company colors or, even worse, the colors in the company logo. If you do, you can end up with an outfit like the one that many Century 21 agents refuse to wear when they are selling, which after all is their business.

• • • • • • • • • • • • • • • • • •

EXECUTIVE INSTINCT

Over a period of years most executives develop what I refer to as "Executive Instinct." This means that they often do the right thing without sometimes knowing the reason. One of the right things executives have been doing for years is dressing themselves in a very specific way and persuading their employees directly, or by indirect pressure or nudging, to do the same. Until now, however, when some disgruntled employee has asked why he must wear a suit, shirt and tie to work, the executive had to fall back on the answer, "Because I say so." Most of those executives have been accused of being medieval, and backward, and out-of-date.

I can give every executive the ammunition he needs to answer such a question. My research shows that if a company or an organization or a profession has an unofficial dress code, it is usually a very good one. For example, print reporters dress terribly. The reason they do so is that in their jobs they are required to question people who are under stress. They want the people to be open and honest with them, and, therefore, the last thing they want to do is appear threatening to them. Their casual, nonauthoritative look helps them get people to relax. It sends the message to the people they are interviewing that they are not going to hurt them. However, if you look at one small corner of almost every newspaper office, you will find a group of men dressed in business suits. They are usually the men who write the business columns. That is the uniform that helps them to get executives to relax. My advice to anyone going into a new job or a new profession is: If you are not sure how to dress, follow the crowd. If everyone in an industry dresses in one style, there is usually a very good reason for it.

My research also shows that executives should wear their pinstripe suits because subordinates in white-collar jobs work harder and longer for bosses who dress in upper-middle-class authority garments. We have proven that company loyalty is based on a sense of security, and that sense of security depends on the concept of the company the employees constantly carry in their heads. This is particularly true for employees who work for small and moderate-size corporations. If you work for General Motors or IBM or any other giant, the concept of the company is predetermined. But if you work for one of the tens of thousands of small corporations, their concept of the company will be based on the size of the building, or the offices in which people work, and on their perception of everyone in the company who outranks them.

To the man pushing a broom, his concept of the company comes from everyone who has a desk; to the man who has a desk, it comes from everyone with an office; to everyone with an office, it comes from every corporate officer.

If company loyalty does not extend down to the lowest employee, then the corporation cannot function at ultimate capacity. And it is only realistic to keep in mind that the executive's ability is of no meaning to the elevator operator who takes that executive downstairs at night. Yet that elevator operator's concept of the top executives is important to the corporation because his loyalty is an asset and because the elevator operator looks to the company to protect him. If an executive of the company looks as if he is stupid or unimportant, then the elevator operator cannot believe in the importance of the company or the value of its protection and cannot give it his loyalty.

• •

IT'S NOT WHO YOU SEE
IT'S WHO SEES YOU

This kicks a hole in the argument of some executives who say, "Look, I know I'm a vice-president of the company, but I work in a corner office and really never see anyone, so I can dress as I choose." Wrong! It's not whether the executive sees anyone, it's whether anyone sees him. Everyone in the company will know that he is a vice-president, and their concept of the corporation will partially depend on how *he* appears before them.

Let me illustrate the importance of executive dress with a story. I had a client on the West Coast who built a multimillion-dollar headquarters. The president of the company was so proud of his new offices that he spent an hour showing me the building.

A year after they moved in, however, he realized that he had a major problem: His salesmen were no longer dressing properly. The minute they moved into the new offices, they started dressing casually. The president assumed they did so because of the laid-back Los Angeles environment, but he was not willing to, as he said, "give up without a fight." In fact, he brought me in to dress up the sales force.

To show me how desperately they needed my services, he walked me through the sales department. When I pointed to one of the fellows, he said, "Don't worry about him, he's our top experimental engineer and they can dress any way they want." In fact, he was head of the engineering department. He wore a short-sleeve shirt with one of those plastic pen holders in the pocket. His pants were baggy, his hair was disheveled, his eyeglasses were down over his nose, and his desk looked like a substation for the Los Angeles garbage dump. The minute I saw this man I knew the company did not need me; all it had to do was move the engineer away from the salesmen or move the salesmen away from him. There was no way a fellow making $35,000 a year was going to dress better than the man in the next department making $150,000 a year.

Within three months of moving the sales and engineering departments away from each other, the salespeople once again were dressing as they had in the past. The company had quickly learned how to enforce a formal dress code for one group of employees, while letting another group dress casually. The answer had been simple: separate them.

• • • • • • • • • • • • • • • • • • •

HOW TO SELL EXECUTIVES ON DRESS CODES

I can hear you saying, fine, we agree that dress codes are important and that dress codes start with executives. But how do we get an executive to observe them? What happens if he fights back?

Well, frankly, I think that most men who are far up the ladder are career-oriented enough to accept the very sensible argument that the way they dress is part of their job, and is, in fact, part of what they are being paid for. One of the basic elements of leadership is example, and they must set a good example for other employees.

In most cases you can let it go at that, and your problem will be solved. If not, then you may be more specific and give them some other reasons that will encourage them even more. One is that it is a fact their executives who dress in conservative upper-middle-class garments are far more likely to succeed than men who dress otherwise. Over ninety-five percent of the successful important men in this country dress in conservative upper-middle-class clothing.

Another reason: Any executive dressed in this manner will find it far more easy to deal with other executives, as well as with subordinates both inside and outside his own company. Most executives come from upper-middle-class backgrounds and tend to distrust—even though not consciously—anyone who looks as if they come from a lower-class background. This is true at all levels of society; even lower-middle-class people tend to distrust other lower-middle-class people, and one of the chief determinants of class in the eye of the beholder is dress. Any executive who decides not to wear the uniform of his position may still be in the race, but he is carrying extra weight and, although he may win, he is working against a needless handicap.

• • • • • • • • • • • • • • • • • • •

HOW TO TACTFULLY ENFORCE DRESS CODES

Once the executives understand that corporate dress codes must start with them, they will enforce dress codes on the people below them. Most executives are right to set such codes, but wrong in the methods they use and the controls they apply.

To establish dress codes for top- and middle-management people, the rules are simple. Do not hire them if they are not dressed correctly when interviewed. If they deviate from the accepted manner of dress after they are hired, tell them. If you are interviewing an executive for a line position, and you expect him to wear a uniform, let him know that and tell him why. Be very clear, leaving no room for future debate.

For those in authority positions below that level—and in this case "authority position" means any employee who has other employees reporting directly to him—there are several basic methods. The best and most obvious, and still the most subtle, is example. It will bring around most employees who possess a sense of responsibility. Recalcitrants should simply be informed, either directly or indirectly that they are in positions of authority and people in positions of authority in the company are expected to adhere to certain dress codes. They are expected to do so because research has indicated that companies with dress codes do better than companies that do not have them.

This is, in fact, true. Some years ago, a stockbroker friend of mine, at my behest, analyzed the stocks of several companies and determined that, by investing in certain groups of companies with very strict dress codes as opposed to those in the same business without dress codes, an investor, in the period of time of his study, earned $3 for every $1 he would have made on the companies with no dress codes.

Establishing and controlling the dress code of general employees, those without authority over others, is a delicate matter, and three levels of employees are involved. First, there is the employee who works on the line and who probably belongs to a union. Often these men will enjoy getting into uniforms because you can point out to them the obvious economic advantage. If you cannot accomplish it this way, you can usually do it through negotiations with the unions. In fact, paying or helping to pay for uniforms is often given as a form of compensation by management.

The second type of general employee is the employee who creates a public image for the company. These fall into various categories, from the repairman who goes out to fix appliances, to the airline ticket agent, to the bank teller—in other words, any employee not in an authority position over other employees, but who must represent your company before the general public.

The proper uniform for such an employee generally creates a positive reaction, but in each case the need and the uniform should be measured specifically. When we speak of uniforms for such employees it should be recognized that a uniform does not have to be what is traditionally thought of as a rigidly standardized, almost military-style, uniform. The only requirement is consistency and coordination of the apparel of all employees of the same sex. Automobile dealers, as I have already mentioned, have successfully dressed their salesmen in gray pants, blue blazers with company emblems on the breast pocket and derivations of the club tie bearing the company logo. Such uniforms are highly effective, although they are not generally perceived as being uniforms.

The third category of general employee is the semipublic employee, the typical officeworker. The office is quite definitely a visual segment of the corporate image, and is the element most often seen by visiting businessmen, clients or customers. It is essential for office efficiency that certain mandatory dress codes be maintained and there are two ways to get them started.

The simplest (and the easiest to adopt) is a written dress code posted on a bulletin board. However, I do not believe this is appropriate in most cases because it creates an impression of the company as a stiff-necked, intransigent intruder on employee privacy. This is neither good employee relations nor good public relations. It also creates the problem of having an affluent fifty-five-year-old male executive with absolutely no notion of fashion telling a nineteen-year-old young woman what to wear. This is impossible and it never works. Most fathers of nineteen-year-old girls can tell you what they do not approve of in their daughter's dress, but they would not dare interfere with it, either. Women in this group, particularly those who are young and unmarried, will often pick up and leave rather than obey a written dress code.

If you want and need a good secretary and good office help, you had best not step too heavily on their toes.

• • • • • • • • • • • • • • • • • • • •

HOW TO SPREAD THE WORD ABOUT UNWRITTEN DRESS CODES

I believe in psychologically sound unwritten dress codes set largely by example. Male employees can be told rather specifically that suits, shirts and ties are required. This is not an unreasonable request. Beyond this there are subtle ways that exist for dealing with any problem of weird colors, patterns and styles, platform shoes, and other inappropriate clothing. God only knows what will be the clothing rage tomorrow.

Making a gift of this book to any employee with a "look successful" problem might be helpful. If that does not work, or if you do not want to give a book to a clerk who has no chance at the executive suite or even a management position, then it is possible to affect him by making certain that everyone else in his immediate environment is wearing proper attire. Generally, men in the office do not create major problems in their dress. If you have those who do continue to have a problem, simply keep mentioning it to them, as diplomatically as possible; they will get the message sooner or later.

• • • • • • • • • • • • • • • • • • • •

HOW TO SET DRESS CODES FOR WOMEN EMPLOYEES

The major problems are created by women for two reasons: In the first place, they look upon clothing as an extension of their personalities, and to let someone else mandate what they will wear is considered by them to be a surrender of part of themselves. Secondly, their concept of what is beautiful and good in clothing is diametrically opposed to the male concept of those qualities. For the same reason that wives should generally not choose their husband's clothing, neither can male executives choose the clothing for women, who will not feel comfortable in what would be chosen. (By the way, fifty-five-year-old female executives are no better, or only slightly better qualified, to choose the clothing of young female employees than their male counterparts.)

The dress code for female employees had best be openly spelled out to the women before they are hired. The code should state that they should be neat, clean and appropriately attired, and in case anyone doubts it, the code should state the same for men. The applicant should be told that any item, such as a skirt that is too short—and I would try to define in advance what too short is—or extreme makeup, will be brought to their individual attention with the expectation that it will be corrected. If the rules are kept general and ambiguous, they should arouse no hostility among female job applicants.

The next step is to have several female executives as close as possible to the age of the average employee single out a few of the female employees to attend seminars directed by experts. Some of the cosmetic companies will undoubtedly be delighted to provide experts on grooming and corporate dress. As an incentive to the women, the experts might offer hair and makeup tips in short courses that can be conducted at lunch hour or after work, but their basic function—to be worked out in advance—is for them to propagandize the female employees to wear exactly what you want them to wear.

At the end of the seminars there should be a consensus period in which the general rules for office dress are defined. If possible, publish as much as you can about the seminars and consensus in the company house organ. The plan is sensible, subtle and has been used successfully for years.

Today there are many more women in management than there were years ago. One does not have to be any more circumspect or diplomatic with these women managers if they dress inappropriately than you have to be with a male manager. You simply tell them what to do. If they are not willing to listen, they can look elsewhere for a management position. I believe in women being treated equally in every way.

• • • • • • • • • • • • • • • • • • •

NEATNESS COUNTS

Research conducted by two companies—independent of each other (one with blue-collar workers, and the other with office workers)—found that employees who were neat and well put together performed better than employees who were not. It may be due to the fact that these employees have a better self-image, and therefore perform at a higher level, I do not know. But I do know that neatness does count and I recommend that companies institute grooming codes as well as dress codes.

Every executive should remember that a corporation's image can be improved very easily, and if it is improved will improve your bottom line. A good corporate image is a bankable corporate image.

17

Dressing Successfully For Job Interviews and a New Job

Before any executive can execute anything, he must have a job. He will have a better chance for a better job at a higher salary if he learns to use clothing as a business tool, beginning with his initial job interview. The rules that apply to clothing and job interviews break down into various levels.

For upper-level industry and government positions, where the applicant is assuredly going to be interviewed by ultrasophisticated, upper-middle-class (in both background and income) heads of corporations or government, he must have several appropriate suits, because he will go through a series of interviews and should never repeat an outfit during the course of these meetings.

Every item of clothing and every accessory must be conservative, traditional and conventional. All items should be elegant and costly and perfectly coordinated. Men who are

347

interviewing for such positions can spot at a glance the difference between a $325 and an $800 suit, and while the $325 suit may be perfectly acceptable once you have the job, the one for $800 will be a good investment in helping you get it. Please understand that this advice only applies to those men who are qualified and seeking jobs in a salary range of $150,000 a year or above, or for men seeking government jobs of great power and prestige. The $50,000-a-year executive or the middle-level government bureaucrat who wears $500 suits will arouse suspicion that he is reckless with his own money and will be no more careful with theirs.

Most men aiming at such positions really do not need me to tell them how to dress; if they do not know how to do it by the time they have reached the point of interviews of that caliber they will probably never learn. I have found, however, that they invariably make one mistake, particularly when they must travel to the interview, and that is they go to the interview directly from the plane in their traveling clothes. Don't! Always fly in the night before; take—but do not wear—your best suit; and have it pressed at the hotel.

The rules for top-level positions in smaller companies and middle-management positions in the larger ones are virtually the same as for the top-management men. You will still need several separate and distinctly different outfits, but they need not be so expensive. If the job you are going for is outside one of the major, relatively sophisticated large cities, then you must be careful, because you could be faced with several types of executives making personnel decisions.

The first type is the man from a lower-middle-class background, who does not know how to dress himself, and who looks at anyone who does dress well as a smart-ass big-city boy. He will be prejudiced about you on the basis of your clothing—in a reverse way. It's called lower-class snobbery.

The other type of executive is the sophisticated man who

may be stuck in the sticks, but who knows clothing, and flies to New York or London to have his suits and shirts made.

The first man will not hire you if you come on too slick, and the second man will not hire you unless you evidence the same awareness of clothing that he has.

If you know in advance whom you will be dealing with, your problems are decreased. If you do not, I always suggest that on the first interview you wear a good solid blue suit, a white shirt and a conservative, nondescript tie. When you get there, look around carefully, and find out whom you are to be dealing with. If there are other men you are to meet after the first interview, ask about their backgrounds. If they sound upper middle class, dress accordingly. If they sound lower middle class, dress appropriately for them.

* * * * * * * * * * * * * * * * * * * *

THE BASIC JOB-SEEKERS WARDROBE

The four suits I recommended for all men seeking upper-middle-level positions are: that very conservative, dark blue suit for the first time in; a conservative, solid gray suit; a conservative pinstripe suit, preferably with a vest, in either dark blue or dark gray (this being your most powerful, most authoritative suit, it should be reserved for wear with the most important man you must see); and, finally, a blue and gray shadow plaid suit for wear if you find the men less conservative in their dress than your other three suits.

Your shirt must be white and you should have a good selection of ties. In Middle America, the traditional rep is acceptable to almost everyone. But just by changing your tie, you drastically change your image. Wear the expensive, small-patterned, Daddy-went-to-Yale, Ivy League tie, and you are saying that you are from a definite upper-middle-class background. But you would not want to wear that in an interview with the executive from a lower-middle-class background whom you will only make uncomfortable by appearing better than he is. Likewise, the Pucci tie or any other expensive, wildly patterned or brightly colored designer tie is a signal that you are very hip and with-it; that tie should be avoided for any industries except the glamour enterprises, where it is expected.

For the man seeking intermediate or future management positions, several conservative suits are sufficient, and they need not be expensive as long as they are well cut and well tailored. But it is essential that these be in keeping with the upper-middle-class patterns and colors outlined in previous chapters.

Interviews for these positions also usually go through several stages. The first is the screening stage where you will meet one or two of the people you will be working directly with or for. This is often a two-part interview; the first part takes place in the office while the second part takes place over lunch or dinner. If you go directly from the office to the restaurant obviously you do not have to worry about what to wear. When you come from home or your hotel you should arrive looking crisp and well put together. If you are being interviewed in another town you should pack a navy blazer and slacks since you may be invited to an outing where a suit would not be appropriate. Naturally, if you receive the invitation to visit the company and they tell you that they are going to take you to the local country club for lunch or for golf, you must bring appropriate sportswear; since you will not only be looking at the club, the club will be looking at you.

If they suggest that you bring your wife, it is not a suggestion. She *must* come and be appropriately dressed as well.

Then there is what is commonly referred to as the

courtesy call on the top man. That is what it's called, but very often that is not what it is. Instead, the top man has said to his subordinates, you select several men whom you think are qualified, and then I'll see them and make the final decision.

You should be very wary of such courtesy calls. Wear your best, most conservative garments, and conduct yourself in an almost formal manner. Regardless of whether or not he is actually going to be making the decision, he's a busy man, and you will not be in his office long. The clothing you wear and the personality you display in those few minutes are going to frame his decision to a considerable degree.

• • • • • • • • • • • • • • • • • • • •

IF YOU'RE JUST OUT OF COLLEGE

What about the young man right out of college, going for his first or second interview?

Usually, his financial resources are limited and his wardrobe suffers accordingly. But large wardrobes, or even expensive wardrobes, are not the issue. The right colors, patterns and styles are. If this man has only one good suit, it should be a dark blue solid. If he can afford a second, it should be a gray pinstripe, preferably with vest. Unless he is applying for a position with a financial institution or Big Eight accounting firm, then his first suit should be a three-piece gray pinstripe and his second suit should be a three-piece blue pinstripe. With those two, and appropriate shirts and ties, he should be able to get through most interviews.

If you land your position, your natural inclination is to take your new-found security and income and start buying stereos and sports cars and start dating expensive ladies. Don't fall for those temptations until you have an adequate wardrobe, even if you have to borrow to get it. I'll tell you why. You may think that your first few years of working are basically unimportant, but the exact opposite is true. In most corporations, you are being watched and tracked. Whether you are to be routed in directions that lead to upper management and success will depend on intelligence, ability and personality, obviously. But it will also depend to a great extent on how you dress.

I know many of the men who make these decisions. I know what they say, and I know what they think. And I know that clothing is an important, if not crucial, element in their decisions. If you do not believe me, go back and read the questions I put to hundreds of these men on pages 37–38.

They are not being unreasonable when they start tracking you at age twenty-four, they are being practical. They want their executives to be approximately forty-two years old and to have gone through a number of work experiences before they reach that age. If they do not start early, they will not make it. And if they do not dress correctly, they will not get started.

• •

WHAT ARE THEY WEARING ALL AROUND YOU?

If you are a young man about to begin accumulating a business wardrobe, I suggest several specific steps before you buy a single item. The first is to undertake a general industry orientation. This simply means that in your chosen industry in your area, you should study the dress habits of as many executives as possible—at least twenty or thirty. Number them, and write them down. Eliminate the most conservative and the most flamboyant from your list. You now should have a realistic range in which the successful men in your industry dress. If you position yourself in the top third from a conservative point of view, and in the top third in terms of neatness, tailoring and coordination, you will find yourself in a most advantageous position.

The most important orientation, of course, is in your own office. Here you should look at all men above you, all who have jobs you would like to have, all who are going to be making the career decisions about you, and determine your own clothing goals based on what these men are wearing. One of the best ways of fitting in with these men is to find out where they buy their clothing and purchase yours in the same store. There is, by the way, no reason you cannot dress better than your boss, as long as you do not make him look like a slob by comparison.

Once you have determined both the general industry and office standards of dress, you should have a solid idea of the acceptable range for successful dress. There is one additional range and that concerns your own physical and emotional characteristics. For this information, I would refer you back to Chapter 8, since that information is as relevant to corporate executives as it is to salesmen.

• • • • • • • • • • • • • • • • • • • •

CLOTHES THAT CAN MAKE YOU MORE LIKABLE

To reemphasize: The overriding essential of all corporate business clothing is that it establish power and authority. If you can accomplish nothing else, presenting yourself as a person who is capable of the job he wants, or has been given, is an acceptable goal. There is one other prime element: whether other people like you, and certain clothing elements tend to make a man more likable. Sounds crazy? I'm sorry, but I have the research to show I am right. Solid suits, for example, make a man more likable than pinstripe suits, although pinstripe suits make him more authoritative. Men are more liked by the upper middle class in gray suits, more liked by the lower middle class in blue suits.

Combinations that increase likability are gray suits with pale blue shirts and maroon solid or rep ties or beige suits with blue shirts. Pale yellow shirts with dark blue suits tend to have the same effect. Soft beige and soft browns are the best colors for plaid patterns if likability is the goal. Anything that is too authoritative, too gaudy or too sharply contrasted creates opposite effects.

Any clothing that reminds the viewer of his youth creates a pleasing effect, and makes the wearer more likable to the viewer. For example, if your boss is thirty-eight, he would be quite amenable to button-down collar shirts, end-on-end shirts and rep ties, because those were worn during his youth. If you don't have a personality that makes you immediately likable, I would suggest that you avoid black suits, avoid lavender or pink shirts, avoid any type of purple, avoid small-patterned ties and avoid any strong clash in either the colors or the lines of your clothing. I also suggest that men with severe personality problems avoid the white shirt because it works for everyone except the man with a terrible personality.

WHY VIRTUE ISN'T EVERYTHING

Many men believe that men receive promotions in business due to their efficiency, reliability and hard work, but this is not always true, not even for the boss's son. More often than not, it is the semblance of these qualities that helps success along, rather than the reality of them. To create the look of these qualities, you, your desk and your office must be as neat and precise as possible. Your clothing must always be perfectly coordinated, in upper-middle-class patterns and colors. You should wear pinstripe suits, white shirts, conservative ties. Never wear loud or gaudy colors. If you work in an office where men take off their suit jackets, then take off yours and roll up your shirtsleeves; this creates the impression of hard work.

If you are permitted to decorate and arrange your office, then you should read and follow the advice in Chapter 13, because a properly decorated and arranged office can help in the creation of this image.

18

Making Your Clothes Fit the Occasion

The truly sophisticated executive realizes that he must appear as if he is a different person on different occasions, and in order to do so must dress accordingly.

Although self-analysis is difficult for most people, we must recognize that some of us are just plain dull. If you are, you can appear to be more lively simply by brightening your clothing. If you are too flamboyant, you can tone down this image by dressing in the most conservative manner possible. If you look as if you are too young for the position you hold, you can dress in the manner of an older man. If you are in a business dominated by men younger than yourself, you can wear designer suits and ties and completely change your image. Although this breaks all my rules, it does adhere to the most formidable one: Always use clothing as a tool.

Use your clothing to help you fit the situation.

To apply this idea to specific situations, let us say that the average executive's week is divided as follows. On Monday, he meets with the president or chairman of the board. On that day he should dress extremely authoritatively and conservatively. On the second day, he meets with department heads, and should dress approximately the same. The third day he spends with his staff and, in order to maintain his working relationship with these people, he should soften his look slightly, wearing lighter colors with less contrast and none of the high-authority garments of the two previous days.

On Thursday, he is seeing an executive of another major corporation and should wear clothing equal to that worn by the man he is going to see. On the fifth day, he goes to see an executive of a minor corporation; he does not want to overwhelm this man—or come on like the same conservative old stick-in-the-mud that everyone in his corporation is supposed to be—so he softens his appearance, brightens it a bit and wears a paisley tie.

This executive would be adhering to my most formidable rule: Always use clothing as a tool. As we have seen, his adjustments are subtle, yet they will profoundly affect his psychological relationships with those with whom he comes in contact.

Another situation that is becoming more and more common to executives is that they are often called upon to speak from a stage. I usually know the purpose for which my own clients are going to be on stage, and I can be quite specific in my advice; for this book, I have simplified the rules to fit more general situations.

1. The first and often the most important statement a speaker makes to his audience is a nonverbal one. Dress to fit your audience's expectations. If you are the president of a corporation you must look like the president of a corporation. If you are selling stock, look like a stockbroker. Now

I understand that there are top-notch salespeople who could sell almost anything dressed in their BVDs if they talked to their propective clients on a one-to-one basis. However, if they dress inappropriately when speaking to a large audience they are going to lose that audience for the first three minutes or so. Then, unless they are one of the world's best speakers, they are never going to get them back. This holds true for anyone in any position.

2. Neatness counts. If a speaker has even one small flaw in his appearance some of the audience will notice it and it will probably hurt the speaker's credibility. The old fly and tie rule—pull up your fly and tie your tie—is not enough. You have to be meticulous about your appearance. Even though you may be some distance from your audience, you are going to be examined as closely as if you were under a microscope.

3. See yourself through your audience's eyes. When you are getting ready to speak stand back twenty or thirty feet from a mirror and look at yourself at that distance. Only then will you see what the audience sees. You will find that many outfits that are beautifully coordinated, even chic at two or three feet, are rather bland at twenty or thirty feet. Most speakers end up favoring outfits composed of solids with high contrast. For example, nine out of ten of the people we spoke to thought they looked better in a navy suit with a white shirt and a deep maroon tie than they did in a beautifully coordinated medium blue suit worn with a blue shirt and a beautiful blue tie. Almost everyone agreed that this very chic outfit made of three shades of blue faded into itself when on stage.

4. Never wear strong patterns. All strong patterns create blind spots in the audience. If you videotaped an audience and counted the number of times each member of the audience blinked, you would find that people in one

section of every audience would blink three to four times more than the rest of the audience. The reason is that there are certain distances at which strong patterns disturb people. Researchers know that when people are blinking they are not paying attention. Therefore, if you wear a strong pattern on stage you will lose at least part of your audience.

5. Never fade into the background. I once saw a very competent woman executive attempt to speak while wearing a maroon dress that exactly matched the maroon curtains hung behind her. Because she was using slides and the lights were dimmed, all the audience could see clearly were her hands, face and feet. The subject she was speaking on was very serious, but the audience was in hysterics from the moment she stepped on stage. Obviously, she lost them. As much as she tried—and she tried very hard—she never got them back. If you ever find yourself in a similar situation, you *must* do something to change it. You can ask that the background be changed; move the curtains or put a screen on stage. You can hide your body behind the podium. You can take off your jacket. You can even walk down into the audience. Whatever you have to do, do *something*.

6. Never be a voice coming out of the darkness. Audiences should be able to see a speaker's face clearly. If the lighting on stage is poor for any reason, you must be sure that your face is well lit and, whatever you do, do not count on the podium light. Podium lights are designed to light up speeches, not speakers. Speakers who attempt to use podium lights create one of two effects: If the light is weak, they look as if they are speaking from the shadows; if it's strong, their face becomes grotesque since it is lit from below. You must be certain that you are lit by an independent light, preferably a spot.

7. Unless the platform and the audience area are both well lit do not wear a three-piece suit on stage. The shirt tends to measure the speaker and since only a very small part of the shirt shows when the speaker wears a vest, he will look small. As a result, he will be less effective.

8. Never stand more than ten to fifteen feet from a demonstration, whether it is a picture on a screen or an object. If you are further away, the audience has the unfortunate choice of either looking at you, looking at the demonstration, or bouncing back and forth between both. If they look at the demonstration and ignore you, you have lost them. If they look at you and ignore the demonstration, you are better off without the demonstration. If they bounce back and forth like a tennis ball, they will soon become tired and stop watching either you or the demonstration.

9. Never use a demonstration the audience cannot see. Walk out into the auditorium before you speak and see if you can make sense of the items you are demonstrating. If you cannot, do not use them. If the item or the picture has print on it, the audience should be able to read that print easily. If they cannot, it doesn't belong on stage. Remember, everything on stage has to be visible from twenty to two hundred feet away. If it's not visible at those distances, it should not be used. Demonstrations that cannot be seen annoy audiences and turn them off.

10. Wear nothing that jingles, crackles, or pops. If you wear cuff links when you are speaking from a podium or a table, and they hit the podium or table next to a live mike, it will sound like a firecracker. If you are a woman wearing jewelry, it must not jingle or clink because next to a microphone it will make you sound like an entire troop of Gypsies. The only snap, crackle and pop you want in your presentation is an emotional one.

11. Smile, smile, smile. This is the most important rule for any speaker. The first message a speaker should send to an audience is, "I am a nice person, I like you, I hope you like me." Audiences do not listen to, or believe, people they do not like. Ronald Reagan is a classic example of how well the smile, smile, smile technique works. His smiling, easygoing style says to the world that he's a nice fellow. He can speak on any serious subject and discuss the most dreadful possible consequences of his actions, yet no one will dislike him. If you want to be an effective speaker, imitate Ronald Reagan, and smile, smile, smile. And, when you are not smiling, tell an occasional joke.

12. When in doubt, scream and shout, jump up and wave your arms about. The most obvious mistake made by most amateur speakers is that they do not understand that when they are on stage they are actors and actresses. Most do have some idea that they should speak with more power than they do on a one-to-one basis, but they do not realize that their verbal exuberance must be matched with a nonverbal exuberance. If you move your hand two inches to emphasize a point when you are speaking to one person, you may have to move it as much as two feet when speaking to a large audience. The general rule is, the bigger the audience, the bigger the motion. This is so difficult for people, particularly businesspeople whose general style is that of understatement, that I suggest they take an acting course before they take a speech course. That way they learn the importance of costuming and body language along with verbal presentation.

The great stage of our society is, of course, the television tube, and every now and then executives are called upon to appear on television. They usually don't do very well. They are unsuccessful for a number of reasons, but the one that I think is most crucial is that many of them are firmly convinced what they say will carry the day, and not how they look. This just is not true. The classic example, of course, is the Nixon–Kennedy debate. Most of the American public favored Nixon before the debate, yet the majority agreed that Kennedy won the debate and it gave him the presidency of the United States. Most of those who viewed the debate thought that Kennedy not only looked better, but also had a better grasp of the information. There were two groups who did not agree with this analysis: those who lived in areas with no television reception, and the English public who heard the debate on the radio. The overwhelming majority of these people thought that Nixon won the debate hands down. The simple fact was Nixon won the verbal debate while Kennedy won the nonverbal debate, and the people who watched gave more credence to what they saw than what they heard. That is why any executive going on television without professional consultation on how he looks is doing himself and his company a major disservice.

A tall handsome paragon of virtue should never wear stripes on television. Although television experts will tell you differently, I can assure you that striped suits and shirts, unless the lighting is perfect, will tend to run. Instead, wear three solids on television: you can never go wrong if they're well coordinated.

Several years ago we advised clients against wearing white shirts on television; today they are not only acceptable but preferable. Cameras today have no difficulty handling a white shirt as long as you get to the studio a few minutes ahead of time so that they know what you are wearing and can make the necessary adjustments.

I suggest that you never wear a gray suit on television

unless you know that you are going to have an upper-middle-class audience: today with satellite communications that is a possibility, but it is a rare one. Most mass television audiences, including those who listen to business programs come from all classes. The best suit to wear on television is a navy or medium-range blue with a white shirt or a blue shirt and a conservative tie.

Do not wear ties with small patterns. If reception is bad at home, the pattern will tend to jump and undulate, and people will not be able to watch you; if they are not watching, they will not be listening, either. Many television experts miss this point because they are accustomed to watching studio monitors, and reception is perfect on studio monitors. I think the real experts on how to handle television are the politicians. Most of those fellow, at least the sophisticated ones, test the suits, shirts and ties they are going to wear on camera, before they go on. If you want to model yourself after anyone, choose a political candidate running for state or national office. You cannot go far wrong.

Remember, too, that a large percentage of the TV audience is going to be women, and many women are turned off by men who look traditional. Therefore, you should avoid conservative attire such as pinstripe suits, rep ties and button-down shirts. So, although most executives have short haircuts, the exception should be the man who must go on television. His hair should be up-to-date and styled. As I've discussed elsewhere, women do not usually say that a man does not dress well; they say he does not know how to dress well, and they will reason that if he does not know how to dress well, he probably does not know how to do other things well either.

When I consult with major corporations, I often suggest that two executives be designated for television appearances; one to handle the general problems and announcements, and one to handle disasters. For example, if you manufacture or sell school buses, one of those buses is very likely going to be in an accident someday. If you are questioned about it on television, you must not only be unhappy about it, but know how to look unhappy as well.

The corporate spokesman who handles disasters on television should be around fifty-five years old and be distinguished looking. He should be dressed in a solid dark blue suit, a pale blue solid shirt and a solid maroon tie. If he is at the site of the accident, however, then he will be most credible if he has his jacket off and his shirtsleeves rolled up, or if he is wearing some sort of work uniform. He must appear as if his primary interest is to help solve the problem, not explain it.

There are times when the president is the only appropriate spokesman for his company. The rules for being an effective salesman are not suspended just because he is president. His nonverbal message must match his verbal message, and he must keep in mind that he is not speaking to other executives. All those signals that have served him so well on his way up the corporate ladder will now only cause him trouble.

There are dozens of examples of CEOs who dressed for business and failed on television. One that comes immediately to mind was the president of a defense contracting firm. The cost overruns on his firm's contracts were no greater than those of any other contractor, but because his company was signaled out by a congressman he felt obliged to defend his company's policies. The message he wanted to convey to the American taxpayer was that his company did not overcharge; sophisticated weapons are costly. He appeared on television sitting behind his mammoth desk, wearing his $400 suit (today that would be an $800 suit) and explained why we taxpayers should cover his losses. Then, accompanied by another executive in another equally expensive suit, and wearing a white safety helmet that had never before been out of his closet, he went into the factory to explain the cost overruns.

He thought he was getting his message across, but he was not. The message the viewers were receiving was: "I'm a superior being, and a member of a superior class, and I want you little people to contact your congressmen and tell them to pay us." The message, of course, went over like a lead balloon.

What the president of that company should have done was to surround himself in a cloak of science and patriotism. He should never have given an interview while sitting behind that desk; he should have arranged to be interviewed in the factory wearing a scientist's smock and a slightly used safety helmet.

If you want to know just how effective a good spokesman can be when handling a negative situation, watch almost any of the new spokesmen for the Russian government, particularly the First Secretary of the Soviet Embassy in Washington, D.C. When he testified before Congress about the shooting down of the Korean airliner, he smiled, was affable, charming, articulate, beautifully dressed and they never laid a glove on him. It is ironic that the Soviet Union should be more adept at handling American television than American corporations are, but it is so.

When you pick your man to deliver the good news on television, he should look like a network anchorman: forty-fivish, masculine, authoritative, credible but not pretty. If you pick someone who looks, acts and sounds like an anchorman, you will not go far wrong.

Going on television, then, means adapting one's appearance to the medium.

· ·

THREE RULES WORTHY OF MACHIAVELLI

In addition to the foregoing, there are three other aspects of executive dress that you should know:

1. In group situations, the effectiveness of any member of the group will be affected not only by his appearance but by that of his associates. Super executive teams know this and plan not only the verbal parts but also the visual parts that their members are to play. For example, at a stockholders' meeting, the key executives of the corporation who are to relate good news should be dressed similarly. Other executives, assigned to tell unfavorable news, should be dressed differently. This is not exactly like pitching cowboys in white hats against the outlaws in black hats, but psychologically it is similar: probably the blue suits (good guys) versus the gray suits (bad guys). By separating the information process visually as well as verbally, the identification of the top executives with the positive aspects of how they are running the business is dramatically increased.

   A more sophisticated way to apply this rule of association is to dress members of executive negotiating teams so that each member of the team visually fits the role he is to play.

   The top man on the team should be immediately identifiable as the leader, merely by his expensive, elegant clothes. The second man, who is usually the spokesman, should look like a second man, but be visually associated in some way with the first, so no one can mistake for whom he is speaking. Any expert on the team should be dressed like an expert in his field; for instance, an accountant should wear a pinstripe suit. If there is to be a balloon man on the team—someone who is going to send up trial balloons to see if they will float—he should be visually dissociated from the leader of the team. If one of the trial balloons catches on and is moving along in negotiation, however, on the day following its acceptance the balloon man should change his dress to bring him visually closer to the rest of the team.

What can I tell you? It's a Machiavellian world, and whoever knows how to play the game wins.

2. Every executive should know that there is an absolute transfer of values between people and the inanimate objects with which they may be identified in an advertisement. If we see a man standing next to a machine our perception of the machine will be colored by our judgment of the man. Therefore, if you let an ad agency choose beautiful individuals in lower-middle-class attire to stand next to your computer or tractor, the buying public may well be pleased by their appearance, but will think less of your equipment. All companies should think a lot more about how the models are dressed the next time they get ready to spring for an expensive advertising campaign.

However, dressing up your people isn't always the answer. Several years ago a client brought me into his office to show me a blowup of a magazine ad that was going to run in all the major publications in America to introduce their new computer. He told me that the woman standing next to his computer in the ad was wearing the very finest clothing because he agreed with my premise that there was a transference of values between people and inanimate objects. When I looked at the picture, however, she somehow did not convince me that the computer was any good.

There were other transferences taking place here as well, so we ran a little test. We took the original version of the ad, with this beautifully tailored woman standing next to the computer, a new version of the ad with a young handsome executive standing next to it, and a third version with a computer operator standing next to it. The ad that tested best was when the computer operator was included. Everyone to whom we showed the three ads said, he's a technician and, yes, that's a great computer. Ultimately, we idealized the computer operator, putting an attractive male model in a white smock next to the computer, and it was a very successful ad.

Evidently, you not only have to dress up a person, you have to dress them appropriately if you want them to sell your product either in print or in person.

3. If you have a son, you are part of his environment, perhaps the most crucial part he will know. If you dress appropriately now and follow the rules I have set forth, then your son will not have to purchase the twentieth edition of this book twenty years from now.

• • • • • • • • • • • • • • • • • • • •

FINALLY, TWO CRUCIAL MESSAGES

Throughout this book, but especially in this chapter, I have attempted to pack a tremendous amount of information into a small amount of space. I have tried to say something to almost every man to whom clothing is crucial for success, individually and/or corporately. If I conveyed nothing other than the message that clothing should be used as a tool and as a weapon, then I have succeeded fully in my goal. If the reader has accepted my second message, that beauty is not the name of the game—efficiency is—then I am a perfectly happy man. If, by chance, the reader has received my third message—that some of my ideas can make him more effective and more successful—then I believe I have made a substantial contribution to the American business scene.

Acknowledgments

First and foremost, I would like to express special thanks to my friend and editor Tom Humber, whose professionalism made the difficult seem easy, and whose sense of style made the heavy seem light throughout *Dress for Success*.

The material in this book leans heavily on the genius of all the great researchers of motivation from Pavlov to Skinner, and to them I am grateful.

In addition, I am indebted to Dr. Ernest Carlson, who first introduced me to the use of the indirect questionnaire in this field, which enabled me to question hundreds of thousands instead of merely hundreds. This research forms the backbone of the book.

I also wish to express my gratitude to the people at Hart Shaffner Marx who supplied the suits and Reis of New Haven who supplied the ties used in the pictures in this book. My thanks also go to the Men's Tie Foundation, which provided me with the best "how to tie a tie" pictures available.

Naturally, I owe special thanks to my clients, particularly the corporate clients, who not only supplied most of the cash needed for research, but also opened up their organizations to me. Without this opportunity to research corporate America from the inside, this book would be meaningless.

Index